# Understanding Schemas
## and Young Children

## Education at SAGE

**SAGE** is a leading international publisher of journals, books, and electronic media for academic, educational, and professional markets.

Our education publishing includes:

- accessible and comprehensive texts for aspiring education professionals and practitioners looking to further their careers through continuing professional development
- inspirational advice and guidance for the classroom
- authoritative state of the art reference from the leading authors in the field

Find out more at: **www.sagepub.co.uk/education**

# Understanding Schemas and Young Children
### From birth to three

## Frances Atherton
### and Cathy Nutbrown

Los Angeles | London | New Delhi
Singapore | Washington DC

Los Angeles | London | New Delhi
Singapore | Washington DC

SAGE Publications Ltd
1 Oliver's Yard
55 City Road
London EC1Y 1SP

SAGE Publications Inc.
2455 Teller Road
Thousand Oaks, California 91320

SAGE Publications India Pvt Ltd
B 1/I 1 Mohan Cooperative Industrial Area
Mathura Road
New Delhi 110 044

SAGE Publications Asia-Pacific Pte Ltd
3 Church Street
#10-04 Samsung Hub
Singapore 049483

Editor: Marianne Lagrange
Editorial assistant: Kathryn Bromwich
Production editor: Thea Watson
Proofreader: Elaine Leek
Marketing manager: Catherine Slinn
Cover design: Naomi Robinson
Typeset by: C&M Digitals (P) Ltd, Chennai, India
Printed in India at Replika Press Pvt Ltd

© Frances Atherton and Cathy Nutbrown, 2013

First published 2013

Apart from any fair dealing for the purposes of research or private study, or criticism or review, as permitted under the Copyright, Designs and Patents Act, 1988, this publication may be reproduced, stored or transmitted in any form, or by any means, only with the prior permission in writing of the publishers, or in the case of reprographic reproduction, in accordance with the terms of licences issued by the Copyright Licensing Agency. Enquiries concerning reproduction outside those terms should be sent to the publishers.

**Library of Congress Control Number: 2012943610**

**British Library Cataloguing in Publication data**

A catalogue record for this book is available from the British Library

ISBN 978-1-4462-4893-5
ISBN 978-1-4462-4894-2 (pbk)

# DEDICATION

To my family and friends with love. FMA

In honour of Chris Athey, whose work has inspired my own. CEN

# CONTENTS

| | |
|---|---|
| Acknowledgements | viii |
| About the Authors | ix |
| Foreword | x |

**PART 1  KNOWING ABOUT SCHEMAS**     **1**

| | |
|---|---|
| Introduction | 3 |
| 1 Schemas and the Youngest Children | 5 |
| 2 Observing Children: Spotting Schemas | 25 |

**PART 2  HOW DO CHILDREN UNDER THREE PURSUE THEIR SCHEMAS? 'ALL ABOUT HENRY'**     **33**

| | |
|---|---|
| 3 Henry's Containing and Enveloping Schema | 35 |
| 4 Henry's Back and Forth Schema | 47 |
| 5 Henry's Dynamic Vertical Schema | 59 |
| 6 Henry's Mark Making and Figurative Representations | 73 |

**PART 3  DEVELOPMENTAL JOURNEYS: TRACING DEVELOPMENTS IN CHILDREN'S THINKING FROM MOTOR TO SYMBOLIC BEHAVIOURS**     **93**

| | |
|---|---|
| 7 Containing and Enveloping Schema | 95 |
| 8 Going through a Boundary Schema | 136 |
| 9 Dynamic Vertical Schema | 150 |
| 10 Stories from Home | 170 |
| | |
| Epilogue | 186 |
| Bibliography | 191 |
| Name Index | 205 |
| Subject Index | 207 |

# ACKNOWLEDGEMENTS

This book exists because of the generosity of the parents and children who allowed Frances to spend time with them. Thanks go to the parents and practitioners who became involved in this study and shared their experiences with her. The children, in particular, allowed Frances to spend time with them and this revealed so much about their astonishing capabilities.

We would like to thank our colleagues at the University of Chester and the University of Sheffield for their support.

# ABOUT THE AUTHORS

**Dr Frances Atherton** is a Senior Lecturer in Early Years and Head of Department in the Faculty of Education and Children's Services at the University of Chester. She has a growing reputation in the early childhood field for her research on children under three and their learning through schemas. She teaches on a range of early childhood programmes including BA Early Childhood Studies and MA Early Childhood. Frances also teaches research methodology and supervises undergraduate students and those undertaking higher and research degrees.

**Professor Cathy Nutbrown** is Head of the School of Education at the University of Sheffield where she teaches on a range of early years courses from undergraduate to PhD. She is author of over 50 publications in the field of Early Childhood Education, including *Threads of Thinking: Schemas and Young Children* (now in its 4th edition). In June 2012 she reported on her independent Review of Early Education and Child Care Qualifications, *Foundations For Quality*, in which she made recommendations to Government to improve the quality of qualifications for those working with young children in early years settings.

# FOREWORD

This book explores young children's learning and development through the identification and understanding of their schemas, repeatable patterns of behaviour and thought (Athey 2007). Over an 18-month period, seven children under three years of age were observed in a day care setting. Using observations of children, the book identifies what they were 'telling us' about their thinking, learning and development when they played. Conversations with parents and photographs of their child at play highlighted consistent patterns in children's actions, speech and representations. During these conversations, parents expressed very positive views about spending time coming to understanding their child's play from a schematic perspective.

This book adds to the growing body of knowledge about how richly varied experiences can nourish schematic development and encourage a co-ordination of schemas where children are able to experiment and explore a range of ideas and concepts as active participants in the learning environment. The role of the adult and the nature of their accompaniment with children in the learning environment are also key features. The place of attuned, matched learning encounters between adults who have a knowledge of schemas and are aware of children's particular schemas and the children is highlighted with the importance of a conceptual response to children's *patterns of thinking* revealed as they played, discussed.

This book is structured as follows:

In **Part 1 Knowing about Schemas**, we consider the importance of the first years in a child's learning and development.

Chapter 1, *Schemas and the Youngest Children*, provides an underpinning for the book, and examines research which supports our understanding of young children's learning and cognitive development. It focuses specifically on:

- The 'preciousness' of early childhood
- Schemas
- The relational nature of learning
- Quality practice in early years settings
- Listening, watching and responding to children
- The child as learner

Chapter 2, *Observing Children: Spotting Schemas*, provides suggestions and examples of how observations can be used to identify children's schemas as part of their individual development profiles and also as an aid to curriculum planning. The chapter includes discussion on:

- Observation
- Photographs
- Conversations
- Stories from home

This chapter also discusses schemas, definitions and implications, and explores the complexity of accompanying children in the learning environment in a way that matches their thinking concerns. It focuses on the nature of relationships in learning and reflects upon how precious the first years of early childhood are in terms of learning and development.

**Part 2 How do Children under Three Pursue their Schemas? 'All about Henry'**, provides a detailed account of the schemas of one child, Henry, over two years in his nursery setting. It includes rich accounts of him pursuing his schemas and his developing interests and language. This is a useful example of the importance of making close observations and indicates how observations of schemas can usefully aid a range of developmental aspects and support implementation of curriculum and assessment policy on children under three.

In Chapter 3, *Henry's Containing and Enveloping Schema*, Henry's containing and enveloping behaviour is evidenced by a series of actions which he sometimes accompanies with talk. These behaviours deepen his understanding of insideness and provide a valuable practical foundation, upon which he builds his later symbolic representations.

In Chapter 4, *Henry's Back and Forth Schema*, we see Henry discriminating in his use of objects to play with. He is fascinated with horizontal movement and his choice of items is sensitised in favour of cars, trucks, vans, bikes, glockenspiels, pizza cutters, soft play cylinders and so on. He reveals the relationship between form of thought and environmental content to be assimilated.

In Chapter 5, *Henry's Dynamic Vertical Schema*, we see Henry distinguishing the possibilities of disparate environmental content. He identifies a conceptual relationship between dissimilar objects and his own existing cognitive structures. Henry is involved in motor-level trajectory behaviours in the vertical plane which are significant as a precursor to symbolic representations, co-ordinations and thought.

In Chapter 6, *Henry's Mark Making and Figurative Representations*, Henry's dynamic thought patterns, his schemas, can be clearly seen in his actions, language, model making and constructions. These important action representations provide a foundation upon which mark making can emerge. This chapter aims to identify Henry's thought patterns as they are represented figuratively in his mark making over a seven-month period.

In **Part 3 Developmental Journeys: Tracing Developments in Children's Thinking from Motor to Symbolic Behaviours**, we cover a number of children's developmental journeys through their schemas. Richly detailed observations depict the movement from motor to symbolic thinking, including evidence of their understanding of functional dependency relationships, the effects of their actions on objects. The observations are discussed to reveal their significance in terms of schemas and of other aspects of young children's development. It identifies how children's behaviour can be interpreted both from a schematic perspective and from a holistically developmental perspective.

Chapters 7, 8 and 9 have at their heart a set of observations of five children aged from eight months to 17 months who are focusing on particular schemas, namely containing and enveloping, going through a boundary or dynamic vertical schema. The observations, taken over a 12-month period, are then discussed to reveal their significance in terms of schemas and of other aspects of young children's development. It begins with a set of schema-oriented observations. This is followed by 'an unpacking', which answers the 'so what?' questions that many people have once they have observed schemas.

Chapter 10, *Stories from Home*, focuses on communication between home and settings. The importance of taking time to talk with parents and carers about their child's learning and development is recognised. In sharing detailed observations, the significance in terms of schemas and other aspects of their child's development is revealed. Instances of schema behaviour in the home are discussed during these conversations, as the opportunity to dwell upon their child's developing thinking is enjoyed.

# PART 1
# KNOWING ABOUT SCHEMAS

# INTRODUCTION

This book explores the schematic underpinnings of learning in a group of seven children aged from eight months to 23 months, over a period of 18 months. The study took place in the collaborative and mutually supportive atmosphere of a Children's Centre where the young children, who became part of the research, attended on a sessional basis.

They busied themselves in an environment filled with tempting activities and opportunities for discovery and exploration. The practitioners paid careful attention to what the children were doing and talked with them as they played, noting many observations of important happenings. They also made time for listening and talking with parents and carers each day, usually at 'picking-up' and 'dropping-off' time, so that significant moments could be discussed. This relational aspect of practice was also imperative in the study. Opportunities to share insights so that understandings could deepen were vital.

The study which underpins this book investigated the schematic behaviour of young children asking the question: How are young children pursuing their schemas? It focused on aspects of thinking, learning and development that young children reveal in their schematic behaviour. In addition, the observations and insights were used to consider how adults can support young children as they pursue their schemas, and the implications of schema identification on the learning experiences of young children.

Observations of children, interviews with parents, and parents' notes and photos of aspects of their children's behaviour at home appear throughout this book. They reveal the depth and complexity of young children's thinking, and the necessary unhurried nature of research with young children. The important aim throughout the study was gradually to 'come to know' Annie, Florence, Tommy, Nell, Patrick, Henry and Greg, and in doing so to capture the minute detail of the astonishing 'thinking things' they were doing. Observations and insights were shared, at appropriate times, with the children's parents and significant others.

Opportunities to talk and listen with the parents about their children, fostering an openness and sense of mutual discovery through conversations where our shared understandings of the child were enriched, were vital. Photographs and written observations became an eloquent means through which familiar actions became better known, differently known. From the beginning, the parents were happy to talk about instances of their child's playful escapades at home, while enjoying examples from the setting. These were opportunities for exchanging understandings, for bringing familiar events about their child together, to come to know them in a different way.

Through an understanding of schemas, children's behaviour may be viewed from an alternative perspective. This complementary consideration enables adults to accompany children as they explore and investigate in a way which attunes to their *forms of thinking* and so provides a match for their conceptual concerns, in priority over their associative preferences.

Children's choices, and their fastidious inclinations towards objects around them in the learning environment, are important and so deserve respect. Adults working with children, however, must observe carefully so as not to let to children's partialities about environmental *content* distract them from identifying the particular ways children *use* similar or dissimilar objects in an exploration of *form*.

This *schematic view* of children's behaviour is necessary if the desire to unravel the intricacies of children's patterns of thinking is to be realised. If children's actions, talk and markings are interpreted schematically, a new and different understanding can emerge. This can allow for seemingly unfathomable behaviour to be reconsidered – even understood. To embrace a knowledge of schemas, and to be open to accept a new interpretation of children's behaviour, is illuminating. Children articulate their thinking expressively in their behaviour and so the challenge for adults is to hear, see and understand what is contained in the subtlety of children's actions, representations and talk.

The essence of the research was – through close and sensitive observations taken over many months – to come to know more clearly what children were thinking. As relationships evolved, Frances became an accepted adult in the Centre and an ease of belonging developed. She made observations of Annie, Florence, Tommy, Nell, Patrick, Henry and Greg over a period of more than 12 months. At the start of the study, Annie was eight months old, Florence was 13 months, Tommy was 16 months, Nell was 17 months, Patrick was 18 months, Henry was 20 months and Greg was 23 months old. Frances's involvement in their setting environment could not be hurried. She made a quiet and careful entry into their domain, and only gradually involved herself more directly with the children.

Once relationships were secure, Frances's imperative was to capture the detail of what the children were doing as they played. In this, a perceptive discernment of their thinking could be more clearly understood and, from this, more carefully matched intervention was the result.

# CHAPTER 1

# SCHEMAS AND THE YOUNGEST CHILDREN

## Introduction

This chapter reviews research on the importance of the first years in a child's learning and development. It also looks at schemas and relationships in learning. First, it considers how precious the first years of early childhood are in terms of learning and development. This is followed by a reflection on definitions of schemas. It explores the individual, isolated nature of schemas along with the relational and social. There is an examination of the characteristics of relationships within the learning environment between adult and child and the place for attuned intervention. The importance of accompanying children conceptually is examined and the complexity of the role of the adult in the learning environment is identified.

This chapter takes as its premise Malaguzzi's claim that children are 'strong, powerful, competent learners with the right to an environment which is integral to the learning experience' (Malaguzzi 1998). Nurse and Headington (1999) acknowledge the 'preciousness' of the first years of early childhood, so this chapter considers the characteristics of young children's physical and social learning environments in an attempt to reveal what may epitomise the best support for young children's thinking and learning. Nutbrown (2001: 66) confirmed the 'crucial importance' of the early years for children's learning, which David and Powell (1999: 2) recognised as 'an important period of change and development in children's thinking and ability to make sense of the world'. Within this context, the distinctive role of well-trained and well-qualified, reflective and evaluative professional practitioners is crucial to dynamic learning, alongside the unique and important role of parents in children's learning and development.

## The 'Preciousness' of Early Childhood

Brierley (1994), drawing on studies of the brain, concluded that the period between birth and puberty was critical in terms of learning but that the first five years are when brain growth is particularly rapid, with the first two years being the time of most rapid growth (Friedman 2006). This 'most critical learning phase' (Shore 1997: 51) is one which 'deeply influences the rest of development' (Gopnik, Meltzoff and Kuhl 1999: 190). It is a 'unique' phase, which Hurst and Joseph (1998: 12) confirmed as the period where learning is at its 'easiest' and much of what is learned 'remains for life'. Smidt (2006) also noted the rate of brain development in the very early years, while Hannon (2003) recognised the importance to brain development of the formation of the connections which Brierley (1994) specified were key in the development of intelligence during the first three years.

Development takes place and important brain connections are made when very young children are actively involved in exploration, discovery and interactions (Learning and Teaching Scotland 2005) and, as Friedman (2006) states, the relationship between appropriate stimuli in the early years and brain development is dramatic. In their work exploring cultural communities, Wang, Bernas and Eberhard (2005) support the imperative of a personal response to children's individual priorities. They note that young children's learning potential was improved when practitioners took into account 'the diversity children bring to early childhood settings [which] enriches the learning environment, both for the teachers and the children' (Wang et al. 2005: 284). If appropriate stimuli are to be a feature of early childhood settings, then practitioners must be aware of what is 'appropriate' for each child. To effect a particular and precise response, the practitioner must take into account what is significant *for* the child, what is unique *about* the child, what makes the child the *person* they are.

Cameron (2005: 597) referred to 'empathic response cues' in her work with young children to elicit children's participation. A physical environment which motivates, supported with a perceptive, comprehending adult, is vital in supporting young children's development. Shore (1997: 51) highlighted the significance of these first physical and social encounters for the young child with 'babies' very first experiences having dramatic impacts on the architecture of their brains', which Schiller and Willis (2008) suggested were reinforced as early experiences were repeated.

Clarke and Clarke (1998: 435), in their exploration of the long-term effects of negative early experiences, acknowledged that 'different processes may show different degrees of vulnerability to adversity … with cognitive the best buffered'. This did not absolve early years educators from accountability in terms of quality practice, but suggested that the perception of these first few years as consequential for the long term may be flawed, concluding that 'early learning effects can fade and disappear, [however] under stress such effects might be reactivated' (1998: 435).

Shore's (1997: 51) warning that 'early experiences – positive or negative – have a decisive impact on how the brain is wired' attached significance to this early phase of life. Sylva, Melhuish, Sammons, Siraj-Blatchford and Taggart's study (2011: 119) affirmed the importance of early years' experiences for young children. Their exploration of the medium- to long-term impact of pre-school quality on children's developmental outcomes found that 'high quality learning experiences at *either* home *or* pre-school setting can boost the development of children, thus acting as "protective" factors'. The influence of the environment on young children in the early years, acknowledged in its broadest connotation, is a significant responsibility to accept if children are to be nurtured appropriately. Understanding the nature of quality – what is encompassed within this and what may comprise a quality experience – is an intricate complexity, one with far-reaching implications.

Experiences impact on the brain such that 'the brain changes in radical ways over the first few years of life. ... It actively tries to establish the right connections ... in response to experience' (Gopnik et al. 1999: 195). This was acknowledged in the Department for Children, Schools and Families' (DCSF) evaluation of the Neighbourhood Nurseries Initiative, which recognised that 'the provision of educational opportunities during the early years is related to later school success' (DCSF 2007: 52).

The suppleness of the brain in the early months of life led Gardner (1984) to challenge those working and caring for young children to be aware of their response to the complex thinking, learning and developmental needs of the young child. He asserted that to 'build upon knowledge of these intellectual proclivities' was essential in practice (Gardner 1984: 32).

Selleck (2001) and Goldschmied and Jackson (2004) reminded us of this astonishing capacity for children under three years of age to learn, and Gopnik, Meltzoff and Kuhl (1999: 189) confirmed this as 'the time when we learn most and when our brains as well as our minds are most open to new experience'. Rosen (2010: 102) also confirmed this in her consideration of children's perceptions of their impact on curriculum development in stating that 'children are viewed by teachers and appear to view themselves as competent and capable – a view that underpins a children's rights approach'. There is a collective understanding of capability and an inferred responsibility here; children appear to know their own competencies and rely on the adults working with them to accept, respect and respond to these proficiencies with sensitivity, empathy and challenge.

In the light of this, Brierley (1994) suggested that early years' policy and practice should be underscored by knowledge of brain and sensory development and went further in outlining a set of principles for the education of young children in different settings. Smith, Duncan and Marshall (2005) support Brierley's (1994) understanding of the capabilities of young children's minds. They stated that 'children clearly have something useful and important to say about their activities and have the competence to tell us'. However, they went on to specify that adults need 'to provide the appropriate scaffolding' (Smith et al. 2005: 485).

Penn (2005: 37) acknowledged the value of early experiences as a foundation upon which later ones can build, but supported Hannon (2003) and Clarke and Clarke (1998) in suggesting that the notion of this being critical may be exaggerated. Penn reminded us of the adaptability of children and the possibility of change 'in all kinds of ways at all ages' (2005: 37). Gardner's (1984: 33) proposal that there were 'points of maximum flexibility and adaptability' implied that the enduring permanency in terms of influence of early childhood experiences may be misplaced. What could be described as critical, however, was an acknowledgement of Nutbrown's (2006) principle that children should be at the centre of the learning environment. Indeed, the curriculum for early years should be driven by a 'learner- and person-centred ethos [which] affords children's minds the respect they deserve' (Nutbrown 2006: 125). This place, with the child at the centre of the learning environment, was reflected in the Department for Education's championing of the importance of play in young children's learning and development (DfE 2012). It recognised the complexity of play, its potential, its enabling function, its countless possibilities, and its essential role in supporting children to be themselves, whatever that may be.

Thus, if we are to capitalise on children's potential in the early years and their ability to learn, which Brierley (1994: 29) described as 'in a state of flood readiness', the message is clear. Do we channel the torrent of young children's potential with a creative curriculum and with adults being attuned to children's needs, or do we dam the flow of possibilities with a focus on irrelevant, meaningless and inappropriate activities accompanied by well-meaning but ill-informed adults?

In considering the 'preciousness' of early childhood, we can see the importance of early education experiences for young children, and this has far-reaching implications. The early experiences which form the foundation for later learning include both the physical activities and opportunities to which the child has access, and the social relationships with the adults the child encounters.

## Schemas

Made popular through the work of Athey since the late 1980s (see Athey 1990), understanding about schemas has become part of practice in some early education and care settings. There are many different definitions of schema but no single characterisation is able to satisfy, as no single definition encompasses the complexity and perspectives which emerge. McVee, Dunsmore and Gavelek (2005: 556) reflected this in highlighting the dichotomy between 'the knower and the known': from one perspective, 'schemas are formed within individuals ... a disembodied, in-the-head proposition', whereas from the other perspective, 'schemas (or cognitive structures or representations) are transformed as a result of transactions with the world'. This discrepancy was acknowledged by Beals (1998: 11), who asserted that 'schemata are not individual, isolated constructions, but culturally shared patterns of organising knowledge and experience', and supported by Rogoff (1990: 27), who confirmed that 'context [is] inseparable from human actions in cognitive events or activities'.

Gardner's (1984) definition of schema appeared to accept the perception of the lone, private endeavour in suggesting that the young child brings their schema to bear upon objects in the environment in an effort to come to know and understand. The child, it could be said, is involved in a personal, particularised and exclusive concern – the business of knowledge construction. Gardner (1984: 64) drew attention to the 'existence of one or more basic information-processing operations or mechanisms which could deal with specific kinds of input', which resonated with Neisser's (1976: 56) description of schema as 'a pattern of action as well as a pattern for action'.

McVee, Dunsmore and Gavelek (2005: 550) supported this active, categorising yet arbitrating notion of schema in drawing a distinction between 'schemas as an organisational feature that the mind imposes on experience and schema as a mental representation that mediates activity', which Beals (1998) confirmed in the mind's search for significant associations where new material was appropriated and made part of oneself. Both Gardner (1984) and Neisser (1976) alluded to this active nature of the schema, the modifying, adjusting characteristic, the simple notion of passive absorption into pre-existing structures rejected in the light of an acceptance of schema as a dynamic reality, a constant cognitive turbulence, a discomfort and disquiet, an unremitting process of transformation and growth.

Bartlett (1932: 85) was forthright – actually emphatic – in his discussion of this, in asserting that:

> It is not merely a question of relating the newly presented material to old acquirements of knowledge ... it depends upon the active bias, or special reaction tendencies, that are awakened in the observer by the new material, and it is these tendencies which then set the new into relation to the old.

Neisser's (1976: 111) classification of schemas as 'active, information-seeking structures ... which accept information and direct action' confirmed Bartlett's notion of dynamism, which Meltzoff and Moore (1998: 229) endorsed in suggesting that the 'initial mental structures' that infants possess 'serve as "discovery procedures" for developing more comprehensive and flexible concepts'. Green (1988: 135) proposed that 'reasoning is facilitated when suitable knowledge structures (or schemata) are evoked'. This is what Bartlett (1932: 85) refers to as 'awakened', and what Neisser (1976: 111) sees as 'accepting'.

All this suggests an attuned sensitivity to *experience* which affords either a 'match' or a 'mismatch' with inner patterns' (Athey 2007: 48).

Cheng and Holyoak's (1985: 135) understanding of the place of environment, that 'individuals reason using context-sensitive structures derived from everyday experience', with the child's organising, categorising, classifying structure (schema) sensitised and receptive to appropriate environmental stimuli, resonates with Athey's notion of 'offered and received curriculum content' (2007: 54). Birbeck and Drummond (2005: 594) noted that 'children report on what they see as important and this is not always congruent with adult interpretations'. They recognised that it was important 'to ascertain the reasons behind responses supplied by children' (2005: 594), which resonates with Athey's (2007) imperative of 'match' in that the actions which children carry out, and in the talk which may accompany this, should be interpreted as the child intends.

The literature on schemas acknowledges the complexity of definition in that no one, particular, definitive meaning has emerged. Definitions which consider the individual and social aspects of schemas have been highlighted. In this book, and in our own research, the significance is for practice, and Athey's definition of 'a repeatable pattern of behaviour' underpins our thinking about schemas and young children's learning. Adults who come to understand the particular schematic interests of young children are better able to respond to children's *forms of thinking* in learning encounters.

During the period of early childhood, Piaget and Inhelder (1969: 4) highlighted children's involvement in the construction of 'action schemes', which they described as the 'organisation of actions as they are generalised by repetition' or, as Donaldson (1978: 134) clarified, schemas as 'organised behaviour patterns which can be used intentionally through the emergence of the process of assimilation and accommodation'. The possibilities of early reflexes, such as the sucking and palmar reflex extending through 'reflex exercise' (Piaget and Inhelder 1969: 7), with early habits 'growing out of an assimilation of new elements to previous schemata', was evident (Piaget 1950: 111).

Piaget recognised the importance of early actions as a preparation for later stages, when 'active experimentation' becomes capable of being internalised. At this stage, the child is no longer necessarily immediately physically dynamic when faced with a problem, but instead 'appears to be thinking' (Piaget 1950: 116). There is 'insight and sudden comprehension' – a mental dynamism it could be said – where sensori-motor schemas are combined and brought forward to be applied to new situations (Piaget and Inhelder 1969: 12).

Gardner (1984: 129) stated that 'for many months, the child's knowledge of objects and of the simple causal connections that exist among them is tied completely to his [sic] moment-to-moment experience'. This confirmed Piaget's (1950: 121) characterisation of sensori-motor intelligence as a co-ordination of 'successive perceptions and overt movements ... like a slow-motion film, in which all the pictures are seen in succession but without fusion'. However, Gardner went on to assert that 'the study of thought should (indeed must) begin in the nursery'. This was an acknowledgement of Piaget's (1959: 283) claim that 'sensory-motor activity constitutes the foundation of symbolism and representation ... that thought proceeds from actions', which underpins Meltzoff and Moore's (1998: 224) view of the powerful young child in that:

> The young infant is not a purely sensori-motor being but a representational one. Although sensori-motor development is essential to infants, preverbal cognition neither reduces to, nor is wholly dependent upon, such development. Pre-reaching and pre-locomotor infants are engaged in detecting regularities, forming expectations, and even making predictions about future states of affairs – all of which are possible because representation allows them to bring past experience to bear on the present.

Piaget and Inhelder (1969: 10) acknowledged that the precise moment when 'acts of practical intelligence' appeared was difficult to specify, but it was the progression from these early reflexes, through the acquisition of habits, towards this which was significant. The complexity of young children's thinking and language development, which was identified through a series of sub-stages, a progression towards an intelligence before language, which he characterised as 'essentially practical ... solving numerous problems of action' (1969: 4), was recognised by Bruner (1966: 16) who confirmed the importance of early action in providing the 'necessary and sufficient condition for progress' towards behaviour which was no longer shackled by action alone.

Grace and Brandt (2006: 249) revealed that certain characteristics were adjudged as most important to kindergarten success. These included dispositions and attitudes to learning, communication and the social and emotional domain where there is a sense of confidence and self-worth. It was interesting to note that areas including cognitive development and general knowledge were viewed as less critical to success. It would suggest therefore that the opportunity for children to immerse themselves in relevant, motivating and provoking environments which allow for freedom and exploration, help inculcate important holistic domains of development.

Corbetta and Snapp-Childs (2009) affirmed the central role of object exploration in the development of perception, action and memory, recognising that by sight, touch and manipulation, infants secure knowledge of physical characteristics which they can later recall and utilise. They specified that 'the successful integration of haptic information with visual information begins only around 8–9 months of age' which correlated with Willattes (1984: 133), who reported that from his experiments, '9-month old infants are able to use a support as a means for attaining a goal ... and are able to co-ordinate two separate actions into an effective sequence'.

Although Willattes (1984) suggested that infants from 9 months were able to demonstrate a strategic expression of purposeful thinking, which Piaget (1950: 111) heralded as 'the transition between simple habit and intelligence', where the end is sought, as it were, by using appropriate means, Corbetta and Snapp-Childs' (2009: 55) acknowledgement that infants 'need many trials to alter response and seem to need even more practice before being able to maintain and reproduce the new response steadily' confirmed the place of early action and experience. Goodley and Runswick-Cole (2010: 506) noted that the intrinsically motivated activities which children involve themselves in can only be described as such if done 'for their own sake', which validates the need for young children to have plenty of time to absorb themselves in their own important discoveries.

Green's (1988: 133) observation that 'typically, individuals seek to explore a novel problem in a rather *ad hoc* manner before embarking on a more planned approach' echoed Bruner's (1966: 16) reasoning in his discussion of the origins of enactive representation, which recognised the importance of early action as necessary for the child to 'objectify' and 'correlate' the environment. However, Piaget (1950) suggested that this did not constitute acts of intelligence themselves, as they are composed of successive movements which lead to an end.

Athey (2007: 49) described the development of symbolic representation from these early motor and perceptual behaviours and identified advances in young children's thinking, with schemas identified as 'patterns of repeatable actions that lead to early categories and then to logical classifications'. She went on to specify schemas as 'commonalities and continuities … in spontaneous thought and behaviour' (2007: 113). This resonated with Meade and Cubey's (2008: 3) 'patterns in children's actions' and Smidt's (2006: 24) 'patterns of actions', which Nutbrown (2006: 10) clarified as a 'pattern of behaviour which has a consistent thread running through it', and is similar to Flavell's (1963) behaviour with an underlying sameness. The successive, recurring notion of pattern here, underpinning children's talk, deeds, musings and makings – that is, Bartlett's (1932: 201) 'active, developing patterns', which Athey (2007: 48) clarified could apply to 'dynamic sequences of action as well as static configurations' – has undoubted professional and parental relevance.

Meade and Cubey's (2008: 3) clarification of schemas as 'forms of thought that relate to cognitive structures … like pieces of ideas or concepts', which Smidt (2006: 24) explained 'can be repeated and that lead to the ability to categorise and then to be logically classified', allowed for an alternative interpretation of children's actions, discussions and representations. As Gardner (1984: 303) maintained, 'the child pursues those activities that for him [sic] have come to be connected with pleasurable experiences as well as those activities that lead to outcomes that he desires'. This was not a pursuit to satisfy private cravings, a display of selfish egoism, but a meaningful and significant cognitive compulsion for the young child as they came to know.

If there is a genuine professional yearning, therefore, to provide learning experiences of significance, then to embrace a knowledge of schema which permits a sight of perhaps hitherto obscured views of thought, a way into children's minds, must be a fundamental consideration, driven by a respectful desire to respond to what is of consequence to them. Sandberg and Heden (2011: 328) acknowledged that adults in learning environments need to reflect upon 'the messages that are conveyed through the encouragement or disapproval of play'. Seen in a wider context, their suggestion infers a deeper, more significant impact on practice in general and intervention in learning in particular. The underlying ethos here is one of acceptance, with the implication that the child's concerns should not need to be implored, but anticipated and received with confidence and esteem.

In this book schemas are defined as persistent patterns which underlie children's spontaneous behaviour. There is a personal and social dimension in that the private aspects of individual minds are made public through actions, language and representations. These tangible insights into children's minds are shaped by encounters with the things around them and the people they meet. To be active in these encounters, in a way which attunes to these seemingly unremitting themes depicting thought, is an opportunity to engage with children in a deliberate way, which understands the challenge of a conceptual meeting of minds.

Much research acknowledges the active nature of children's learning. The importance of supporting young children to be both physically and mentally active in learning is key. Environments that stimulate and challenge, and have adults working in them who are able to respond to what is of consequence to the child, are vital if children are to flourish.

## The Relational Nature of Learning

Carr, Jones and Lee (2005: 137) highlighted the key element of environment in their recognition of the strength of an educational agenda which focuses on 'reciprocal and responsive relationships in that it encourages education to be explained in terms of the interactive process of teaching and learning rather than in terms of individual psychology'. Rogoff's (1990: 27) insistence that 'there are neither context-free situations nor de-contextualised skills' understood the shared nature, the relational nature of the cognitive encounter, a meeting of mind, people and place.

Siraj-Blatchford, Sylva, Muttock, Gilden and Bell's (2002: 10) definition of pedagogy included the 'instructional techniques and strategies which enable learning to take place'. However, they went on to assert a significantly more complex consideration which included in the definition pedagogy, 'the interactive process between teacher and learner'. Elfer (2007: 169) drew a distinction between the kinds of relationships which appear in the home and professional setting. He described family interactions as 'intimate and spontaneous' and those in settings as 'more professional and planned'. In a pedagogical context, if Siraj-Blatchford et al.'s (2002) characterisation of relationships is interactional, then Elfer's (2007) depiction of family intimacy should be acknowledged in the professional setting too. If there is to be a genuine egalitarian, reciprocal interaction between child and adult, then the professional distance which Elfer inferred in his description of setting interactions may not be appropriate.

To secure relationships in the learning environment which enable children to feel emboldened, important and free, is to create relationships of trust and respect which are slowly forged and founded upon a real sense of wanting the best for the child. There is a responsiveness here which avoids Elfer's notion of 'planned' in favour of a more reactive kind of engagement. To be able to react to, anticipate, understand and nurture the nuances of children's thinking encountered during playful meetings, needs acknowledgeable adults who can forge intimate professional relationships which continue those which may exist at home.

Elfer (2007) understood the professional adult's role in an early years setting as that which includes specialist competencies as well as more heartfelt qualities. He knew the complexity of the role that Nutbrown and Page (2008: 177) capture in their description of the kind of adults that babies and young children need, including:

> Adults who know about children's needs, know about children's minds, understand different theories of learning, understand emotional literacy as well as literacy and numeracy, and are highly developed in their skills and attitudes which support the healthy and holistic development of children's minds, bodies and souls.

Underpinning professional capabilities is a philosophy which describes an adult who seeks to connect with the essence of a child – their character, their spirit, what makes them the person they actually are. Within learning environments, babies and young children deserve to be with adults who want to spend time with them, responding, supporting and challenging. If professional adults afford babies and young children's minds, bodies and souls the respect they deserve through genuine ethical accompaniments, a true 'person to person' encounter becomes a real possibility.

Within this context, the qualities of professional adults can be understood as both objective and subjective. Arnold (2010: 11) inferred this dual characteristic in her observations of children's schemas in proposing that understanding schemas and understanding emotional events in children's lives were closely linked. She accepted that schemas were 'not necessarily prompted by emotions', but drew links between 'schemas explored and emotions experienced' (2010: 21). There is little evidence to suggest that understanding schemas supports emotional development, but what is clear is that close relationships between professional adults and young children in the learning environment is vital if bodies, minds, hearts and souls are to be cared for.

Lahman's (2008: 282) portrayal of 'joyous, inter-subjective, meaningful relationships' achieved 'with thoughtful, consideration' demonstrates the complexity of developing relationships in settings between adults and children. Broadhead (2004: 131) took this further in her discussion of observation in early years settings, urging practitioners to embrace a more challenging approach to practice, in moving from simply watching children towards reflection, where 'thinking and talking about understanding their learning' is a part of practice. To understand children comes from time spent with children where there is a steady, smouldering closeness which reveals insights easily missed with a more cursory approach.

Kjorholt, Moss and Clark (2005: 176) highlighted the imperative of watching children and being part of their daily lives in that it allows for 'a deeper insight into the "unspoken words" and the complexities of different meaning-making processes'. A literal understanding of words communicating meaning here, it could be said, is rejected in favour of understanding 'unspoken' as a deeper, conceptual articulation of thinking expressed by the child through their preferred holistic medium. For as Athey (2007: 55) confirmed, 'mental representation cannot be studied directly, but it can be construed', thus emphasising the imperative of attentive observation.

Rinaldi (2005: 18) urged adults in the learning environment to question how children can be enabled 'to find the meaning of what they do, what they encounter, what they experience'. This suggested that there is a need to understand children's explicit expressions of thinking and to have an awareness of their implicit representations. Rinaldi inferred an essential reflexive element in 'questioning' which proposed the place of a personal and collective consideration of process in learning. This level of professional scrutiny, a necessary dissection of practice, enables encounters within the learning environment to be of consequence.

In the light of this, Rogoff's (1990: 204) characterisation of the adult/child relationship as one of 'intimate partners' painted a picture of cherished warmth and closeness from which there can be 'a complex sharing of ideas with people who do not require much background to be explained in order to proceed with a new thought'. Intimacy here is to be understood as comfortable familiarity, a compassionate, knowing and perceptive insight, and a considerate acceptance, where meaning is demonstrated or quietly understood.

Kinney (2005: 114) asserted that 'children not only [have] the right to be heard but [have] important things to say and tell us ... that we would learn more about them as a result of engagement'. This supports an embodied perspective of schema modified within and as a result of the relational and social.

Research acknowledges the importance of the shared and relational nature of cognitive encounters. The implication for practice is for adults to acknowledge a more egalitarian relationship with children in their learning environment, and this may require a significant shift in perception to allow for a more reciprocal, responsive accompaniment in learning.

## Quality Practice in Early Years Settings

The quality discourse is not a recent phenomenon but one with deep historical roots. This can be also seen within key influential policy documents of the recent past. Two decades ago, *Starting with Quality*, the Rumbold Report (DES 1990: 31) recommended that attempts be made to overcome 'barriers to the achievement of quality' in addressing issues which impact on the context of young children's learning experiences, including staffing, policy, parental involvement and curriculum. The Report challenged that 'all providers … know what constitutes quality provision' and, furthermore, are accountable for the standards they achieve. This theme continued in Ball's *Start Right: The Importance of Early Learning* (1994), which catalogued what constitutes high-quality provision. Most recently, the *Foundations for Quality* report (Nutbrown 2012: 2) stated that:

> Learning begins from birth, and high quality early education and care has the potential to make an important and positive impact on the learning, development and wellbeing of babies and young children, in their daily lives and the longer term.

All adults working with young children need an understanding of how children learn and develop. This includes the development of relevant and challenging learning environments, careful and respectful observation, timely intervention and a sensitivity not to interrupt. Knowledgeable practitioners and the place of collaborative partnerships in the learning environment are essential.

Athey (1990: 57) warned that 'effective means of evaluating the day-to-day educational progress of young children needs to be found. Until such formative evaluations are refined, starting points will continue to be ascertained by summative evaluation.' There is a challenge here for practitioners to have a much more sophisticated, nuanced understanding of how they may come to know the children in their care. Patiently cultivating sensitive, accepting, gentle, reciprocal relationships within the learning environment, with respectful observation, accompaniment, genuine receptiveness and a willingness to respond, demonstrates the altogether more complex comprehension specified by Athey (2007). As Athey asserted:

> Descriptions of quality must precede attempts to measure it. Measurement without description and conceptual understanding can capture only the organizational, surface or trivial features of situations. The co-ordination of trivial examples from children set within an illuminative theory provides useful explanations. It is the power to explain that makes pedagogy so important. (2007: 27)

Government documents, which related to our youngest children, testified to the ubiquitous notion of quality in terms of learning, development and care.

The *Birth to Three Matters Framework* (DfES 2003: 3) asserted that 'high-quality childcare is a crucial step towards ensuring that all children arrive at school ready to learn' and that when they do, 'high-quality care and education by practitioners' is a prerequisite for the 'effective learning and development' of young children (QCA/DfEE 2000: 12).

The *Every Child Matters Change for Children* programme (DfES 2004b) extended the implication of quality in attempting to address every facet of children's lives in its drive for improvement. The five outcomes highlighted were: being healthy, staying safe, enjoying and achieving, making a positive contribution and achieving economic well-being. These outcomes identified a co-ordinated basis from which the nature of quality and its necessary encompassing composition could be more clearly acknowledged.

The 10-year strategy for childcare (HM Treasury 2004: 1) appeared holistic from the outset, stating that it was the government's vision 'to ensure that every child gets the best start in life', including increased choice for parents in terms of childcare. Crucially, the government recognised that quality early years provision and a highly skilled early years workforce were key (DfES 2005). It is interesting to note the recurrent themes which appear when policy seeks to characterise what quality in the early years ought to look like, and the complexity of attempts to define 'quality' should be recognised.

The Department for Education and Skills' *Statutory Framework for the Early Years Foundation Stage* (2007b: 8) continued to challenge for quality in early years settings in maintaining that:

> Every child deserves the best possible start in life and support to fulfil their potential. A child's experience in the early years has a major impact on their future life chances. A secure, safe and happy childhood is important in its own right, and it provides the foundation for children to make the most of their abilities and talents as they grow up. (DfES 2007b:7)

The document went on to specify areas where provision must be of the highest quality, including: the physical environment, response to individual need, content characterised by a relevant and stimulating play-based approach to practice, appropriately qualified staff with opportunities for continuing professional development, occasions for sustained shared thinking and effective monitoring of information, including children's progress.

The Department for Education and Skills (DfES) in their evaluation of the *Neighbourhood Nurseries Initiative* (2007a: 66), highlighted key important influences on quality provision. It referred to the *Infant/Toddler Environmental Rating Scale* (Harms, Cryer and Clifford 2003) to measure different dimensions of quality. These categories included aspects of the physical environment, including space, furnishings and resources, the activities and opportunities to which the children have access, personal care routines, the extent of collaboration with parents and training opportunities for staff. In addition, the quality of the social environment was taken into account. The extent and nature of interaction, of listening and talking with children, and how children's learning was supported, were the key dimensions of quality identified in the report.

The DCSF's document, *The Children's Plan: Building Brighter Futures* (2007: 53), noted similar themes which have an impact on young children in the early years. It acknowledged the key role of parents in supporting their children's learning as 'an essential foundation for achievement'. This was affirmed in *Play Strategy* (DCSF 2008a: 5), a commitment from the Children's Plan which outlined the five principles underpinning the Children's Plan. The acceptance that parents, not government, 'bring up' children, and that there needs to be more support for parents and families to do this, was clearly articulated. *Next Steps for Early Learning and Childcare* (DCSF 2009b: 39) also conceded that 'in the early years the quality of early learning and childcare is second only to parenting in determining children's outcomes – both short and long – term'.

Nutbrown (2011: 119) acknowledged the intricate nature of quality and the difficulty in finding one single, acceptable, representative meaning. She did, however, assert that if an early childhood setting were to be deemed of good quality, 'then the extent to which the provision is meaningful and appropriate to those who use it is key'.

The concept of quality, therefore, must be understood as having complex divergent and convergent implications. Divergence here is not a conflicting dilemma but an acknowledgment of the scope which the notion of quality attempts to define. These multifarious strands intertwine and shape the provision. This tapestry must have the young child and how they are supported in their formative years, in practice and in the home environment, woven into the very centre of the pattern.

The understanding of the place of the child was audible in government documents at the time, which accentuated the imperative of attuned responsiveness. The DCSF *Next Steps for Learning* (2009a: 39) outlined the need for learning experiences 'adapted to each individual' and resonated with the earlier *Children's Plan* (DCSF 2007: 53), which championed 'tailored teaching', a concern for the individual reflected in approaches to learning with young children. Those founded on 'excellent play-based learning' (DCSF 2009a: 39) which Play England clarified as play experiences 'which follow a child's own ideas and interests, in their own way and for their own reasons' (DCSF 2008b: 11) were acknowledged as being of key significance for young children and were embedded into the current curriculum documentation used with our youngest children (DfE 2012).

Samuelsson, Sheridan and Williams (2006), in their comparative consideration of five pre-school curricula, recognised the difficulty in characterising quality as a concept and acknowledged the ambiguity of understanding, defining and meaning in the context of early childhood education and care. They speculated about the existence of a 'common core of values and objectives' and pondered the question of stakeholders, in questioning the meaning of quality, asserting that it depends purely 'on the situation and the context in which it is used and/or on the perspective of the user' (Samuelsson et al., 2006: 14).

Bennett's (2003) emphasis on the definition, realisation and evaluation of quality as 'participatory and democratic [engaging of] staff, parents and children' resonated with the stakeholder perspective of Samuelsson, Sheridan and Williams' (2006) and Bush and Phillips' (1996), yet definitive indicators of quality remain unclear. Sheridan and Schuster (2001: 109) confirmed the uncertainty of characterisation, admitting that how quality is 'concretised' and evaluated is indistinct.

Dahlberg, Moss and Pence (2007: 5) noted an historical emphasis in early childhood settings to explore quality in terms of relationship between various 'resource and organisational features', 'an essentially technical issue of expert knowledge and measurement'. However Penn (1994: 25) asserted that 'it is impossible to uphold a values-free and context-less definition of quality in early years services'. The intricate pluralism of the concept is elevated if we include the more abstract notion of values in our effort to define quality. 'Why' practitioners work with, care for and support children in certain ways influences 'how' this is achieved, which reflects Athey's (2007) challenge that practitioners should be able to eloquently articulate their professional role.

Rosen (2010) accepted the multifarious nature of quality in early childhood in affirming the place of collaboration. She understood the complex nature of quality in noting not only overt characteristics, 'the practices, and environment of the preschool' with the need for engagement in critical dialogue about ideas of 'curriculum and education', but the more significant, covert, philosophical aspect of 'purpose'. For significant adults to come together with common intent, to determine the kind of life a young child has, is an understanding which extends beyond the practical. Rosen's 'purpose' may be derived from the tenet of measurable achievement or from the more challenging perspective of accepting a personal responsibility for shaping childhoods.

The kinds of relationship forged in early childhood, therefore, is fundamental for children's well-being. Sellers, Russo, Baker and Dennison (2005) noted the significant role which professional adults have in the lives of young children and recommended the need for communication with parents. This is echoed in Nutbrown and Page's (2008: 37) later clarification that 'issues of practice in relation to children's cognition and learning development' can be considered if assured relationships between children and practitioners exist. However, the importance of secure relationships *between* the adults in a child's life, and not just between the adult and the child, is appropriate, if their influence not only on their learning and development but on their life is understood. If the tension felt by practitioners in Grace and Brandt's (2006: 250) work, in terms of their reluctance to embrace more collaborative relationships with parents, is to be overcome, then Woodhead's (1998) inference of a shared ethos which determines to foreground the child's needs and interests must be accepted. To know children more fully demands that all those who are involved in their care and education should unite to deepen this awareness.

The complexity of what constitutes quality in the early years is acknowledged in research, in practice and in key, influential policy documents of the recent past. The ubiquitous nature of the themes associated with 'quality' practice is significant in that their recurring presence recognises important features which cannot be disregarded. In this book, the place of stimulating and challenging environments, adults who cherish children and encourage their learning, and who seek to establish collaborative relationships with parents, are vital. These key elements of practice are deeply rooted in research, practice and policy of early childhood.

## Listening, Watching and Responding to Children

Conroy and Harcourt (2008: 159) confirmed the responsibility adults had in providing 'respectful and legitimate contexts' in which children's concerns can be expressed. In the context of learning environments, there is a recognition that for genuinely co-operative relationships to be realised, opportunities for deep-level involvement, enabling collaborative understandings to evolve, are essential.

Rinaldi (2006: 84), knowing the competency of children and their desire to share understandings, noted that they are proficient in attaching significance to particular happenings. This supports the place of adults who celebrate the capabilities of young children and who are able to co-operate cognitively in relationships which intensify these capacities, in mutually beneficial partnerships. Thought-provoking, nurturing and understanding relationships require attuned, synchronised, professional adults. In the context of this book, the dialogues between children and adults were antiphonal,[1] reciprocated interactions which listened to and responded to what was seen and heard.

In the light of this, and if Bronfenbrenner's (1970: 133) implication that children are 'the most "contagious" models' is accepted, then Jenkins, Franco, Dolins and Sewell's (1995) understanding of toddlers' expectations about relationships should worry adults working with young children. Haudrup (2004) suggests that the adult role in conversations with children should be reconsidered, with a repositioning of roles towards a more equitable understanding in the relationships which form: of parity, not oppression.

The Researching Effective Pedagogy in the Early Years Project (REPEY) (Siraj-Blatchford, Sylva, Muttock, Gilden and Bell 2002) revealed that positive

---

[1] A verse or song to be chanted or sung in response; a psalm, hymn or prayer sung in alternate parts. In the context of this book, we use this word to describe the exchange between adult and child in the learning environment when accompanying the child in play.

outcomes for children in terms of learning were directly linked to these adult–child interactions, which involved sustained, shared thinking. It is a process of dynamic cognitive encounters between the child and the adult, where learning is extended through co-construction. It is a partnership involving a collaboration of ideas, where there is an opportunity for 'teasing out' and unravelling, a chance to try things out, to make mistakes and wonder why, to try a new approach, something different, to talk things through while undertaking a learning journey together.

Nutbrown (2011: 34) confirmed that 'watching children and listening to children are essential to understanding their learning'. Sylva and Taylor (2006) verified this in their analysis of the importance of positive relationships between children and adults. They stated that this led to cognitive and social progress. This was also recognised in Sheridan and Schuster's (2001: 120) evaluation of pedagogical quality in early childhood education, where 'splendid interactions and sustained communication with children' were characteristics of quality.

Davis (2011) distinguished a particular kind of interaction in describing the practice of open listening:

> The philosophy and practice of open listening is not just about being nice or tolerant, and nor is it the kind of listening that looks for the repetition and affirmation of the already known ... it means opening up the ongoing possibility of coming to see life, and one's relation to it, in new and surprising ways. Open listening might begin with what is known, but it is open to the understandings one has of self and other, and the relations between them, creatively evolving into something new. Open listening opens up the possibility of new ways of knowing and new ways of being, both for those who listen and those who are listened to. (Davis 2011: 120)

The implicit ethos underpinning Davis's characterisation of 'open listening' is a dedication and devotion that speaks of personal openness. Adults are challenged to reposition themselves in their relationships with children so that an unrestricted sense of freedom of expression can evolve. Samuelsson, Sheridan and Williams (2006: 18) echoed this obligation in their assertion that 'to understand each child and his or her experience is no longer a question of just having a knowledge of child development', which is an altogether more searching obligation.

This type of convergence, which has a positive impact on young children's outcomes, in settings depicted as excellent where sustained shared thinking is encouraged, emerged as a key finding in the Effective Provision of Pre-School Education (EPPE) Project (1997–2003) (Siraj-Blatchford et al. 2003). Stephenson (2009: 139) also accepted that spending sustained periods of time with children 'might be the route to understanding a little more of the complex reality of their lives'. She recognised that if children's agency – their intention and purpose – is to be distinguished, then the unpredictable nature of the learning arena where children and adults co-exist must be acknowledged.

Sustained, shared understanding (Siraj-Blatchford et al. 2003) may therefore evolve in relationships where adults take time to notice what is important to children and are responsive to this. As a result, children come to know that what is of consequence to them is where *company in learning* begins. For the adult, this is much more than a meeting of minds; it is a witness of a professional ethical philosophy.

In this book, we highlight the importance of open, accepting and flexible pedagogical approaches when working with children, where adults reposition themselves in their relationships with children to one of learning partner, displaying a more closely shared and reciprocal quality. Though this may well be professionally challenging, it opens up the prospect of a more complementary accompaniment – a better learning 'conversation' and a deeper learning experience.

## The Child as Learner

To characterise learning as a process reveals a certain standpoint which influences how the child is viewed. In a review of early learning approaches and their impact on later development, Sylva (1994) argued that success in early education did not hinge on the transference of facts or skills from adult to child with the child viewed as a receptacle for transmitted appropriate experiences. She affirmed the significance of children as active learners and stressed the importance of process in the learning experiences of young children (and not exclusively the content to be learnt), stating that the 'learning-orientation rather than performance-orientation' was crucial (Sylva 1994: 10). A focus on content obscures the view of the child as an active learner, which Abbott (1999: 75) supported in confirming that learning is 'a deeply reflective activity' where new ideas are 'internalised and used to refine, or to change or to upgrade, earlier more naïve understandings'.

Hohmann and Weikart (2002) confirmed the importance of the child being active in the learning environment, where creativity and purpose, resourcefulness and independence, are nurtured. Wood and Attfield (1996: 80) suggested that a learning environment which included 'learning initiated by the child' rather than that which is always predetermined by the adult must be embraced. Forman and Fosnot (1982: 190) upheld the view that young children deserve rich learning environments which challenge thinking and encourage active exploration and discovery but drew a distinction between action and activity, stating that 'one can be mentally active yet physically passive'. This aligns with Nutbrown's (1999: 112) assertion that 'play rightly has a prominent place in young children's learning and development … [in fact, it] is at the centre stage of learning'. Forman and Fosnot (1982) were merely cautioning practitioners in their clarification that more meaningful learning takes place in response to a child's 'own self-generated and self-regulated questions'. It is the significantly more crucial notion of activity, the mental activity underpinning action, where children themselves reflect, question and experiment, which impacts on learning, not simply action in a physical sense.

The observations taken in the Froebel Early Education Project (Athey 2007) identified patterns of behaviour in young children aged between two and five years. The project documented developmental sequences of behaviour from acquiring early motor skills through to the thought level, as revealed in action and figurative representations. The project gave an insight into specific aspects of thinking, learning and development, and suggested how schemas may be nourished. Athey (2007: 209) affirmed that one of the most important outcomes of the project was the collaboration of parents with professionals as they all 'watched and listened with ever-increasing interest to what the children were saying and doing'. As a result, the responses made by parents and practitioners to the children were deeply significant.

Nutbrown's (2011) study also revealed the powerful nature of children's minds, in particular, the exploration of 'match' between *form* and *content* and the impact of this on the kinds of interaction which can evolve. The importance of nurturing children's thinking in cognitive encounters resonated in the work of Whalley (2001), Meade and Cubey (2008) and Arnold (2010), who identified how an informed understanding of schema theory can have a rejuvenating effect on curriculum design and adult engagement in the learning process, both in the setting and home environment.

The opportunity to develop an approach to learning and development which evolves in response to identified schemas should not be missed. A richly resourced physical environment with adults who work closely with children in a supportive, encouraging and stimulating manner is essential. However, the extent to which adults may respond to children's thinking depends on their own professional knowledge, skills and understanding, and adults need to try to understand what children *know*, what children are *focusing their attention on*, so that the intricate nature of distinct behaviour patterns which support their learning and development may be appreciated. Children's thinking, which is represented by and evident in their everyday behaviours, is easily obscured by lack of understanding.

An informed understanding of schemas gives practitioners insight into the richness of children's thinking and helps adults to be thought-provoking in a relevant way as they unite with children on their learning journeys. Piaget's (1959: 272) description of young children's thinking, where the notion of egocentric learning, rather than being a negative concept, can be viewed as an expression of the way young children are intensely interested in their own 'questions', and how they continuously strive to share their thoughts with those around them, have 'no verbal continence' (1959: 39) and seek many ways to make sense of the world around them through communication. It is a complexity which, if understood, enables a more attuned and insightful understanding of young children's thinking. This was seen in

Piaget's (1959) unravelling of the complexities of children's 'why' questions, which seek explanation, purpose or motive and justification, as young children search for sense and meaning. In so doing, practitioners do what Nutbrown (2006) calls 'rich justice' to children's capacity to think through what they encounter. Fostering the type of relationship the child has with the adult and the kinds of interchanges which characterise this are vital in the support and nurturing of thinking and learning.

## Conclusion

This chapter has highlighted the importance of the early years for children's learning and development and the significance of realising children's astonishing potential during this key phase of life. Definitions of schemas and the importance of adults coming to understand children's thinking, through their repeated patterns of behaviour, provide an underpinning for the rest of this book, which seeks to show the children it features as competent and capable, recognises the importance of practitioners who understand children's capacities and are able to attune their interventions to the thinking concerns of each child they teach.

## Reflection

Professional learning encounters between young children and their practitioners can be rich, deep and meaningful. The research indicates the importance of high-quality learning encounters in fostering children's developing minds. Readers may wish to reflect on the skills they have in understanding young children's learning modes. The following questions may be useful starting points for individual reflection or for conversations with colleagues:

- What do you already know about young children's schemas?
- What kinds of learning conversations do you have with the youngest children?
- How do you 'come to know' them and their learning?

## Further Reading

There are two books which underpin much of this book and we recommend that readers add them to their 'must read' list.

Athey, C. (2007) *Extending Thought in Young Children* (2nd edition). London: Paul Chapman Publishing.

Nutbrown, C. (2011) *Threads of Thinking: Schemas and Young Children Learning and the Role of Education* (4th edition). London: Sage.

# CHAPTER 2

# OBSERVING CHILDREN: SPOTTING SCHEMAS

In this book, the voices of all the participants, the children, parents and professionals, as well as our own, come together to paint a picture of children with intense 'colour' and rich 'depth,' picking up Verma and Mallick's (1999: 78) suggestion that the focus is 'discovery of meaning'. This book contains many observations and conversations. The observations are both written and photographic. The written observations consist of narratives made over a period of 18 months of children in the day care setting of a Children's Centre. Sitting, waiting watching, listening, photographing and talking were the means by which, over time, incidences of similar patterns of behaviour were identified in the Children's Centre and at home.

## Observation

*Patrick is working at the painting easel. He mixes a colour and makes marks on the paper starting at the top of the paper and going downwards with his paint brush. He takes the paint pots to the table and stands them on top of each other. 'I've got two paint pots' (he has two pots at the time). 'It's high, it's big.'*

**Figure 2.1** He painted lines

**Figure 2.2** Paint pot tower

**Figure 2.3** Enveloping hands

**Figure 2.4** Hands covered

*Patrick gets the paint brush and begins to cover his hand with paint.*

  Patrick: *'I paint my hand.'*

  Adult:   *'All covered in green paint.'*

  Patrick: *'It's all diggy.'* (sticky)

  Adult:   *'Sticky hands.'*

Observation generates insightful views of the subtle, complex detail of children's schematic behaviour revealed in their own actions, speech and representations. Being open to what the children may bring to the learning environment, accepting in terms of how children can enlighten us about their thinking through their behaviours, impatient for understanding, and showing a readiness, if not a conviction, to reflect on and evaluate practice in an effort to respond to what has been seen.

Lahman (2008: 286) warned that 'even the most understanding, sensitive, early childhood researcher cannot fully achieve a relationship that is not Othered between adult and child, researched and researcher, due to inherent differences. In essence the child will remain *always Othered*' (emphasis in original). Lahman's position here suggests a discrepancy of power between those doing the observing and those being observed. From the child's perspective, the 'other' may be the adult or the researcher, but in this study it was important that neither the child nor the researcher remained 'othered' for this suggests distance and not a relationship. Rather, I take the view that children are 'other-wise' (Nutbrown 2011).

The emphasis on evolving relationships with both parents and practitioners was an essential part of the study reported in this book. A 'coming to know' each other, to allow trust and openness to develop, was essential if, as Flewitt (2005: 555) stated, we are to 'demystify the research process' and, in so doing, 'empower the participants rather than making them the objects of research'.

Flewitt's (2005) view of her young participants emphasised the need to gradually draw the participants into the research, to hear their perspective, to slowly feel comfortable enough to share in the process. Hastrup (1993: 174) acknowledged the value of longitudinal immersion in the field when she stated that 'to "know" another world, one must associate with the natives, even possibly become one of them, at least temporarily'. However, it is important to identify the importance of gradualness in this process.

Gradualness in this research was characterised in different ways when considering the children, parents and practitioners – Hastrup's 'natives'. In the observation of the children, it was a vital strategy in field entry as the children were so young. The continuum of participation in the initial stages was at the extreme of non-participation. In fact, it was non-observation at first; it was simply just being there, a new person in the room – a new person in their world. To allow children to adjust to an unknown adult in their setting was imperative, but gradually perceived caution and suspicion evaporated as familiarity developed.

Christensen (2004) acknowledged this initial guarded approach in her ethnographic research with children, but maintained that its attentive nature rejects any idea of passivity. If the children were to start to feel secure and comfortable in the presence of a new, unfamiliar person (the researcher), a reserved and lengthy courtship was required. This measured approach was vital if ultimately a relationship was to develop that would allow for what Einarsdottir, Dockett and Perry (2009: 229) called opportunities 'to promote mutuality in interaction as researchers and children share focus and attention'. To be able to do this, there needed to be a level of comfortableness with each other that would enable a reciprocal, relaxed meeting to be a reality.

Brewer (2000) recognised the necessity of trust in research relationships and commented on the unhurried, measured nature of developing trust. Ethnographers need to secure a confident reliance from research participants by demonstrating a commitment to understand what is of importance to them. The requirement in the research underpinning this book was that Frances should 'edge her way' into the field by joining in appropriate, accepted setting routines, playing in a solitary way or in a parallel role, tidying up, setting activities up, supervising alongside practitioners, brushing up after snack-time and so on. While she did these things, it allowed the young children in this study to become accustomed to the presence of a new and unfamiliar adult.

Relationships with the parents, too, were characterised by a gradual and evolving approach, although face-to-face meetings with the parents were not gradual, necessarily occurring informally during pick-up or drop-off times or when a more formal arrangement was made for Frances to talk with them. The need for openness, collaboration and dialogue was a requirement from the start and was one that Fetterman (1998) asserted is built on genuine sincerity. He went on to state that this was cemented in the field by the behaviour of the researcher, who must assure the participants that the research will be carried out in an atmosphere of confidentiality, protection and respect at all times.

The observations throughout this book were made following the principle that the depth of scrutiny that they deserved was a prerequisite. In the light of what the observations had portrayed, this was a requirement if a cursory disservice to the children involved was to be avoided. The essence of this research was to come to know children's thinking more clearly. Through painstaking observations taken over many months, children became better known. These relationships between researcher and the children were forged by gradual recognition and acceptance and became ones of familiarity and ease. They were friendly acquaintances of intimate understanding.

Time spent reflecting on the observations and photographs was a way of 'coming to realise' what the moments captured in them could be revealing about a particular child's learning and development, viewed from a schematic perspective. The meticulous observations allowed an understanding of the children to evolve and strengthen; in watching, listening and being with them, details were revealed.

## Stories from Home

**Figure 2.5** Stick into hole

**Figure 2.6** Finger into hole

LeCompte (2002) was aware of the importance of adopting a variety of strategies in the research process when it came to understanding the views of participants. In the desire to draw in these different voices, and to capture aspects of the child's behaviour at home with the parents, 'Stories from Home' were used. These 'Stories from Home' were intended to encourage parents to be part of the research process, to know that their contribution was wanted and valued. The 'Stories from Home' were designed as a tool for conversation which, subsequently, parents could take to the home environment and reflect upon as they observed their child. Visual and written prompts included in the 'Stories from Home' were designed to alleviate possible anxiety about wondering what the study might be seeking to do and as a support in terms of how to look at and respond to what their child may be doing in the home environment in a different way.

Swanson, Raab and Dunst's (2011: 66) research on early childhood intervention and capacity-building, which was intended to promote parents' or other caregivers' skills, abilities and confidence to provide children with development-enhancing learning opportunities, resonates with this study. Working with parents to develop their knowledge of schemas through conversation and interpretation of observations and images together, helped Frances to secure a different understanding of their child's behaviour and facilitate a changed involvement in their play. Swanson et al. (2011) noted that 'capacity-building intervention practices strengthened families' abilities to provide their children with interest-based everyday natural learning opportunities and had caregiver competency-enhancing effects (2011: 5). Swanson et al.'s description of an 'interest-based' response is significant in this book as the interests which the children reveal are based in thought. For parents to be able to respond to their child's thinking patterns is significant and appropriately meaningful for the child.

Nutbrown (2011: 17) suggested that looking at children's behaviour from a schematic perspective gives 'a focus to observational details which might otherwise become a list of disconnected events'. In the light of this, the study reported in this book used photography to capture images of children immersed in playful activities, where strands of repeating patterns of behaviour caught 'on film' could be drawn together to enrich the depiction of their schematic stories. The detail which visual images offer can transcend the narrative and provide a more holistic illustration, which was essential in this research in its attempt to capture children's learning journeys in a respectful way.

The photographs in this book can sometimes stir an emotional connection with the viewer, provoking an intensity and depth that may penetrate the surface view and suggest, even reveal, personal characteristics of the viewed. This requires a genuine engagement with the visual image, a recognition of its worth as a distinct medium in the research process, and is demanding of the viewer in terms of a responsibility to gaze and not just glance.

However, Blaikie (2001) argued that photographs could not stand alone without explanatory narrative as there was opportunity for misunderstanding to emerge. Riley and Manias (2003: 3) confirmed this in their study, suggesting that the inclusion of the visual image in research 'relies upon other cognitive and sensory faculties for interpretation'. Stanczak (2007: 11) acknowledged that 'the meaning of images resides most significantly in the ways that participants interpret those images, rather than as some inherent property of the images themselves'. Stanczak appears to support Athey and Nutbrown's inference that knowledge (in this case of schemas) may influence the viewer's perspective of the image. How photographs are interpreted and their meaning is understood are subjective in that they are dependent on the viewer rather than the viewed. Photographs are pauses in action; they hold a moment which has gone but can still be seen. They recall a tiny instant in time which can be re-viewed, although the way viewers 'see' is variable, particularly if Flewitt's (2005) suggestion in using photographs – that all participants should have the opportunity to view and comment on them – is taken into account. In the case of the photos in this book, parents, children, practitioners (and us as authors) inevitably saw the images from their own perspectives and brought their own understanding to the images. It was not until the conversations with parents about the images and their schematic inferences that new understandings about what was depicted could be seen.

Denzin's (1997: 44) notion of 'situatedness' took many forms in this research. The visual representation of a child's lived experience, captured in a setting, could be simply described as geographically situated. The visual portrayals in this research, which glanced at a moment now passed, were more of an insight into the theoretical situatedness of the researcher, in the conscious choice to represent certain seen experiences, which evidenced existing, or new understandings.

The unique social situatedness of this study, which sought an understanding of activities and social interactions of children, parents and practitioners in a day care setting, employed the visual image as part of the representation. This provided a more complete illustration of the thinking and learning experiences of the child and their interactions.

## Conversations over Photographs

*Tommy's mum said that he was 'a very quick and clever boy', that he had 'amazed her with his learning capabilities and speed'.*

*Patrick's mum shared that 'he had always been a big climber. Cots, washing machines, anything that looks like a "step higher"'. She also said that 'he had always climbed into things as well', that she would 'often find him sat in a toy box or a plastic basket that we kept cars in'.*

To draw the children, parents and practitioners into the research, to actively enable their voices to be heard, was vital in coming to understand the complexities of the observations captured, from the perspectives of all those involved.

Cruickshank and Mason (2003: 21) acknowledged that photographs 'are not capable of talking for themselves, the information has to be teased out of them, interpreted and de-coded'. The photographs in this book did indeed speak for themselves in representing specific moments in time, but what they 'said' was significantly more meaningful when contextualised by the interpreters and de-coders, those doing the teasing out, specifically, the parents, children and the researcher.

Using photographs with parents acknowledged the strength of this visual medium as a powerful multilayered tool for discussion. The photographs provided a catalyst for conversation where the one-dimensional, visual-only nature of photographs, which Dicks, Soyinka and Coffey (2006) conceded, became part of a multifaceted understanding. In the study underpinning this book, the photographs, narratives, conversations and comments meant more when used together. They had a synergy, with each contributing their significant worth to provide a more vivid picture of the children's *forms of thought*.

Although the children did not take the photographs themselves, they were still authoritative when considering the visual images and did so with adult support. During the sharing, they were able to enjoy them and communicate meaning where they felt able and where they wished to do so. In weaving together the interpretations from the children, parents and practitioners, a more eloquent and holistic telling of the child's thinking and learning story is achieved.

## Conclusion

Building relationships with children through sustained observations and responding to natural behaviour in familiar situations, where children were not removed from known environments or expected to participate in any unusual, unexpected or contrived activities based on a research agenda rather than that of the child, was essential in this study. To more fully portray what children were saying about their thinking and learning, depicted when they played, photographs were taken to enrich the narratives and conversations, and more fully convey the children's stories.

The need to understand young children's *forms of thinking* more clearly is the starting point for this book. How to come to know children more deeply so that their thinking concerns become visible is a key pursuit. This means putting the child and their concerns at the centre of the process at all times.

In the next part of the book, we focus on Henry and his schemas. Using Athey's (2007) schematic theory, observations and photographs of Henry are presented. Over an 18-month period, seven children under 3 years of age were observed in a day care setting. What children were 'saying' about their thinking, learning and development when they played was observed.

## Reflection

This chapter has focused on different ways of watching young children so as to learn about the schematic behaviours that underpin and stimulate their learning. It has also focused on ways of using photographs to gain further insights into what children are doing and to share with parents. The sharing of 'stories from home' means that parents have an opportunity to tell practitioners what they know about their children's schematic behaviours and the learning moments they have identified as significant.

Practitioners might wish to consider the following questions:

- Are the observations I make of young children sufficiently 'open and deep' and attuned to children's concerns so as to be meaningful in developing real pedagogical understanding?

- What processes are in place to share accounts of children's learning with parents and to hear parents' accounts of their children's schematic behaviour and their learning?

## Further Reading

Two useful readings on involving young children in research, making observations and using photographs to observe and interpret children's learning are:

Flewitt, R. (2005) Conducting research with young children: some ethical considerations. *Early Child Development and Care*, 175(6): 553–565.

Lahman, M.K.E. (2008) Always Othered: ethical research with children. *Journal of Early Childhood Research*, 6(3): 281–300.

# PART 2
# HOW DO CHILDREN UNDER THREE PURSUE THEIR SCHEMAS? 'ALL ABOUT HENRY'

This middle section of the book provides a detailed account of the schemas of one child, Henry, over two years in his nursery setting. It includes rich accounts of him pursuing his schemas and his developing interests and language. This is an illustration of what we mean by 'making close observations' and also indicates how observations of schemas can usefully aid a range of developmental aspects and support implementation of curriculum and assessment policy on children under three.

*Note*: Frances Atherton made the observations of the children and these chapters are therefore written in her own voice. The 'I' refers to Frances, throughout.

# PART 2

# HOW DO CHILDREN UNDER THREE PURSUE THEIR SCHEMAS? ALL ABOUT HENRY

# CHAPTER 3

# HENRY'S CONTAINING AND ENVELOPING SCHEMA

Henry was 20 months old. He lived with his mum and dad and attended the day care setting of a Children's Centre on a sessional basis. His nana, mum and dad took it in turns to bring him to the setting and collect him. Henry was an only child at this time but his mum was having another baby. He appeared contented, always eager to continue the busyness of his day on his arrival at the setting. He tried things out and appeared to consider and ponder as he went about his explorations. He was purposeful in his work, confident and determined. As I came to know Henry through observations, underlying patterns in his thinking emerged.

Henry maintained his industrious endeavours in the day care setting as he played with the things around him. Henry's (1 year 10 months) 'containing and enveloping' behaviour was evidenced by a series of motor level actions, including: putting spoons inside cups, knives inside teapots, spades and scoops in buckets, raisins into milk, stones into bottles, mixed objects (elephant, horse and policeman) inside the stable together, all represented his prevailing *form of thinking*. He also regularly placed assorted objects (sand, soil, stones, dry pasta, crayons, toy animals, Lego, chalks) into a variety of containers and enclosed himself within or underneath a range of items. All of these actions were his chosen, purposeful explorations.

Henry's actions were accompanied with attuned speech, when appropriate, which was compatible with his *form of thinking* and not directly focused on the substance of his play. The adult working with Henry suggested possibilities including: 'Can your hand fit inside the little green cup?', 'You've covered your hands with sand, I can't see them', 'We can tidy up all the spades into one bucket, will they fit?', 'Do you need a big spade to fill the big bucket?', 'I'm going to use the little spoon to fill the big yellow bucket, I think it will take me a long time'.

**36** UNDERSTANDING SCHEMAS AND YOUNG CHILDREN

Figure 3.1　Chalks and paper inside the book box

Figure 3.2　Filling the book box, but not with books

Figure 3.3　Spoons and knives inside teapots and cups

Figure 3.4　Spade into bucket

Figure 3.5　Scoops and spades inside a bucket

Figure 3.6　Henry's hand inside the green cup

The accompanying narratives used by the adult were not ones of holiday trips to the seaside, rides on donkeys, paddling, arm bands, rock or sandcastles. Henry's accomplice sought a conceptual complement, intended to provide *language of form*. To talk genuinely with children when they play demands a familiarity which can induce recall and enable relaxed probing. This, entwined fundamentally with *language of form*, can embed conceptual understanding in a significant and relevant way for the child.

Bruner's (1999: 12) thorough rejection of children's minds as 'tabula rasa, a blank slate ... a passive receptacle waiting to be filled' is appropriate here in that an adult with a prospective view sees an active, thinking child and endeavours to nurture, not in a cushioning, comforting way but through support which bolsters and empowers. Kellmer Pringle (1986: 36) recognised that the child 'is enabled through mutually rewarding relationships, first with his mother and then with others who become significant to him'. Kellmer Pringle's notion that things 'become significant' can be seen as almost cautionary in suggesting that the adult role when working with young children can be an inconsequential, tepid and superficial one and therefore insignificant in terms of intervention. The journey towards significance is one some may not choose to set out upon, or indeed recognise the need for. The destination of conceptual reciprocation is never reached.

To become Kellmer Pringle's 'significant adult' a person needs to be acutely aware of the nuances of the soul in their presence. It is not someone who disrupts children's thoughts and actions with clumsy, intrusive, mis-matched comments. In order to offer a fitting response to children's thinking, actions and talk, the adult, in turn, accepts Bruner's (1999: 19) characterisation of the child 'as an active, intentional being', with whom adults can construct and negotiate knowledge. The adult is aware of Donaldson's (1978) determination for relevance in the learning environment. It is a challenging responsibility, which those working with young children should not refuse for, as Winnicott (1971: 65) revealed:

> It is creative apperception more than anything else that makes the individual feel that life is worth living. Contrasted with this is a relationship to external reality which is one of compliance, the world and its details being recognized but only as something to be fitted in with or demanding adaptation. Compliance carries with it a sense of futility for the individual and is associated with the idea that nothing matters and that life is not worth living.

For Henry, there should be no understanding of compliance or obedience in terms of his thinking and his significant adults should not be expecting acquiescence. This is not a mandate for chaos but a championing of individuality, where children do not feel thwarted by adults who may appear to them to misunderstand. Significant adults are those who do

**Figure 3.7** Elephant, horse and policeman inside the stable

**Figure 3.8** Inside the soft play den

**Figure 3.9** Blocks inside the truck

not see children's efforts as 'futile', but as powerful expressions of vigorous minds.

Henry's 'significant adult' is able to recognise his exploration of insideness with his own body and with a variety of environmental content. In the observation of his play with the zoo animals, he appeared not to want to play with them as one might conventionally expect, for example, making roaring noises with the lions, poking giraffes' heads into tree tops or swinging monkeys around, but took an elephant and put it inside the farm stable alongside a horse and policeman (Figure 3.7). It could have been anything in the stable. The objects were not of consequence, they were just conveniently to hand. The essential aspect seemed to be that they *could be contained*.

These motor level actions helped deepen Henry's understanding of insideness and provided a valuable practical foundation upon which to build later symbolic representations. They intensified his grasp of higher order concepts which he came to know in these playful occupations.

## Containing and Enveloping Schema: Symbolic Representation

Henry (age 1.11) was playing with the mobile people, furniture and cars. He tried to put the doll inside the car.

Henry: In car.

Adult: She's inside the car. [*The doll falls on the floor.*]

Adult: Oh no, she's fallen out.

Henry put the doll back inside the Mobilo car.

Donaldson (1978) warns that when children become 'learners at school' the freedom and spontaneity to pursue what is important to them, to focus attention on particular, personalised interests and express these in their own precise ways, can often be lost:

**Figure 3.10** Doll inside the Mobilo car

> The child's attention is drawn to something that interests him and expresses it in whatever form comes most readily to him. He is never required, when he is himself producing language, to go counter to his own preferred reading of the situation – to the way in which he himself spontaneously sees it. But this is no longer necessarily true … when he becomes a learner at school. (Donaldson 1978: 74)

Henry's interest and attention appeared to be focused on ensuring that the doll was inside the car (Figure 3.10) as he persisted with this action and, upon completion, attached appropriate talk 'in car'. Although it could not be assumed that he then occupied the position of Donaldson's 'listener', his seeming 'preferred reading of the situation' – that of exploring the inside-ness of the car – was recognised by the familiar adult who maintained the *thread of thought* with corresponding remarks. The encounter was harmonious and did not 'counter' Henry's apparent schematic pursuit with tactless, out-of-place comments which could deflect from important thinking.

It's snack time but Henry (2.1) was working and far too busy to stop to eat.

Henry: Hello.

Adult: Would you like some water or milk?

Henry: Milk [*pointing to the jug*].

Henry gazed into his cup and started dropping the raisins inside one at a time. After a few went in, he tipped the bowlful of raisins into the cup of milk.

Adult: Your cup is full of raisins now. Why don't you tip them back out so you can have more milk?

**Figure 3.11**  Henry gazed into his milk

**Figure 3.12**  Picking up raisins, one by one

**Figure 3.13**  In they go, all at once

**Figure 3.14**  The last raisin can fit in

**Figure 3.15**  Henry empties out the milk and raisins

When the last raisin had dropped inside the cup, Henry tipped the milk into the bowl and the raisins onto the table. He then picked the raisins out of the bowl and started to drop them inside the empty cup.

Henry got some more milk and started to drop the raisins into the new milk.

Adult: Why don't you drink your milk now and eat your raisins? You must be hungry.

Henry: I'm finished [*and drinks his milk*].

Through observation, Donaldson (1978: 18) recognised that 'each participant needs to try to understand what the other knows already, does not know, needs to know for his purposes, wants to know for his pleasure ...' for a conversation to go smoothly. Henry did initiate conversation with a greeting but did not talk about what he was doing. The notion of conversation here could be seen in a more encompassing sense, that of encounter between adult and child. Henry's thinking, demonstrated in his actions, is understood by the familiar adult who redefined Donaldson's definition of smooth conversation and took her turn responding to what was seen and not heard. The attuned suggestions seemed to provoke unspoken thoughts which Henry seemed to make apparent. His part in the 'conversation' was dynamic and non-verbal.

In interpreting children's behaviour schematically, Athey (2007: 144) identified a 'satisfactory' perspective, in that a 'wide range of behaviours' are embraced and 'interpretations are positive ... instead of attributing naughtiness'. Although the raisins and milk episode may appear to be an inconvenient and roguish exploit, from a schematic perspective Henry could be seen engrossed in a purposeful and focused enterprise. Although undesirable in the reality of practice, to be conscious of Henry's calculated deliberations was liberating in terms of response. However, Henry's conscious ponderings must be acknowledged in a measured and respectful way. In this instance, a sensitive curtailment was required, with alternatives for enclosure and emptying offered.

A proposal, a suggestion to lead Henry towards other environmental possibilities to continue his conceptual investigations, was necessary. More acceptable, yet equally stimulating possibilities were a must for, as Winnicott (1971: 64) stipulated, 'to afford opportunity for creative impulses, motor and sensory, are the stuff of playing and on this basis is built the whole of man's experiential existence'. Parker-Rees (1999) recognised the power and place of playfulness. Winnicott's 'creative impulse', it could be said, was not play as *activity* but a significantly more intricate understanding of self, a way of being. Through their own epistemic explorations, children may challenge adult perceptions of appropriateness, yet Parker-Rees (1999: 64) asserted that this allows for 'richer, more subtle and more complicated interpretations'.

Forman's (1994) consideration of the physical properties of various media and how these properties may influence thought is resonant here. He acknowledged that different media have different properties that mean some concepts are more effortlessly conveyed than others. How easily children can transform media is an 'affordance' (Forman 1994). Forman used the example of the twisting property of clay which children could use, for example, to represent anguish. He went on to state that 'an affordance is the relationship between the transformable properties of a medium and the child's desire to use that property to make symbols'. Henry was using the milk and raisins to explore insideness. 'Affordance' in the milk and raisins example allowed Henry to represent his conceptual thought. He was not transforming the physical *properties* of the media, he was transforming their *use*.

Forman (1994: 38) went on to discuss the inevitable transformative limitations of the properties of media, which, he asserted, leads children to 'develop a biased perspective to their work' in that the bias is in what the medium enables children to express. Forman viewed this as a strength because it allows children 'to view the world from an unusual perspective'.

Athey (2007: 200) acknowledged that 'the content of representation' appeared to have varying degrees of potential in terms of matching a child's existing schema. Athey's 'content' and 'match' were arguably Forman's 'media' and 'affordance' in that a child could be sensitised to the potential of specific aspects of the environment, be aware of certain possibilities and attracted to the prospect of what could be. Nutbrown (2006: 35) verified that 'in each apparently unconnected activity [children] sometimes find (and understand) important cognitive links'. Henry appeared to recognise the affordance of raisins and milk. Although Henry's use of the milk and raisins appeared not to be symbolic, his desire to use these to represent his thinking, his schematic concern, was evident.

Forman (1994) proposed that 'each affordance provokes a special orientation to the problem to be solved'. To *provoke* is to *rouse*, which has dynamic connotations for practitioners and children. How practitioners tender environments of suggestion to children and respond conceptually within this is a concern, as is how children feel *roused* within environments to follow their own cognitive significances. For practitioners, the capability, confidence and willingness to sustain children's own concerns and for children to encounter this in their everyday business is bolstered by Rinaldi (1994: 50), who proposed that 'it is not so much about *how* to teach children, but to ask ourselves *what* and *how* children can learn *from* a certain situation'. The perspective of constructivism is significant here as it moves away from transmission towards negotiation.

The requirement for adults to relinquish a level of control within the learning environment can be an unwelcome challenge. There is not advocacy to surrender responsibility but, more significantly, the suggestion to accept a different kind of responsibility. An obligation to acknowledge the notion of control can be said to be a characteristic of responsibility, necessarily understood and essentially embraced.

Winnicott (1971: 57) described an encounter between therapist and patient and warned that 'the patient's creativity can be only too easily stolen by a therapist who knows too much.' A cautionary thought indeed when seen in the light of the practitioner/child relationship in an early years setting.

## Containing and Enveloping Schema: Observations

Henry (2.5) tried to post carrots through the gap in the side of the toy oven (Figure 3.16). It would not fit through the gap as he tried the fat end of the carrot. He turned the carrot around and pushed the thin end of the carrot through the gap. The whole carrot fitted through the gap and dropped inside the oven.

Through a functional dependency relationship, Henry appeared to understand that in order for the carrot to fit through the gap, he needed to rotate it around to fit the thinner end in first. He identified a mathematical problem involving shape and space and invented a solution. Henry could be seen using developing mathematical ideas to solve practical problems (DfE 2012). He appeared to be exploring variation in size (one end of the carrot is fat and one end is thin). Henry was not using language here to accompany his actions and therefore it could not be assumed that he was thinking about comparative size – that 'this end of the carrot is fatter than that end'. It must be observed as an exploration of 'will this go in here?'

**Figure 3.16** **Posting carrots**

In this observation, Henry could be seen trying to fit and enclose objects. Through these explorations, Henry was furthering his understanding of a range of concepts, including: width (the carrot will only fit through the gap in the oven lengthways and not sideways), length (the carrot increases in thickness along its length), trajectory (the carrot will slide through the gap starting with the thin end first), orientation (the carrot will only fit through the gap if I turn it around and put the thin end in first). This short observation indicates a busyness of thought upon which increasingly complex concepts could be built.

Henry (2.9) was playing at the water trough. He submerged the bottle to fill it with water. He dropped a lolly stick inside the bottle.

Adult: What did you do with the stick?

Henry: Put it inside the bottle.

Henry: I putting this [*holds up bottle with water*] into there [*points to watering can*] to do that [*tips out water from the watering can*].

Henry: Put some water in the kettle. Make a cup of tea.

Adult: The kettle's full.

Henry again dropped a long object inside a container and this time accompanied his actions with language. Henry's intentions were made clear as he represented his *form of thought* in action and speech. Henry realised that in order for the watering can to be able to be tipped out, water from his bottle needed to be poured in.

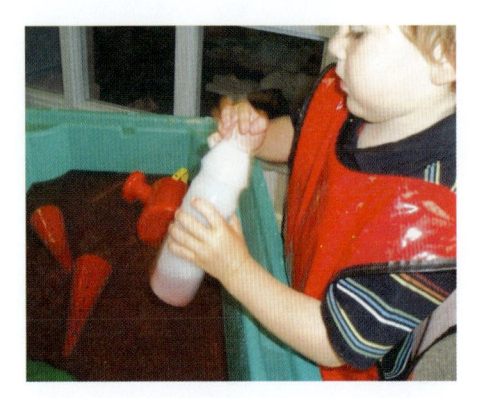

**Figure 3.17** Dropping sticks inside the bottle

He was able to co-ordinate sentences in sequence about cause and effect but could not yet be described, on this evidence, as a conserver. In this observation, through a functional dependency relationship, Henry realised that he must fill the watering can in order for it to work. However, Athey's (1990: 70) clarification that functional dependency relationships 'immediately precede conservation' must be acknowledged.

In this observation, Henry revealed his schematic explorations in several ways. His selection of the things around him (watering can, bottle, kettle), his actions (stick inside bottle, tipping out, pouring in) and his speech (inside, into there, full) suggested a schema of 'containing and enveloping'. The opportunity for Henry to reveal his ability as a conserver, however, was missed.

If Henry was a conserver, Piaget and Inhelder (1969: 98) would expect him to understand particular concepts. When Henry was playing at the water trough, pouring water from the bottle to the watering can and back again, he was experimenting, at a motor level, with important concepts, as summarised in Table 3.1.

Table 3.1 Henry and the water trough

| Concept | An interpretation of what Henry might have been thinking |
| --- | --- |
| Simple or additive identities | 'It is the same water ... nothing has been taken away or added.' |
| Reversibility by inversion | 'I can pour the water from this watering can back into the bottle where it was before.' |
| Compensation or reversibility by reciprocal relationship | 'The water is lower in the watering can and the bottle is wider but it's the same amount.' |

## A Moment's Speculation...

Would Henry have been restricted to a discussion of 'gross quantity, quantification restricted to the immediate perceptual relationship' (Piaget 1952a: 11) or would he have been able to acknowledge the unchanged quantity of water yet account for the lower level in the watering can as a result of its greater width compared with the bottle? This, as Piaget and Inhelder (1969: 99) clarified, was a feature of conservation where 'operatory level reactions were based on identity or reversibility by inversion or reciprocity'.

If Henry had been unable to reason that, irrespective of the change in water level in the can, the quantity remained the same as before (when it was in the bottle), it would be evidence of Piaget's (1952a: 12) characterisation of young children's inability to decentre. Piaget asserted that children were unable 'to reckon simultaneously with the height and cross-section of the liquids to compare'. Donaldson's (1978: 62) discussion clarified Piaget's argument that young children concentrate 'on one feature of the immediate situation and neglect others ... failing to think back to how things were before'. Piaget and Inhelder (1969) confirmed that reversibility in thinking was one of clearest indications of a child having reached the stage of concrete operations.

As a result, could Henry have been enabled to travel more freely between different points of view? Could a more searching intervention during the water trough play have yielded a deeper understanding of Henry's level of thought? Piaget (1959: 286) confirmed that it is in both the sense of 'inter-individual co-operation and of intra-individual co-ordination that this system of operations constitutes a true instrument for adjustment, which will set the individual free from his initial ego-centrism.' This is an acknowledgement for the place of both individual and social construction of knowledge, where children interact with their physical environment and the people within. This is not about children simply accumulating more knowledge but, in a metacognitive sense, it is a coming to know different ways of thinking, different perspectives of thought.

Donaldson's (1978: 83) notion of 'disembedded thinking' was resonant here and was supportive of Piaget's consideration of reciprocal and solitary processes. Although she stated that 'this calls for the ability to stand back from life', she acknowledged that when this is accompanied with action, greater treasures were revealed. Here, action arguably encompassed both physical acts and relational encounters.

Nutbrown (2006: 133) reminded us that 'it is only when practitioners seek to understand the meanings behind what they have seen that the real worth of observational practices [is] realised.' The distinctiveness and individuality of Henry has been revealed by Henry himself. His unique character peeped out from the sand, water, blocks, raisins, milk. These mundane objects were employed in his own significant cognitive adventures. As Winnicott (1971: 54) has stated, it is 'in playing and only in playing that the individual child is able to be creative and to use the whole personality, and it is only in being creative that the individual discovers the self'.

To question how Henry's creativity had been liberated and his sense of 'self' and 'personal identity' inculcated in the everyday encounters captured here, through observation, was important. It should be a dynamic and motivating accountability. Within the observations, there was an honesty in what Henry described. He was working from the heart and head, faithful that his openness and spontaneity was met with cherished acceptance and nurturing approval. Learning environments are places where children are vulnerable to suppression and control. Therefore, practitioners who delight in children for the astonishingly capable individuals they actually are, are in a powerfully prospective position from which to journey in learning.

## Reflection

Think about the children in your setting and reflect on the following questions:

- Do any seem to show repeated patterns of behaviour like Henry? How might staff come to know individual children's schematic pursuits?
- How do staff share their knowledge and understanding of individual children's endeavours?
- To what extent does knowledge and understanding of children's schema inform planning for learning?
- What additional experiences can be provided to support children's containing and enveloping schema?

Now think about Henry's actions with the raisins and milk:

- To what extent does understanding a child's particular thinking concerns inform your intervention?
- How might knowledge of a child's containing and enveloping schema influence approaches to pedagogy?

## Further Reading

Arnold, C. (2003) *Observing Harry*. Buckingham: Open University Press.
Athey, C. (2007) *Extending Thought in Young Children* (2nd edition). London: Paul Chapman Publishing.
Meade, A. and Cubey, P. (2008) *Thinking Children: Learning about Schemas* (2nd edition). Wellington: New Zealand Council for Educational Research and Institute for Early Childhood Studies, Wellington College of Education/Victoria University of Wellington.

A further account of a child's containing and enveloping schemas can be found in:
Nutbrown, C. (2011) Jeanette: containing and enveloping schemas, pages 61–68 in *Threads of Thinking: Schemas and Young Children Learning and the Role of Early Education* (4th edition). London: Sage.

# CHAPTER 4

# HENRY'S BACK AND FORTH SCHEMA

## Back and Forth Schema: Motor Level

Henry continued in his playful endeavours at the day care setting. As I came to know him more, through sustained observations, further underlying patterns in his thinking appeared. Henry (1.11) pushed a variety of wheeled toys along the floor – fire engines, trucks, trains, diggers and cars – and in so doing he was furthering his exploration of horizontal movement.

In the play house he went back and forth to the cupboard collecting knives, spoons, teapots, forks and cups, and stacked them on the table. Henry displaced a wide range of objects, toy animals, soft shapes and small wooden blocks and made piles with them on completing a particular 'back and forth' trajectory. His main concern was that he could move them, and they could be heaped, lined up and joined together. He displayed a 'transporting' schema.

Figure 4.1  Objects along the floor

Figure 4.2  Beads around the frame

**Figure 4.3** Beater along the glockenspiel

**Figure 4.4** Blocks banged together

**Figure 4.5** Rolling the soft play cylinder

Inhelder and Piaget's (1964: 18) definition of 'graphic collection', where 'the spatial arrangement of the elements to be classified plays an essential part in the eyes of the subject', can be seen in Henry's repeated actions. He was not accumulating objects based on similarity, yet his heaps and bundles could be recognised as the precursor to later classification. As he pursued his dynamic back and forth schema, Henry was coming to know the 'intensive' properties of objects in that shared attributes were realised.

The essential trait of the mounds Henry makes is what Athey (2007: 125) calls 'transportability': the objects are able to be collected, moved and bunched together. This 'primitive collection' contained items which to Henry are clearly related in that they are moveable and, what's more, that *Henry* could move them.

Henry selected objects from the environment which allowed him to pursue his fascination with the horizontal, including the glockenspiel, pizza cutter, frame with beads and the soft play cylinders.

He used content to pursue his *form of thinking*. For example, in bringing the red blocks together he connected them through dynamic 'back and forth' trajectory movements.

Henry immersed himself in important investigations and enquiries. While it is inappropriate to 'put words in Henry's mouth', it seemed that, as he pursued his schema, he contemplated objects in the environment as if asking 'What is this and what can I do with it?' With the soft play cylinder, Henry discovered that 'this thing moves if I touch it'. He could have been thinking, 'I wonder what would happen if I give it a push?', 'If I give it a big push, it might roll right over there'.

In the absence of speech, it would be an erroneous characterisation of Henry's thinking. Athey (1990: 68) considered this in her discussion of behaviours classified at motor level as those which 'do not appear to have representational significance'. Her caveat of 'even though they may have' was clarified in later work, which specified that 'intention and meaning were clearer when utterances were made in context' (Athey 2007: 169).

In the outside environment, Henry pushed himself along on wheeled toys and pointed his finger at vans when they are parked where he could see them. He kicked and rolled objects and ran after them, repeating the process.

Henry spent time lining objects up, cars, animals and trains. The dynamic aspect of lining up objects could easily be missed on viewing the completed static configuration. The dynamism is seen in the child making connections involving trajectory behaviour: an exploration of beginning and end, start and finish, an adding to, a representation which required movement to compose. Through these trajectory behaviours, an understanding of higher order concepts such as length, distance, connection and addition germinates.

Scrutinising children's actions can reveal early conceptual tussles. The child may invite or hope for participation or intervention from an understanding, compliant partner; compliance not in a submissive context, but as a respectful response to the thinking concerns of the child. An adult who may unknowingly resist, conflict or disturb this may pass by or, worse, interrupt a child's persistent explorations.

**Figure 4.6** Kicking objects along the floor

**Figure 4.7** Lining up objects

**Figure 4.8** Cars, trains, blocks, made longer

## Back and Forth Schema: Symbolic Representation

**Figure 4.9** Pushing cars along

**Figure 4.10** Rolling cars along in the paint

Henry (1.10) held up a train and named it 'tain' and a tractor 'ta te'. He was using language to label the things he was using. He held up a toy car and said 'brumbrum', he pushed a fire engine and shouted 'nee nor nee nor'. Henry's imitative vocalisation 'nee nor nee nor' was the differentiated signifier for the signified something (the fire engine). This 'verbal evocation of events not occurring at the time' was a behaviour characteristic of the semiotic function, which Piaget and Ingelder (1969: 54) suggested constituted the beginning of representation.

He picked up a lorry and says 'I go orry' (I've got a lorry) and a car, 'I go ca' (I've got a car). Later, Henry (2.0) picked up different sizes of cars, 'a big car', 'a little car', 'a big bus'. He could also be said to be experimenting with higher order concepts of absolute size in referring to cars which were 'big' and 'little' with references to comparative size not yet present.

It is interesting to note that Henry was discriminating in his use of content in revealing the relationship between *form of thought* and environmental content to be assimilated. His fascination with horizontal movement sensitised his selection, seen in his favouring of cars, trucks, vans, lorries and so on, and in his actions, which were accompanied with appropriate schematic-related speech.

Henry (2.7) brushed paint across the paper. He said to the adult 'put car in', 'I've got one car'. He pushed the car along the paper in the paint.

The utterances – 'brumbrum', 'I go orry', 'I go ca' – suggest that Henry's talk is Piaget's (1959: 17) speech as monologue, intended to 'accompany, to reinforce, or to supplement action' but not as a social tool. However, the fact that Henry held up his train and tractor before naming them and asserted 'I go orry', 'I go ca' suggested a transition in the purpose of his language, where Henry actually wanted the adult to *listen*. He appeared to be attempting to engage the adult, to tell her something, to actually 'make his hearer listen', which Piaget (1959: 20) distinguished as a characteristic of socialised speech, 'adapted information'. The aim of which was to make the hearer aware of his thinking.

Henry's command 'put car in' when he played with the cars and paint was socialised speech made explicit in that there was a definite attempt, a determination to draw the adult into the activity. Henry's use of side-to-side movements with the paint brush was a further physical exploration of a dynamic back and forth schema.

## Back and Forth Schema: Functional Dependency Relationships

When Henry (1.11) was playing with the police car and blocks, he shouted 'beep beep' and moved blocks out of the car's way, realising that in order for the police car to maintain its trajectory along the block road, the obstruction needed to be moved.

Henry (2.0) was outside on the bikes, pushing himself along, getting on and off different-sized bikes.

He walked to the car and said 'stuck'.

**Figure 4.11** 'Beep beep'

Adult: I'll pull the car out and move the big bike out of the way.

Henry: Big scooter, big car.

Adult: What are you riding, Henry?

Henry: Red bike.

Henry got off the red bike, picked up a ball and kicked it.

Adult: The ball's rolled away.

Henry got on a scooter and rode off.

The adult accompanied Henry's dynamic back and forth schema with

**Figure 4.12** The big bike

appropriate language (car, bike, riding, pull, move, rolled away). She accompanied his schematic action (riding the bikes, kicking the ball) with language which linked meaning and *form of thought*. The opportunity for this kind of appropriate connection must not be missed for, as Piaget and Inhelder

(1969: 86) clarified, when referring to symbolic functioning 'it detaches thought from action'. Athey (1990: 72) confirmed this in highlighting that 'adult speech, meaningfully linked with a child's actions, helps "action" to become symbolic'.

This observation suggested a cognitive competence in terms of Henry's use of speech and in his understanding of cause-and-effect relationships. In saying 'stuck', Henry was informing the adult present of his predicament, which required assistance in order for him to continue his actions. This attempt to influence the adult is a characteristic of Piaget's (1959: 10) socialised speech in seeking to elicit a response. By attracting the adult's attention by shouting 'stuck', Henry demonstrated an understanding of functional dependency relationships: in order for him to use the car, it would have to be pulled out and the big bike moved, i.e. his use of the car was functionally dependent on obstacles being moved out of the way.

Henry, again through a functional dependency relationship, realised that when he crashed his blue car into the pram he has to back up in order to continue on a forward trajectory. As he pushed himself along, his accompanying schematic speech, 'crash', 'ready, steady', 'faster, faster' appeared essentially egocentric; however, when he shouted 'watch', conversation was initiated. The richness of Henry's early experiences emerged as he represented language heard before appropriately in his play. The fruits of his past encounters were seen here in his present endeavours.

**Figure 4.13** Henry pushed himself along

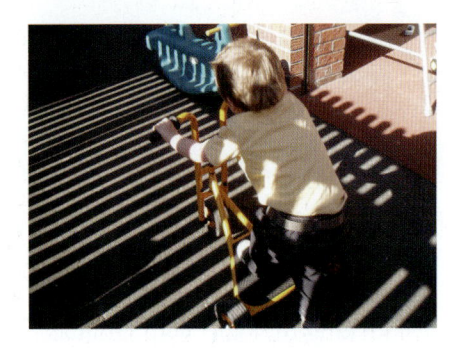

**Figure 4.14** 'Ready, steady, faster, faster'

Henry's playfulness suggested that he could be experiencing higher order concepts, including speed ('faster, faster' as he pushed the scooter along), distance and force (the vigour of pushing impacting on the extent of ground covered), direction (reversing the car backwards after the crash, walking the car forwards) and position (the pram is in front of the car and the car has crashed into it).

Tovey (2007: 32) suggested that 'many key mathematical and scientific concepts, such as height, distance, speed, energy, space, gradient, gravity, can only really be experienced outdoors'.

Athey (2007: 54, original italics) supported the imperative of early action, stating that '*seriation* and *classification* have their origins in early actions applied to a wide range of objects and, later, to events'. Rogoff's (1990: 140) suggestion that 'the model of most effective social interaction is to attempt to understand' is notable in that she acknowledged the importance of coming to know the child, the thinking child, better, seemingly irrespective of location.

Tovey's (2007: 32) proposal that key concepts could be 'experienced' inferred the possibility of passiveness in terms of a child's level of engagement. Concepts described here are almost as content, to be assimilated or not. However, Athey seemed to present an alternative consideration in referring to the *application* of early action because recognition of a child's cognitive structures (their schemas) and subsequently how children applied these to environmental content (both outdoors and indoors) enables adults to exceed associative interventions.

Athey (2007) and Tovey (2007) acknowledged the place of environment in stimulating learning, but Athey asserted that it was arguably not the outdoors which was significant, but the potential for the children to be confronted with challenging surroundings which was more fundamental. This confrontation sees a potential for responding and extending children's own ideas and understandings in different situations, though Tovey's suggestion that the outdoors lends itself to certain explorations is useful in that the space and dynamic offered by challenging outdoor environments can be more enriching than more confined (or limited) inside spaces. Clarke's (2005: 45) view of children as 'competent communicators' should be accepted by adults who are willing to watch knowingly and react appropriately.

Henry fully communicated his schematic concerns in action, speech and representations. Athey's (2007: 56) reference to the problem of the 'slip between what is offered and what is received' is worth restating here. Henry offered the accompanying adult a clear glimpse of this thinking. Although Athey's reference was about the match or mismatch in children's knowledge and understanding, it seems relevant here to adults who may not understand what a child offers, or who may not receive this information about their own ideas and understanding and therefore may be unable to respond appropriately.

In a later observation, Henry (2.9) was playing with the toy steamroller on the car mat.

> Henry: Near the home, round the corner, a big steamroller's here, nearly here, it's here.
>
> Adult: The steamroller's on the way to a job, along the road it goes.

Later Henry made a steamroller with modelling resources.

Henry's earlier trajectory behaviour – where he first displaced himself, then transported objects from one point to another, making heaps – was recognised by Corbetta and Snapp-Childs (2009) as early practical foundations and essential for later recall. Henry has pushed objects along the floor (cars, lorries, trains, tractors, fire engines, soft cylinders), he has kicked balls and watched them roll and he has added things too, to make things longer. He appeared to be building upon these early trajectory behaviours in the steamroller play.

Henry (2.10) accompanied his dynamic action as he pursued his back and forth schema with appropriate language: 'steamroller'. The adult also attuned and accompanied conceptually – 'along the road it goes' – instead of digressing with 'flattening', 'squashing' and 'making things smooth' comments about steamrollers.

Henry pursued his dynamic back and forth schema actively and figuratively. Where he pushed the toy steamroller around the mat he was beginning to use everyday language related to time (DfE 2012) in that he was ordering events. In saying 'here, nearly here, it's here', Henry appeared to have an awareness of time passing. The steamroller did not simply just arrive at the destination, it was not just 'here'; it was a gradual happening.

Henry also appeared to be exploring distance in a practical sense. He used vocabulary in this observation which suggested addition. He was pushing the steamroller a bit further ('here'), a bit further ('nearly here'), a bit further still ('it's here'). Through a functional dependency relationship, where the arrival of the steamroller at the destination was dependent upon it being pushed, Henry seemed to be exploring the concept of additional distance. Additional pushes, punctuated with language, made the steamroller go a little further, consequently taking more time to arrive, an action which suggested that Henry was engaging with notions of distance and movement.

Punctuating the flow of action with language was also an important practical foundation for Henry's developing understanding of early writing and sentence construction. He was not beginning to break the flow of speech into words (DfE 2012), but appeared to be exploring segmentation which could be carried forward to his later literary endeavours. Meade and Cubey's (2008: 117) findings also suggested that enriching experiences 'helped to lay the foundation for writing and reading'. They referred specifically to outdoor experiences to do with aspects of mathematical understanding, for example, shape, comparison and direction. However, arguably, the essential aspect is the inspirational nature of any environment we offer to the child.

This short observation of Henry pursuing his back and forth schema enabled an examination of several significant higher order concepts, which Athey (2007: 126) suggested was one of the functions of symbolic representation: specifically, 'to reactivate original experiences, thus leading to stability of knowledge'.

Table 4.1 identifies specific concepts and relates these to Henry's actions. It highlights what Henry actually did and makes links between these actions

## Table 4.1 Henry's work with the steamroller

| Concept | What Henry did | An interpretation of what Henry might have been thinking |
|---|---|---|
| Position | Henry pushed the steamroller along the car mat. | 'The steamroller can't go in a straight line on the car mat, as the round bends around, it's got to go round the corner.' |
| Force | Henry pushed the steamroller. | 'I've got to push the steamroller to make it move.' |
| Velocity | Henry pushed the steamroller fast and slow. | 'The faster I push the steamroller, the quicker it will reach the end of the road.' |
| Estimation | Henry kept pushing the steamroller. | 'I've got to keep pushing as I'm not at the end of the road yet.' |
| Direction | Henry moved the steamroller forward. | 'I'm pushing the steamroller forward. I hope I don't meet another car as I'll have to reverse.' |
| Friction | Henry moved the steamroller off the mat and onto the floor. | 'The car mat is rougher than the floor. I need to keep pushing so that it will move. If I put it on the floor and give it a push, it will roll on its own.' |

and particular concepts in suggesting what Henry might have been thinking while involved in his work.

Henry (2.10) displaced the toy steamroller in this dynamic play through back and forth trajectory movement (Figure 4.15). Later, he made a steamroller. He appeared to have internalised the displacement of objects in symbolically representing a steamroller using an appropriate signifier (Piaget and Inhelder's (1969: 51) 'signified something [a steamroller] by means of a "signifier" which serves a representative purpose [the cylindrical container]'.)

**Figure 4.15** The steamroller

Henry (2.2) was playing in the clay (Figure 4.16). He squeezed a lump of clay with his hands.

Henry: Sausages.

Henry rolled his hand over the clay to roll it out.

> Henry: I made a big sausage.
>
> Adult: Yes, a big, long sausage.
>
> Adult: I've made a small, thin sausage.

He then got a very big lump of clay.

> Henry: I've made a big sausage.

Henry went to the clay tools and selected two shaped sponges: 'car, van'.

> Henry: I've made a big sausage.
>
> Adult: Look at my thin sausage.

**Figure 4.16 Clay sausages**

Henry broke a bit off his sausage and said 'thin sausage'.

He went back to the clay tools and selected a pizza cutter and rolled it along the top of the table.

Henry was pursuing his schema dynamically (rolling the clay), figuratively (making a model of a sausage), in the language used to accompany his work ('sausage') and in the content assimilated (pizza cutter; car, van sponges) which related to horizontal back and forth trajectories. This holistic engagement with schemas can be heard in Nutbrown's (2006: 64) writing about the importance of creating times for mathematical discovery. She reminded us that 'young children must create their own wheels and watch them turn and roll before they truly understand what the "wheelness" of wheels really is'.

In Henry's explorations in the clay, he appeared to be busy coming to know the 'bigness' of things through a symbolic representation of his dynamic back and forth schema. He seemed interested in the effects of his action on the clay and continued to experiment with this through sustained testing. He appeared to deduce that if he had a large lump of clay, he could make a bigger sausage. Although he was using language of absolute size, he was aware that a bigger lump of clay could make 'a big sausage'. He was not articulating comparative mathematical language but was involved in the practical foundations for this.

The adult was encouraging Henry to think mathematically in drawing his attention through action and language to different ideas and understanding, for as Nutbrown (2006: 71) continued, it is through observation of children *as they work* which is essential in detecting and relating to their current thinking. Athey's findings recognised the importance of acute attention during observations. She highlighted that 'speech used by project children reflected prominent schemas as well as content assimilated to schemas' (Athey 2007: 167). An unfocused (or unaware) practitioner may not discern the schematic essence of a child's particular musings and could unwittingly proceed to interrupt with suggestions which intrude into, rather than elaborate upon, their own important deliberations.

Henry was not toiling or labouring in these observations. He was playful. There was no sense of drudgery, chore or task. He brought together known understandings and was able to secure these in a self-motivated way where things were relevant to him, meaningful to him, significant to him, worthwhile to him, and in context. Nutbrown and Page (2008) acknowledged the significance and place of playtime, which Laevers (1976) suggested allowed for an involvement of total focus and intense mental activity. This is an inspirational yet challenging motivation for early years practice in general and for Henry's day-to-day business in particular.

## Conclusion

This chapter has focused on Henry's dynamic back and forth schema evidenced in a series of motor and symbolic behaviours. Henry could be seen using objects in his surroundings to further his understanding of movement in the horizontal plane. In the pursuit of his dynamic back and forth schema, he could be seen experiencing higher order concepts which were captured in observations of his actions, speech and representations. Through perceptive, knowledgeable observation, the adult in the learning environment was able to adjust to the nuances of Henry's thinking and therefore support him conceptually as he busied himself with his own important investigations. Accompaniment of this nature is vital if interventions in learning with children are to be of relevance. The role of the adult working alongside the child is dynamic in that it demands a constant modification to respond to the distinctions of the individual child.

## Reflection

Observations of children taken over extended periods can reveal richly detailed accounts of their schematic pursuits.

- How can these observations inform planning for learning and development so that what is offered is attuned and relevant for children?

- Do children in your setting display seemingly unfathomable patterns of behaviour? Could these apparent inscrutable incidences be understood differently if viewed with a schematic lens?

- How might a knowledge of schemas enrich your understanding of the children in your care?

## Further Reading

Athey, C. (2007) *Extending Thought in Young Children* (2nd edition). London: Paul Chapman Publishing.
Elfer, P., Goldschmied, E. and Selleck, D. (2003) *Key Persons in the Nursery: Building Relationships for Quality Provision*. London: David Fulton.
Meade, A. and Cubey, P. (2008) *Thinking Children: Learning about Schemas* (2nd edition). Wellington: New Zealand Council for Educational Research and Institute for Early Childhood Studies, Wellington College of Education/Victoria University of Wellington.

A further account of children's consistency, continuity and progression in thought can be found in:
Nutbrown, C. (2011) Consistency, continuity and progression, pages 37–53 in *Threads of Thinking: Schemas and Young Children Learning and the Role of Early Education* (4th edition). London: Sage.

# CHAPTER 5

# HENRY'S DYNAMIC VERTICAL SCHEMA

## Dynamic Vertical Schema: Motor Level

Henry (1.10) spent time reaching up and putting objects (dinosaurs, toy cars, farm animals) on different steps of, or on top of, the soft play den. He climbed or crawled up the steps and pushed or threw the objects on to the floor. He then ran, walked, slithered or slid down the slide.

Henry's movements were accompanied with attuned speech when appropriate, as he negotiated the soft play furniture:

You are climbing up to the top of the steps.

What can you see up there?

You're at the top now.

Do you want to come down?

Are you going to slide down to the floor?

Figure 5.1  Henry reached up

Figure 5.2  Henry pushed, threw things down

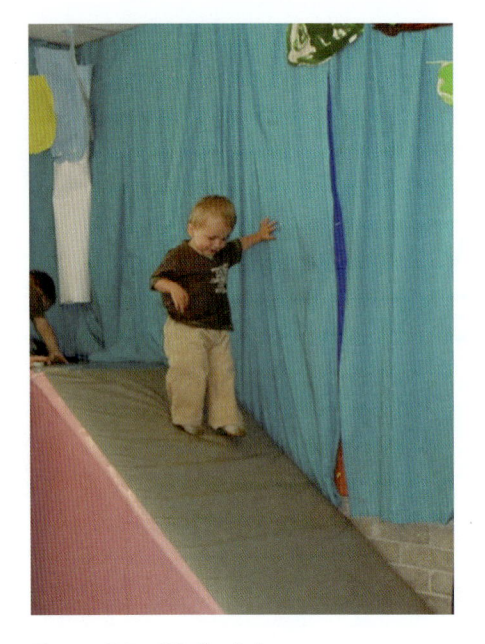

**Figure 5.3** Walked down

**Figure 5.4** Slid down

All recognised Henry's exploration of the vertical, for, as Nutbrown (2006: 40) stated, 'children are more likely to assimilate language used by adults when what they say matches children's interests'. Athey (2007: 164) confirmed the significance of this for practitioners in that 'a match [should] exist between existing forms of thought and appropriate speech' in learning encounters with young children.

A note about the timeliness of intervention must be emphasised, and an understanding of if – when and certainly how – acknowledged. Children

**Figure 5.5** Bowl on cup

**Figure 5.6** Pegs pushed

should not be overwhelmed with an incessant, unremitting torrent of questions and comments during their work, and certainly intervening with Henry in such a way during his investigations of the soft play would have been inappropriate. Instead, a learning accomplice who is compatible, like-minded and able to gently provoke challenge and wonder, at just the right time, should be the goal.

**Figure 5.7  Tambourine up-ended**

Hofer, Hohenberger, Hauf and Aschersleben (2008) proposed that these sensitive interactions can support the early development of particular cognitive capabilities. De Lisi (2002) also recognised the place of co-operation rather than constraint. Relationships founded on mutual respect are a prerequisite in the learning environment. Understanding and respecting the child's own concerns facilitates 'interesting' and, much more importantly, 'appropriate' learning experiences (Bruce 2005: 72). Gopnik, Meltzoff and Kuhl (1999) validated the importance of appropriateness in terms of adults being in step with a child's thinking. They maintained that 'just one salient instance and babies will internalise a word forever' (Gopnik et al. 1999: 115).

Henry put his bowl on top of his cup and pushed pegs down on to the washing line, a continuing acquisition of trajectory motor experiences.

Henry (1.10) explored verticality with his own body and with a variety of things around him. He did not appear to want to play with the tambourine but persisted in standing it up on end. It seemed that it was not the noisy potential of the object which fascinated Henry; it was the dynamic vertical characteristic which captured his imagination.

Henry (1.10) pushed the cars and watched them roll down the yellow slope of the garage. He picked up the cars and pushed them up the red slide.

Henry (2.3) picked up the pieces of melon and dropped them on to the floor, watching them fall (Figure 5.9). Although this may not have been the behaviour to encourage at snack time,

**Figure 5.8  Cars rolled down**

**Figure 5.9** Melon dropped

the purposefulness of it for Henry in furthering his understanding of movement in the vertical plane was important. Akin to the well-known behaviour of babies dropping toys from their prams, it would be more appropriate to suggest alternative possibilities for this further pursuit! His established schema distinguished the possibilities of disparate environmental content. Cars rolling, melon dropping, pegs being pushed down, bowls on top, his body sliding, and climbing up all represented his prevailing *form of thinking*.

These motor level examples of trajectory behaviour in the vertical plane were significant as a precursor to symbolic representations, co-ordinations and thought, with children able to bring forward embedded earlier experiences. Though dropping some of the materials (like the melon) was not deemed to be socially acceptable, viewing this schematically does, as Athey encouraged, move us away from a view of children as naughty, or even 'sinful', and towards an understanding that they use whatever they have to hand to pursue their schemas. The role of the adult is to provide flexible materials to allow for socially acceptable experimentation and discovery.

## Dynamic Vertical Schema: Symbolic Representation

**Figure 5.10** The chime bar

Henry (2.2) said 'up' as he lifted the chime bar beater above his head and 'down' as he pointed the beater towards the floor (Figure 5.10). Two different directions in the vertical plane were evident in Henry's speech as he accompanied his actions. He continued this exploration when he described the chime bar beater, 'it's a hammer', and proceeded to get a drum and bang the beater up and down on the drum. Henry's *form of thinking* was evident in action and speech when he referred to the beater as 'hammer' – a tool requiring vertical dynamism to be effective.

Athey (2007) assumed in the Froebel project that there was some specific conceptual understanding if a child consistently attached appropriate language to actions. Here, Henry supplied an appropriate commentary ('up', 'down') to his action (upward and downward trajectory movements) on the object (the beater), evidence of Piaget's (1959: 17) ego-centric speech (a monologue): while serving 'no social function', it is intended to 'accompany, to reinforce, or to supplement action'. Nutbrown's (2006: 52) recommendation, therefore, to use 'appropriate descriptive language, language of *form* as well as appropriate content descriptions', is relevant when accompanying children in their play, and supports them in making this match.

**Figure 5.11 Toy aeroplane flew**

Henry (1.10) picked up the toy aeroplane (Figure 5.11), lifted it above his head and vocalised 'bruuummm'.

He climbed on to the see-saw and pushed himself up and down on it and sang 'see saw, see saw'.

Outside, Henry (2.6) piled the large blocks on top of each other (Figure 5.12).

Henry: I'm making a bouncy castle I'm jump on.

Adult: Jump on it up and down?

Henry: A big bouncy castle.

Adult: You can jump up into the air and down again.

Athey (2007: 55) highlighted the place for 'conceptual rather than associative' accompaniment when responding to children in the learning environment and Neisser (1976: 57) verified this in recognising that 'the perceiver engages in an act that involves information from the environment as well as his own cognitive mechanisms. He is changed from the information he picks up'. Neisser's (1976) acknowledgement of the place of environment must be realised in its fullest, most far-reaching, all-embracing, influential and richest implication.

**Figure 5.12 A bouncy castle of blocks**

**Figure 5.13** Cylinder towers

An adult playing alongside Henry outside with blocks should resist an appealing, yet incompatible, conversation about castles, kings and queens, knights, battles and other such associations (such language can be experienced by children when they share the richness of stories with adults) in favour of what Athey (2007: 152) described as 'precise language' – in other words, a dialogue of conceptual correspondence. The significance of this play was not (it seemed) Henry's fondness for blocks, but the opportunity for assimilation of relevant environmental content into his prevailing cognitive structures.

Henry (2.7) was in the soft play area. He stood a cylinder on end and tried to balance another cylinder on top (Figure 5.13). He said 'put it there'. It fell off. He climbed on top of the cylinder and jumped off: 'jump, big jump'.

Henry (2.7) was outside with the ball and kicked it to the adult.

Adult: Can you throw it up into the air? [*Henry threw the ball into the air.*]

Henry: My big ball ... up in the air ... you kick it to me.

Piaget (1959: 39) proposed that young children strive continuously to share their thoughts, that they have in fact 'no verbal continence' and seek many ways to make sense of the world around them through communication. As speech becomes gradually more socialised, where children try to involve and influence those around them by entering into collaboration or dialogue, the motive for communication shifts towards the need to be understood.

When Henry issued the instructions 'put it there' and 'you kick it to me' to the accompanying adult, evidence of Piaget's (1959: 10) socialised speech could be distinguished. Henry 'exchanged his thoughts with others' and attempted to manipulate the behaviour of others in drawing the adult in to assist him in his play, his schematic endeavours.

Piaget (1959: 263) went on to assert that it is the responsibility of the adult 'to reduce the child's soliloquy to a satisfactory proportion and to develop dialogue'. And Howard (1987: 176) stated that 'to relate information taught to students' existing schemata' must be kept in mind. This was not a matter of making concessions to social convention in the learning environment with children, but an altogether more significant protocol. Howard's stress on seeking to 'relate' must be understood as a necessity in working with children because to 'relate' is to connect to, or associate with, the child.

To relate is not to inform or convey, but has a much more co-operative connotation. It compels the adult to identify with the actual thoughts of the child. In so doing, Piaget's (1959: 263) challenge to 'develop dialogue' with a child is a requirement to respect and value by listening and understanding what is heard and seen. This willing investment can lead to astonishing reward. To listen is an acute task and real comprehension is a skilful proficiency. It requires a capacity for attunement and asks much of the early years practitioner.

**Figure 5.14** The trampoline

Henry (2.8) was jumping up and down on the trampoline (Figure 5.14). He shouted to another child, 'Harry, are you jumping?'

Piaget and Inhelder's (1971: 366) definition of 'scheme' as 'a generalization instrument' was appropriate as Henry identified a conceptual relationship between dissimilar objects – the wooden blocks, trampoline, soft play cylinders and aeroplanes – which for him were proximal. He was discriminating in his use of content and revealed a relationship between this and *form*. He appeared sensitised to specific experience as he assimilated disparate environmental content to his existing cognitive structures.

Henry and Nell were playing with the Lego (Figure 5.15). Henry (2.10) observed: 'Yours is higher'. Nell (2.7) replied: 'Mine's going higher, I'm making a tower, bigger, bigger'. Henry retorted: 'I'm building it bigger … mine is bigger, look two big towers.'

Piaget's (1952a: 10) discussion of the principle of discrimination between quantity and quality and the essential relationship between the two can be seen in Henry's actions and language. His 'big jump' provides evidence of Piaget's 'symmetrical relation expressing resemblance', where Henry attributed appropriate description to his own action in classifying his jump as 'big'. Later, we saw Henry in the Lego referring to his tower as 'higher … bigger' – Piaget's 'asymmetrical relation expressing difference' – indicating what Piaget defined as 'the germ of quantity'.

Henry's exploration of the comparative appeared to be confined to the immediate in that his language and

**Figure 5.15** Building higher, bigger

action were commentaries on the directly perceived. However, he can be seen engaging with cause and effect, which Athey (1990: 70) terms more precisely as a 'functional dependency relationship' and defined as 'the effects of action on objects or material'. His language – 'Yours is higher … I'm building it bigger' – suggested a functional dependency relationship, and when he realised that in order for his tower to be higher, bigger than Nell's he needed to add more Lego suggests a migration of mind. He described both his action ('I'm building it bigger') and the figurative effect of this action ('Two big towers').

Henry brought forward earlier schematic behaviours – his previous exploits and encounters (up, down, sliding, climbing, building, dropping…) – and applied them to new proceedings, thus resonating with Gardner's (1984: 129) reminder that 'the study of thought should (indeed must) begin in the nursery'. This substantiated Piaget's (1959: 283) claim that 'sensory-motor activity constitutes the foundation of symbolism and representation … that thought proceeds from actions'.

There was evidence in these observations, presented schematically and not chronologically, of Henry's representations. Piaget (1969: 356) identified the 'figurative and operative aspects of knowledge', where 'figurative' relates to perception and mental images and 'operative' refers to action. Both aspects of Henry's representation are presented and correspond to Athey's (2007) findings: both dynamic thought patterns emerging from action and figural representations related to perception were evident. Athey specified that materials of figural representation included drawings, block constructions (Henry's bouncy castle, Lego towers and soft play tower), clay and models with recycled materials.

## Dynamic Vertical Schema: Further Investigations

Henry appeared to be actively trying things out, exploring possibilities, practising and making discoveries, as he pursued his dynamic vertical schema. Many of Henry's experiences were related to a developing understanding of mathematical concepts which could be seen in his encounters in the learning environment.

> Early awareness of shape, space and measure grows from their sensory awareness and opportunities to observe objects and their movements, and to play and explore. (DfE 2012: 35)

Henry appeared to be exploring height and balance as he put the dinosaurs on top of the soft play den. He stretched his arms above his head and, through a functional dependency relationship, seemed to realise that in order to reach the top of the den he had to stand on 'tip-toes' and balance using his other hand to achieve his goal. An examination of different positions appeared evident in dinosaurs 'on top', tambourine up-ended, bowl 'on top of' cup, and staring down as melon pieces fell to the floor.

Nutbrown (2006: 66) alerted practitioners to recognise 'the validity and relevance of these kinds of experiences in terms of their potential for learning'. An environment which freed Henry to build 'bigger, higher towers' with a range of objects and materials was the necessary practical groundwork to secure Henry's later conceptual thought. Henry appeared to realise, through a functional dependency relationship again, that more and more blocks were required if a tall structure was to be constructed; an early practical engagement with the later concept of addition.

Henry pressed pegs down on to the washing line. This short observation indeed captured Henry's activity at the time. The careful selection of task, the persistence and determination to succeed, and the meticulous precision demanded for such an intricate task could be lost if considered in such a cursory way as just pressing pegs down. Henry's apparent understanding of forces (seemingly understanding 'I have to press this peg down to make it stay on the washing line') builds upon these early tangible activities, and is evidence of Piaget's (1969: 309) 'schemes of action, principal sources of concepts'. A timely warning for adults working with young children is that if authentic observations are not captured, understood and acted upon, 'the detail of children's activities and their thinking can be lost' (Nutbrown 2006: 67).

Henry spent a long time walking or crawling up the soft play steps and running, sliding or walking down. In so doing, he engaged in a real and actual exploration of similarity and difference as he experimented with velocity. Although the steps and slide were the same height, walking or crawling up the steps took longer than sliding or running down the slope. Henry's play was giving him a practical experience of an asymmetrical relationship, equivalence of distance, and ascending and descending gradients affecting speed, regardless of whether his exploration was intentional investigation of these concepts or not.

Bruner's (1966) enactive child, objectifying and correlating the environment, is apparent here. Piaget and Inhelder (1956: 453) confirmed this when they stated: 'thought can only replace action on the basis of the data which action itself provides'. Although the context of Piaget and Inhelder's discussion was the child's understanding of the properties of shape, their conclusion that experimentation was more than a physical 'coming to know' is pertinent. Henry was not just physically active, but mentally dynamic. He was physically active as he involved himself in a range of mathematical discoveries, but Piaget and Inhelder (1956: 454) confirmed that it was more than this, as 'in the course of such an experiment, the child also learns something of the way his actions are co-ordinated and how one determines another', and this is evident in Henry's investigation of different slides and wheeled toys.

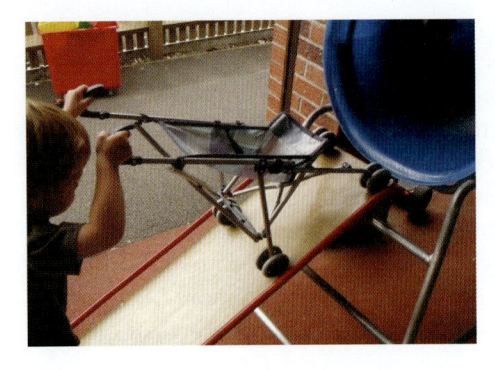

**Figure 5.16** Henry and the pram

**Figure 5.17** The bike and the slide

Henry (2.10) was outside with the pram. He pushed the pram up the big slide.

> Adult: You've pushed the pram right to the top of the slide. Is it too big to fit inside the tunnel?

Henry pulled the pram back down the slide. He went and got a bike and attempted to ride up the slide.

> Adult: The slide is very steep.

Henry got stuck at the bottom of the slide. He got off and started to push the bike up the slide.

> Adult: You'll have to push hard, Henry, to get the bike up that steep slide.

He got so far and pulled the bike back down the slide. Henry then took the bike over to the plastic frame and started to push it up this slide. Henry persisted until he had pushed the bike up and into the frame. He then pulled the bike down the slide and rode off.

Henry's thinking appeared to be in line with what Piaget (1950: 121) termed the sensori-motor child, whose intelligence was characterised as a co-ordination of 'successive perceptions and overt movements … like a slow-motion film, in which all the pictures are seen in succession but without fusion'. Henry's repeated actions demonstrated his seeming inability to see an overall picture, to imagine whether the pram or bike would fit inside the tunnel without actually testing.

He appeared to be functioning within 'the restricted boundaries of sensori-motor action' (Piaget and Inhelder 1969: 91), where 'for many months, knowledge of objects and of the simple causal connections that exist

Figure 5.18  The bike and the plastic frame

Figure 5.19  In it goes!

among them is tied completely to moment-to-moment experience' (Gardner 1984: 129).

As Henry's pram and bike explorations unfolded, 'accommodations, or steps forward in knowledge' could be inferred (Athey 2007: 51). Through a functional dependency relationship, which Athey (1990: 70) defined as 'the effects of action on objects or material', Henry realised that the pram required pushing in order to get to the top of the slide. He seemed to be experiencing force (the pram is light so requires minimal effort to push), ascending and descending trajectories (moving up and down the slide with the pram), height (the pram is above his head and his arms are raised, position (up to the top, down to the bottom), weight (the pram is light and can be pushed to the top of the slide easily) and size (the pram is too big to fit inside the tunnel).

When he selected the bike to ride up the slide, he appeared to be responding to the suggestion of the adult concerning the size of the pram, in estimating that the bike was smaller. An emerging awareness of the volume taken up by the pram in relation to the capacity of the tunnel could have influenced his selection of a smaller object to test. When he tried to push the bike up the first slide, he appeared to realise that the bike was too heavy to push up the slide. He seemed to be thinking that, irrespective of the amount of force he may be able to exert in this case, it was not going to be enough to succeed in getting the bike up the slide.

Piaget and Inhelder's (1956: 404) correct assertion that 'co-ordinating actions is no part of the physical experiment, but a part of intelligence mechanisms' was significant here in that Henry's focus shifted from the steep slide to the plastic slide. The difference between the two slides was size (the plastic slide was smaller) and incline (it was less steep). The similarity, however, was not so much that it was another slide but that it enabled Henry to continue his thought process. He continued his exploration of the dynamic vertical, his *form of thinking*. 'What is "known", that his action could have an effect on an object, that the force he exerted on the pram resulted in it being at the top of the slide, led to what became "better known"' (Athey 2007: 51).

'Better known' could be the link between volume and capacity (this small bike fits inside this big frame but the pram wouldn't fit inside the tunnel). The capacity of the big frame accommodated the volume of the small bike. 'Better known' could be the relationship between increased weight and required force (this little bike is heavier than the pram so I have to push it harder to get it up the slide). 'Better known' could be the comparative relationship between objects (this bike is heavier than…, the plastic slide is shorter than…, the frame is bigger than…).

To return to Piaget and Inhelder's (1956: 454) clarification of action, where 'in the course of such an experiment, the child learns something of the way his actions are co-ordinated and how one determines another' is noteworthy, for as Henry succeeded in pushing the bike up the plastic slide and into the frame at the top, functionally dependent on rotation and his changing position and grip, his understanding of gradient and speed, weight and force, height, volume, capacity, size and trajectory was becoming established.

Henry's exploits with the bike and pram could be seen as purposeful, meaningful endeavours when considered in the context of Athey's (2007) optimistic characterisation of children's schematic behaviour. Instead of mischievous deeds, she asserted that schematic explanation 'embraces a wide range of behaviours and interpretations are positive … instead of attributing naughtiness' (Athey 2007: 144). Although Henry was motivated and industrious in this play and certainly not busy cultivating delinquent tendencies, it suggested that further outlets for his schematic pursuit through sensitive resourcing was needed, as not all adults working with children may be in a position of such acceptance. Were Henry in a setting where bikes were only for riding and slides were only for sliding, he would have been thwarted from his bike and slide exploration.

Athey (2007: 153) put forward the notion of 'clusters' of schemas. Although clusters prevented a developmentally hierarchical classification of the schemas themselves, they showed how schemas could be co-ordinated. Athey stated that these 'develop into systems of thought'. Nutbrown (2011) also identified continuities in actions through her observations of children in a nursery, suggesting consistencies in patterns of thinking. She clarified that although dominant schemas were recognised and highlighted, other schemas were also part of children's repertoires. In these co-ordinations, Athey (2007: 50) asserted that 'the environment is comprehended at higher levels by the child'.

In the light of this, Henry appeared to be co-ordinating different thought patterns in his block play. Meade and Cubey (2008: 155) recognised this in their work, where children were making 'connections between schemas to form new ideas (concepts)'.

**Figure 5.20** Blocks inside lorry

**Figure 5.21** Blocks moved over

Henry seemed to be representing his dynamic vertical schema figuratively in his block play. Although classified as a motor level observation in the absence of accompanying talk, he seemed to be experimenting with different concepts.

Although observations could only be inferred, it could be seen that Henry might have been involved in important co-ordinations. He appeared to be experimenting with different emerging concepts in his investigations with the coloured blocks. He was not stuck in pursuit of one schema but engaged in complex, synchronised enquiry. This required time and timeliness; time for the play to evolve and timeliness in terms of intervention from an adult who recognised these important conceptual endeavours and took them as the cue for engagement.

Table 5.1 identifies specific concepts and relates these to Henry's actions. It situates what Henry did and what was observed in a conceptual framework. It aligns actions with concepts and interprets what Henry might have been thinking while he was busily involved in his investigations and explorations.

## Conclusion

This chapter has revealed Henry's dynamic vertical schema as evidenced in a series of motor and symbolic behaviours. He used the things around him to further his knowledge of movement in the vertical plane and, through these schematic explorations, experienced several higher order concepts. It is the responsibility of those working and caring for young children to come to know the thinking concerns of children through such observations. It is a professional duty for practitioners to be able to attune and match their interventions with the cognitive concerns of young children.

Table 5.1 What Henry might have been thinking

| Concept | What Henry did | An interpretation of what Henry might have been thinking |
|---|---|---|
| Size | Henry chooses the small blocks to take into the sand. He piles them up. | 'I can make a big tower.' |
| Addition | Henry put blocks on top of blocks. | 'My tower gets taller when I put more blocks on top.' |
| | Henry piled the blocks up in one corner. | 'If I move my tower over, I can fit another one next to it.' |
| Height | Henry stood the blocks on end. | 'If I stand the blocks up this way, my tower goes higher.' |
| Position | Henry balances the blocks on top of each other. | 'This block fits on top of this one.' |
| Classification | Henry chooses cuboids to build with. | 'I'll get these long, straight blocks not those round ones as they'll roll away. I'll just use the ones like bricks today.' |
| Capacity | Henry put the blocks inside the truck. | 'My tower fits inside the truck.' |
| | Henry piled the blocks up in one corner. | 'The lorry can fit another tower in if I move this one over a bit into the corner.' |
| Shape | Henry picks a triangle and puts it on top of the blocks. | 'This looks like a roof. I'll put it on top of my tower.' |

# Reflection

Think about Henry's use of the tambourine (seen in earlier in the chapter).

- Do you take account of the spontaneous *form* of children's thought and the environmental content children may use?
- Do children in your setting with particular schemas select certain things to play with? Do they appear to be sensitised to particular environmental content?
- What additional experiences can be provided to nourish children's dynamic vertical schema?

# Further Reading

Donaldson, M. (1978) *Children's Minds*. London: HarperCollins.

A further account of children's developing concepts of functional dependency through schematic pursuits can be found in:

Nutbrown, C. (2011) Functional dependency relationships, pages 71–72 in *Threads of Thinking: Schemas and Young Children Learning and the Role of Early Education* (4th edition). London: Sage.

# CHAPTER 6

# HENRY'S MARK MAKING AND FIGURATIVE REPRESENTATIONS

## Mark Making

This chapter aims to identify Henry's thought patterns as they are represented figuratively in his mark making. The observations of Henry's mark making were taken over a seven-month period and those captured during this period are presented here. Piaget (1969: 356) suggested that 'all knowledge has to do with structures' and identified two kinds of cognitive patterning, specifically *figurative* (linked with early perception) and *operative* (linked with action). Henry's dynamic thought patterns could be clearly distinguished in his schematic pursuits, as could his emerging perceptual patterns, which Athey (2007) considered to be represented in children's two- and three-dimensional representations – including drawings, model making, constructions and clay.

Henry's fascination with dynamic vertical movements could be seen within many aspects of his play. Observations of Henry have included him performing a number of actions: reaching up, putting things on top of, climbing and crawling up steps, sliding, slithering and running down slopes, pushing or throwing objects on to the floor, standing objects up, rolling objects down and building structures. All such actions were evidence of one of his prevailing *forms of thinking*, represented in dynamic action, specifically his dynamic vertical schema.

Henry has also been observed investigating dynamic horizontal movements in the pursuit of his dynamic back and forth schema, including lining objects up, rolling or pushing objects along the floor, kicking balls and riding wheeled toys along. His investigation of insideness was also apparent in repeatedly putting objects inside a variety of containers and enclosing himself inside structures, evidence of his dynamic containing and enveloping schema.

Piaget and Inhelder (1956: 43) recognised the relationship between perception and movement, stating that children are able 'to recognise, and especially represent, only those shapes which they can actually reconstruct through their own actions', a point which Athey (2007: 75) confirmed in her acknowledgement that 'mark and model making are abstractions from the child's own movements'. There appeared to be a relationship between Henry's dynamic schemas, represented in action, and his subsequent mark making. He demonstrated a perceptual correspondence to *form* in his mark making using a variety of materials and tools which were synchronic with his dynamic actions.

Athey (2007) found that straight-line trajectories preceded circular trajectories, which was also evident in Henry's mark making. Henry (1:10) used vertical scribble (vertical action of the hand) and horizontal scribble (Figure 6.1 and Figure 6.2). Piaget and Inhelder's (1956: 77) confirmation that mark making derived from physical action, that it was 'based originally upon a sensori-motor and ultimately on a mental, representational space determined by the co-ordination of these actions', was verified by Athey (2007: 78), who described early marks as the 'figurative outcome of bodily movement'.

## Henry (1.10) Making Marks

Lowenfeld and Brittain (1982: 172) supported this developmental route of early scribbles in their classification of 'disordered scribbling', or what Piaget (1969: 63) referred to as 'aimless scribble'. Scribbling is common at Henry's age, where there was no 'representative intent … no attempt to portray the visual environment'. It is in fact what Piaget and Inhelder (1969: 63) described as 'a play of exercise'. Plaskow (1972) and Kellogg (1969) had an altogether more prospective view of young children's scribblings. Although they defined the most rudimentary efforts as 'basic scribbles', they did not use the term in a derogatory or dismissive way and acknowledged that they 'are the building blocks out of which all graphic art, pictorial and non-pictorial, is constructed' (Plaskow 1972: 4). Kellogg (1969: 15) concurred in identifying the natural fundamental capacity of young children to draw, which 'permits a detailed and comprehensive description of the work of young children'.

**Figure 6.1** Henry (1.10) Horizontal scribble with vertical lines

Henry (1.10) was seen making marks corresponding with Kellogg's (1969: 16) classification of the basic scribbles, specifically 'multiple ones resulting from rapid back and forth movement' (Figure 6.1) and 'single line versions' (Figure 6.2). Athey (2007: 62) referred to these as 'continuous horizontal and vertical scribble' and 'horizontal [and] vertical lines', which were synchronic with Henry's dynamic action during this time.

**Figure 6.2 Henry (1.10) Horizontal and vertical lines**

He spent time reaching up and putting objects on different steps of, or on top of, the soft play den, climbing or crawling up steps, pushing or throwing objects on to the floor and running, walking or sliding down the slide in his exploration of dynamic vertical movement. At this time, Henry was also observed collecting objects, moving them, making heaps, lining objects up and joining things together in his fascination with dynamic back and forth movements. He pushed himself along, kicked and rolled objects and selected content which required dynamic horizontal movements to make them connect. Lowenfeld and Brittain (1982: 175) had observed that 'controlled scribbling' emerged when children discovered a 'co-ordination between visual and motor activity', which led to enthusiastic scribbles including horizontal, vertical and circular lines.

Athey (2007) distinguished 24 different marks which she subdivided into *straight lines* and *curves*. These straight lines and curves were further subdivided into 11 *space orders*. Henry's dynamic back and forth and side to side schema behaviour were evident in his motor actions – rolling, pulling, pushing, lining up and so on – and though it is not possible to claim for certain that these early drawings were in fact symbolic representations of his action schema represented figuratively, what was clear was that his actions and his mark making were similar in style and seemed to match.

Kellogg (1969: 35) clarified that her classification of mark making 'is a descriptive convenience and not a hypothetical sequence of development'. Athey (2007: 64) acknowledged the sequential nature of drawing development in her identification of distinguishable marks, which she suggested 'could be listed in *lines*, *curves* and *space orders*'. She did, however, concede that generalising about the ages at which schemas appeared as a result of environmental influence was inappropriate. An environment of physical stimulation and challenge and appropriate social interaction could have an important positive nurturing influence.

Henry (1.10) was also observed putting objects into a variety of containers – spoons inside cups, knives inside teapots, spades and scoops in buckets, raisins into milk, stones into bottles, mixed objects (elephant, horse and policeman) inside the stable together. Evidence of Henry's motor level containing and enveloping behaviour was found in observations of Henry purposefully putting assorted objects which had no apparent connection (sand, soil, stones, dry pasta, crayons, toy animals, Lego, chalks) into a variety of containers and enclosing himself within or underneath a range of items. These examples were also important action representations which provided a foundation upon which mark making could emerge.

## Henry (2.1) Making Marks

Henry (2.1) continued to make horizontal and vertical lines (Figure 6.3) but began to make circular marks which corresponded with Athey's (2007: 63) 'circular scribble' and 'concentric circles' and Kellogg's (1969) circular basic scribbles. There also appeared to be an emerging deliberateness about Henry's mark making which Kellogg (1969) identified as 'emergent diagram shapes'. Henry could be seen making a circular enclosure (Figure 6.4), which must have required him to lift up his paint brush to make a different enclosure.

Figure 6.5 shows what Kellogg (1969: 36) described as 'centeredness markings', which, although no single shape was clear, suggested a purposeful movement towards forming shapes. When Henry placed the circular scribble and spiral adjacent to each other (Figure 6.5), this was suggestive of Athey's (2007) categorisation of space orders, which she specified were related to the spatial relationship between things represented. In this case, there was proximity between the marks Henry made. This was the first of Athey's *space order* relations – Piaget and Inhelder's (1956: 48) 'most

**Figure 6.3** Henry (2.1) Horizontal and vertical lines

**Figure 6.4** Henry (2.1) Circular scribble with spiral

**Figure 6.5** Henry (2.1) Circular enclosures

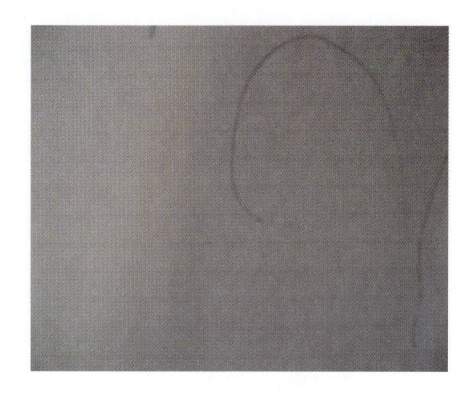

**Figure 6.6** Henry (2.1) Open semi-circle

elementary spatial relationship' – and was found, Athey claimed, most frequently in younger children.

It could be suggested that Figure 6.5 indicates Kellogg's (1969: 15) 'multiple-line circumference circle' confined to one diagonal half of the paper, which Kellogg described as a placement pattern requiring eye control. In the observations of Henry's mark making it could be suggested that there was evidence of increasingly conscious positioning, as seen in Figure 6.6 where he appeared to place the open semi-circle in a quarter of the page. For this to be a more secure judgement, and not an observation of random placement, further evidence would be needed.

These circular marks also became more apparent at a time when Henry had been occupied co-ordinating dynamic vertical and horizontal movements with actions of containment and envelopment. Evidence of what Athey (2007: 63) categorised as 'circular enclosure curved marks placed in proximity with each other' is shown in Figure 6.5.

## Henry (2.2) Making Marks

There seemed to have been a developing precision about the location of Henry's marks. For example, in Figures 6.7 and 6.8 in particular, he positioned his marks in specific places on the paper. These are either centred or in one vertical half of the paper and take a distinct form. There was evidence of Athey's (2007) circular enclosure and core and radial marks with proximity between both types of mark.

To suggest a link with his dynamic representations at this time, which included an exploration of insideness in dropping raisins inside his cup of milk, is possible. Henry was absorbed in an intense investigation with the raisins and milk. He appeared to be exploring 'containment', evident in his gazing examination of the insideness of the cup. Henry's marks in Figure 6.7

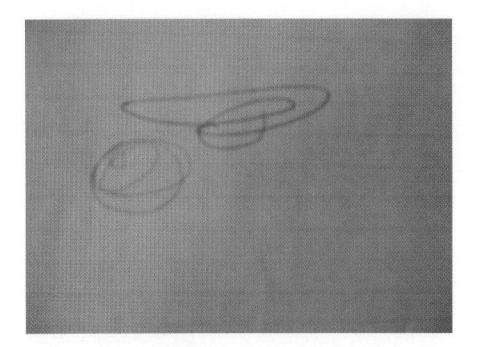

Figure 6.7  Henry (2.2) Enclosures and proximity

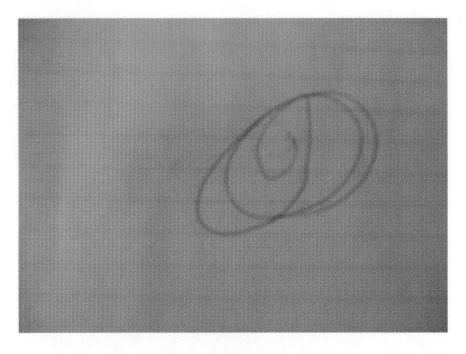

Figure 6.8  Henry (2.2) Single enclosure

could be classified, therefore, as a figurative representation of 'containing and enveloping', with its foundations in the dynamic exploration of the same *form of thought*, using the content of raisins and milk.

Holliday, Harrison and McLeod (2009: 244) acknowledged that 'drawing may be an appropriate non-verbal method for "listening" to children's ideas and recording their perspectives'. Dockett and Perry (2005: 512) confirmed this in their work in describing drawings as 'nonverbal avenues of expression'. Henry's marks in Figure 6.7, which related to concurrent dynamic actions observed at the time, are evidence which suggests that Coates' (2002: 26) assertion that 'we are not in the position to know the thinking behind them' (talking and drawing) could be questioned. Henry's persistent patterns of behaviour observed figuratively and dynamically have the same underlying *form*. They are indications of his thinking concerns, evidence of his schemas, which give insight into his mind.

Concurrent with the marks in Figures 6.7 and 6.8, Henry was observed co-ordinating dynamic back-and-forth and containing movements as, for example, in the following observation made when he was 2 years and 2 months.

> An observation of Henry using play dough:
>
> Henry rolled the pastry cutter along the table.
>
> Adult:   The wheel is going round and round.
>
> Later that day Henry was outside on the bike. He began to spin the bike around in a circle.
>
> Henry:   Round and round.

Piaget and Inhelder (1956) and Athey (2007) confirmed the influence of physical action and the co-ordination of these on the child's ability to use drawings for representative purposes. Henry was busy pursuing his schemas and representing them dynamically. He was accompanied in this instance by appropriate language from the adult who joined him during his play with the dough. He later repeated this language in a different environmental context but with similar conceptual threads. The underlying *form* is 'enclosure', seen *in action* (the pastry cutter wheel going around) and *in speech*, from both the accompanying adult and later from Henry himself when he said 'round and round'.

Coates and Coates (2006: 221) acknowledged the importance of children's talk when they make marks: 'children's simultaneous utterances might potentially inform the nature and content of the work and help elucidate their intentions and processes of thinking'. In the light of this, Henry's figurative representations (Figures 6.7 and 6.8), made on the same day as the dough and bike endeavours, showed a similarity in *form*, that of 'enclosure'. To extrapolate symbolic meaning from these marks is inappropriate in the absence of speech, but the correspondence with how Henry was using environmental content to pursue dynamic thought patterns is strong. Henry's thoughts were not articulated through speech, but his purposeful intentions were to be perceived in his dynamic and figurative behaviour.

It was interesting to note Henry's use of lines within his enclosures (in Figures 6.7 and 6.8), which appeared to divide the space. Kellogg (1969: 51) described 'attempted combines' where the child tests out the connection of figures. Although Henry had not combined two separate drawings (e.g. two ovals or two circles), he could be said to be investigating combinations in that his drawings appeared to show evidence of division. A reflection on Henry's dynamic actions reveals an involvement in a range of activities which seemed to include an exploration of various higher order concepts, including (in Figures 6.9 and 6.10) an investigation of height, addition, capacity and position.

In relation to Kellogg's (1969: 51) classification of 'attempted combines' and Athey's (2007: 62) recognition of the link between 'assimilated environmental content' and form in graphic schemas, Henry's placing of the tower in one half of the lorry appeared intentional. He knew there was room inside the yellow truck (Figure 6.9) for two towers, as he had placed blocks in there,

**Figure 6.9** Henry (2.1) Tower inside the yellow lorry

**Figure 6.10** Henry (2.1) Tower inside the orange lorry

side by side, already. He could be considering a division of space inside the orange truck (Figure 6.10) as well, so that two towers could fit in, as there was an obvious gap. This exploration of 'enveloping' space in action, where subdivision of space was implied, is a step forward in a child's thinking. Athey (2007) confirmed that representations of 'enveloping' spaces evolved into representations of subdivided spaces. These may well form the practical foundations for other higher order concepts, including fractions.

Henry's use of lines within his enclosures in Figures 6.7 and 6.8 are suggestive of a continuation of the spiral action staying within the 'enclosure'. In his action representations, Henry was co-ordinating several schemas, which Athey (2007: 50) clarified as 'more complex amalgamations' and Nutbrown (2006: 22) confirmed as 'mark[ing] an important progression in learning'. Henry was able to secure a deeper level of conceptual understanding through these co-ordinations.

**Figure 6.11** Henry (2.2) Curves and lines

In the light of this, although there are suggestions of core and radial patterns in his marks in Figure 6.11, these do not appear deliberate enough and are more likely to be continuations of the spiral. Henry's action representations at the time were not restricted to the pursuit of one dominant schematic *form*. He combined aspects of enclosure and containing and enveloping with dynamic back and forth and vertical action. These action schemas are important experiences which support figurative representations.

## Henry (2.3) Making Marks

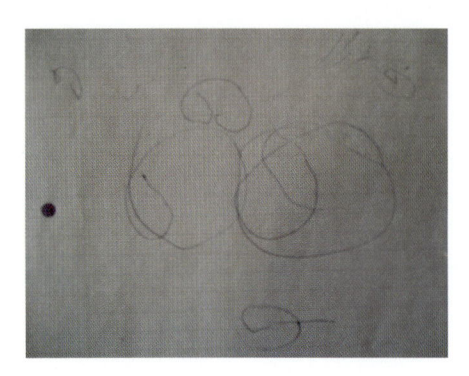

**Figure 6.12** Henry (2.3) Enclosures and curves

Henry did not ascribe meaning to his marks (Figure 6.12), but there was evidence of circular enclosures and open semi-circles. He was also exploring several space order schemas, including 'proximity' and in 'vertical and horizontal order between figures'. Kellogg (1969: 52) recognised 'aggregates' in children's drawings as 'units of three or more diagrams', which relates to Henry's representations. In Figure 6.12 he used ovals and circles placed across the paper from one edge heading towards the other edge in a purposeful and meaningful way.

## A Moment's Speculation...

Piaget and Inhelder (1956: 453) stipulated that 'perception cannot be separated from its sensori-motor context', thus drawing attention to the importance of action as a foundation for evolving and developing understandings.

In Figure 6.12 Henry could be using graphic schemas to represent earlier and concurrent experienced environmental content, for example the big bike play (Figure 6.13). Henry's drawing could be a figurative representation of earlier dynamic action:

| | |
|---|---|
| Circular enclosures | The wheels of his bike. |
| Oval | The handlebars. |
| Proximity | The wheels of the bike are near to each other. |
| Vertical order | The handlebars are arranged above the wheel. |

Henry (2.0) used language – 'big scooter', 'big car', 'red car' – during the big bike play but did not accompany his drawing with language. While the figurative representation in Figure 6.12 could be linked with Henry's perception of a bike, it cannot confidently be identified as such because Harry did not say this. However, what is clear is the similarity of form between his marks and the bike.

In Figure 6.14, several of the basic scribbles identified by Kellogg (1969) are evident in imperfect circles, spirals and lines but it is in the placement of these scribbles, mainly in the vertical half of the paper, which seems to indicate Henry's developing perception of shape.

**Figure 6.13** **Henry (2.0) The big bike**

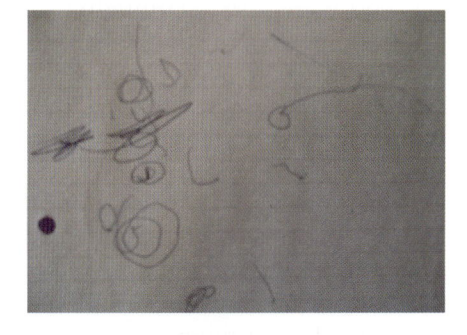

**Figure 6.14** **Henry (2.3) Core and radials**

Kellogg (1969: 38) suggested that 'children deliberately place markings so that the *total* configuration implies a shape'. This is relevant in Figure 6.14, in which a vertical rectangle can be inferred. Although Kellogg confirmed that combinations of scribbles are frequently seen, the opportunity to intervene genuinely with children during mark making is missed. She insisted that:

> No questions need ever be asked, and comments that teachers make can be restricted to such constructive ones as 'very interesting', 'nice colours', 'I like that', 'good work', 'a nice scribble', 'pretty'. ... Such remarks can be made quietly and sincerely. No extended comment is usually required. (Kellogg 1969: 156)

Athey (2007: 169), however, recognised that 'intention and meaning were clearer when utterances were made in context'. This was relevant to both figurative and dynamic schema behaviour and underlines the key role of the adult in accompanying children with appropriate talk. This enables 'links between *forms of thought*, the content of thought and appropriate speech' to be made. To recognise and match children's *form of thought*, and so enable a more conceptual accompaniment, appeared to be disregarded by Kellogg, who seemed to have focused specifically on the mark making and not the influences and alternative meanings. This disregard neglected to recognise the potential for nurturing and extending children's thinking as they engage in the learning environment. Athey's (2007) work and the observations of Henry lead to the belief that the recognition of *match* is much more important than suggested by Kellogg. *Match* offers huge potential for cognitive connections to be made in the learning environment, a correlation between a child's *form of thinking* and an adult's accompanying conversation.

Coates (2002: 26) noted the importance of conversations 'as an essential ingredient to the drawing process' and went on to warn that if the drawn product is the only aspect interpreted and the talk used in the process of drawing is ignored, 'utterances which could aid understanding are ignored' (2002: 23). Angelides and Michaelidou (2009: 27) discovered the importance of accompanying conversations with children while they were drawing in revealing that 'children's drawings and simultaneous discussion with the creator of the drawing can help us develop a richer understanding'. In their work, it was an understanding of marginalisation; in Henry's work, it was an understanding of particular *forms of thinking* that children revealed.

Fargas-Malet, McSherry, Larkin and Robinson (2010: 183) also expressed the place of process in drawing, rather than an over-emphasis on product, in emphasising the importance of the 'child's explanation of what the drawing was about'. To take time with children while they work is essential if a real understanding of the nature of their thinking and their particular concerns is to be understood.

Henry again used graphic schemas and space orders in his work (Figure 6.14), but it is not possible to say whether they represent assimilated environmental content. There are curves, core and radials, spirals and lines, specifically vertical and horizontal. There is also evidence of space order schemas in the proximity between some of the marks, a suggestion of vertical order between figures and connection in that some of the shapes were connected but some remained separate. Athey's (2007: 65) acknowledgement that 'the shift from "motor" to "symbolic" functioning was clearest when children describe the content they are expressing through marks' is important in confirming the place of the knowledgeable adult in supporting children to make this transition. Although Henry did not ascribe meaning to the marks made in Figure 6.14, these do find a parallel in some of his dynamic actions in observations made around the same time.

Henry (2.3) was picking up pieces of melon and dropping them on to the floor, watching them fall (although this was not encouraged by staff). He also accompanied his own dynamic action with appropriate speech 'up' and 'down' when using the chime bar. Various other motor level examples of trajectory behaviour in the vertical plane have been previously discussed.

Rolling cars down a slope, pushing pegs down, climbing up, sliding down and putting his bowl on top of his cup were evidence of contrasting content but comparable *form* of this vertical schema. Henry was representing his 'vertical trajectory' schema dynamically, in speech and, it could be suggested, figuratively (Figure 6.14). This similarity of *form* can be detected in Figure 6.16 where marks again have been placed in a way which implies vertical rectangular shape.

Cox (2005: 123) noted that 'drawing thus becomes a constructive process of thinking in action, rather than a developing ability to make visual reference to objects in the world'. Henry did not attempt to draw slopes, cars rolling, chime bars and did not appear to attempt to capture a particular image. However, his mark making (in Figure 6.16) did suggest a depiction of the same *form of thinking* evident in his dynamic actions concurrent at the time.

Figure 6.15  **Dropping melon**

Figure 6.16  **Enclosures, spirals, core and radials**

Anning (2003: 30) recognised children's ability to represent their thinking in a variety ways, referring to the 'multi-modes of signing, physical actions and graphical representation'. Henry depicts his thinking through a variety of seemingly unrelated actions and marks. If there is to be a cohesive understanding of children's thinking, one where Anning's 'multi-modes' are not seen as a collection of isolated incidences, an informed understanding of what is being observed is needed. Henry's multi-modal approach to representation is consistent in its *form*.

## Henry (2.4) Making Marks

Figures 6.17–6.20 show evidence of lines and curves, including vertical lines, straight parallel lines, horizontal lines, core and radials, and enclosure. There was also a relationship between space, in the proximity between the marks and in the vertical order. Kellogg (1969) specified that these emerging diagram

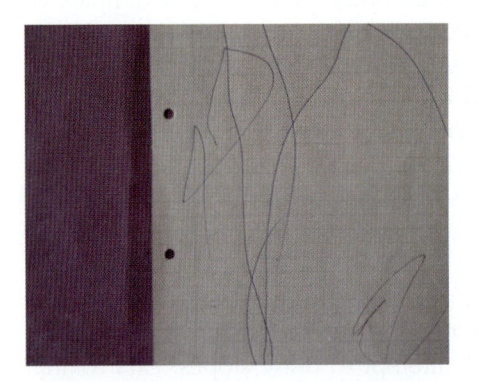

Figure 6.17   Henry (2.4) Vertical lines

Figure 6.18   Henry (2.4) Parallel lines and horizontal

Figure 6.19   Henry (2.4) Vertical lines and enclosure

Figure 6.20   Henry (2.4) Vertical lines on card

shapes may be produced with an element of eye control but suggested that the parallel line crosses (evident in Figures 6.17–6.20) may be as a result of uncontrolled rhythmical dynamism, which is often evident in the marks made by younger children.

Seen in isolation, the apparently uncontrolled nature of these drawings could be accepted. However, viewed from a schematic perspective and considering Piaget and Inhelder's (1956) recognition of the link between sensori-motor movement and figurative representation, they propose a much more holistic, over-arching and connected interpretation of Henry's behaviour. The drawings presented in this chapter have a static configuration; they are end-products. The action precursors, the antecedent behaviours, which are essentially dynamic in nature and which led to the production of these figurative representations, are unseen.

Henry's drawings (in Figures 6.17–6.20) could be interpreted as a figurative representation of Henry's dynamic vertical schema. In the absence of speech, however, it can only by concluded that marks and preferred actions match. Anning (2003: 32) recognised the importance of careful observation of children's dynamic and figurative behaviours in coming to a more holistic understanding of the child. She warned that the 'children's agenda and purposes for their representations are rarely taken seriously' and went on to say that, in fact, 'their meaning making is relentlessly towards school versions of literacy and numeracy'. Henry's drawings in Figures 6.17–6.20 suggested underlying *patterns of thinking* in his actions, which were evident to a careful, knowledgeable observer. The patient and informed observer, who understands and accepts the significance of children's schematic behaviours, may be able to nurture these thinking concerns with appropriate and meaningful accompaniment. This kind of practitioner may not be intent on trying to shape Henry's meaning making into something it was not, but rather wants to understand his meanings.

Henry's emerging symbolism had been observed in the pursuit of his dynamic back and forth schema. He had played with a small toy steamroller on the car mat and used language to accompany his actions of pushing the steamroller along (dynamic back and forth). Later, he made a model and called it 'steamroller' (Figure 6.21). Henry pushed a variety of wheeled toys along (motor displacement of objects). He said 'near the home, round the corner, a big steamroller's here, nearly here, it's here' (internalised displacement) and made a model calling it 'Steamroller' (symbolic representation).

**Figure 6.21** **Henry (2.10) 'Steamroller'**

## Henry (2.5) Making Marks

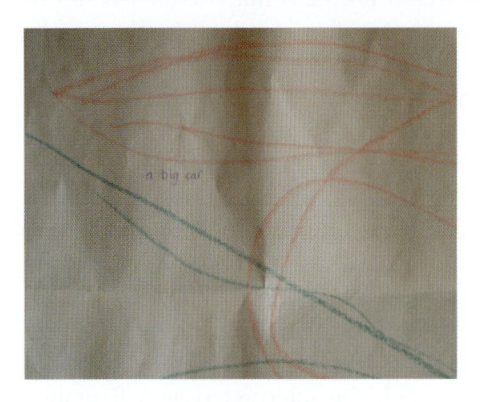

**Figure 6.22** Henry (2.5) A big car

In making the drawing in Figure 6.22 Henry used language to ascribe meaning to his marks – 'big car'. Lowenfeld and Brittain (1982) would suggest that this was an important step in thinking. Henry was making a connection between the marks he had made and the world around him. In early representations, Athey (2007: 81) also identified a link between what children drew and what they could see around them, stating that 'content had a perceptual equivalence to graphic form'.

In Figure 6.22 Henry appeared to be co-ordinating two schemas – trajectories and enclosures – and named it 'big car'. He used an oblique line which corresponded with previously experienced environmental content in his sliding, walking and slithering down use of the slide in the soft play (Figures 6.23 and 6.24).

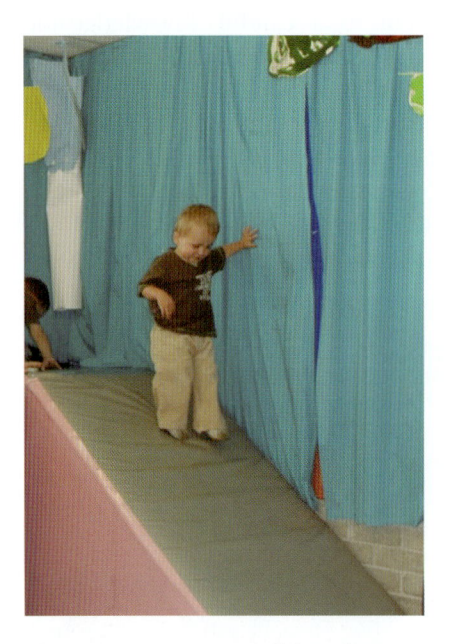

**Figure 6.23** Henry walking down the slide

**Figure 6.24** Henry at the bottom of the slide having slid down

Athey's (2007: 90) confirmation that 'graphic representations are based on schematic form combined with personal experience' can be seen in the way Henry brings together dynamic exploits and appeared to draw upon them in his representation of 'big car'. In the pursuit of his dynamic back and forth schema, Henry had pushed a variety of wheeled toys along the floor, including fire engines, trucks, trains, diggers and cars. He had gone *back and forth* from the cupboards to the table collecting knives, spoons, teapots, forks and cups and stacking them on the table. He had displaced a wide range of objects, toy animals, soft shapes and small wooden blocks and made piles with them on completing a particular trajectory. His apparent sensitivity to specific environmental content in the pursuit of this *form of thought* had seen Henry using the glockenspiel, pizza cutter, frame with beads and soft play cylinders. The exploration of horizontal trajectories was brought forward in his representation of 'big car'.

Henry named his drawing but did not describe specific elements within it and it could be argued that an adult could have engaged in conversation here in an attempt to extend this. Kellogg's recommendation was to 'supply descriptive terms that do not have pictorial connotations'. This overlooks the possibility of a conceptual response, specifically the opportunity to invest a child's marks with meaning both of *form* and related content. To let Henry hear language in an encounter which complemented his *form of thought* is appropriate. This requires a certain accord with the child and an ability on the part of the adult to describe what they see and not what they think they see the child doing. This is not a cursory, shallow endeavour, but a preparedness to work with the child, from the child, to enrich the child.

If the conversation with Henry, while drawing his 'big car', was limited to 'I like red cars too', 'your road is blue', 'what kind of car does your daddy have?', it could be said that there had been a missed opportunity. To understand what it was that Henry was busy thinking about as he made his drawing was the essential defining feature of attuned accompaniment. This required an adult who had been conscious of Henry at other times, who had seen him occupied with other important explorations. It required an adult who recognised and applied this knowledge to make relevant connections with him, using language which resonated with his *form of thinking*. This, combined with additional associative talk, which is not at the expense of conceptual discussion, is fruitful.

Nutbrown (2011: 45) notes the importance of both *content* and *form* in language used to accompany children's play, emphasising the place for matched correspondence. She clarifies that in order for this match to be realised, the adult joining the child in play needs to pay particular attention to the *form* of the play so that, through 'attentive listening', underlying thought patterns are not 'unknown and unnoticed'.

Henry used graphic schemas and space order schemas in his drawing of 'big car' (Figure 6.22).

Oval enclosure: The big car.

Separation: The big car is separate from the oblique line beneath; it does not touch it.

The configuration of Henry's drawing 'big car' (Figure 6.22) cannot be said to suggest what Athey (2007: 109) observed as 'the shift from *topological* to *projective* space notions used by children'. Henry had represented one object (the big car) on top of another mark (oblique line), but in the absence of further speech, there was insufficient evidence from this observation to suggest an experimentation with projective space. If Henry had attached additional descriptive language to his drawing and named the oblique line 'road,' then a more secure understanding of this shift would have been made clear.

Piaget and Inhelder (1956: 467) clarified that 'the essential feature of this process was the entry of the observer, or the "point of view" in relation to which figures are projected'. Henry would have demonstrated an ability to '*rotate* [himself] mentally around an object as well as *rotate* objects in the mind' (Athey 2007: 111). If Henry, in drawing his 'big car', had said 'that's daddy's door with the steering wheel, you can't see mummy's, it's on the other side', it would have implied an exploration of projective space. However, this sophisticated concept is likely to emerge with greater maturity.

Henry knew that cars move along on top of roads. He had experienced this, played with this (Figures 6.25 and 6.26) and represented it graphically. He had not, however, displayed an ability to decentre. He had not yet, as Piaget and Inhelder (1956: 468) required, 'with the addition of a perspective

Figure 6.25 Henry (1.10) pushing objects along the floor

Figure 6.26 Henry (2.6) pushing himself along

viewpoint ... embraced relative orientation'. If the adult had pursued the conversation to enable Henry to reflect on his drawing, he might have been able to point out that 'you can't see my car seat, it's inside the car, behind daddy', thus demonstrating a level of symbolic functioning where static configurations can be negotiated mentally. However, it must be acknowledged that Henry, at such a young age, would not be expected to be able to do this.

Henry, in his drawing of 'big car' had not represented the rotations figuratively or in speech but had attached a label. He had also attached a name to his drawing 'Crayons, Paper, Spider, Sun, Prickly Bush' (Figure 6.27).

**Figure 6.27** Henry (2.5) Crayons, Paper, Spider, Sun, Prickly Bush

Kellogg (1969: 98) recognised that the labels children attached to their scribbles may be as a result of the child realising 'the adult's wish for evidence of pictorial meaning in child work' but that they might not use these pictorial labels 'until the adult uses them' (1969: 138). This is significant in terms of conversation with children about their work in general and graphic representations in particular. Intervening comments from well-meaning adults, intended to support and enable, may in fact be received as distracting irritations by children, who feel obliged to satisfy the adult in providing what children think the adults want. Heywood (2001: 9) acknowledged this in describing childhood as ostensibly 'a function of adult expectations'.

Henry, in drawing 'Crayons, Paper, Spider, Sun, Prickly Bush', attached the labels spontaneously and this could be the graphic equivalent of the collection of chalks, books etc. collected together in a box discussed previously (Figure 3.1). The adult did not initiate an associative *content-related* exchange about creepy crawlies, favourite colours, sun hats or plasters on scratched fingers. The opportunity to explore the underlying *form* within the drawing, however, was also missed.

Coates and Coates (2006: 221) alerted adults to the importance of being aware of the potential of children's drawings and mark making, which can reveal 'the quality and depth of young children's spontaneous and self-taught visual expression ... [and is] evidence of their conceptual and creative development as well as the richness of their fertile imagination'. The potential of this drawing episode was overlooked when the adult missed the opportunity to take the exchange further. Until then, Henry had been soliloquising in naming his marks and the opportunity to explore *form* was neglected.

Athey (2007: 80) identified a 'close relationship between mark making and an increased perception of objects in the environment that have a figural equivalence'. It could be argued that most of the names Henry attached to this drawing have a perceptual equivalence to graphic *form* in his use of lines to represent spiders, crayons and prickles. Henry did not represent prickles with enclosures. To extend Henry's thinking, an environment enriched with content which allowed for a dynamic and figurative exploration of vertical and horizontal (and emerging interest in core and radial forms) was important, as was the presence of an understanding adult.

An approach to intervention consistent with children's intentions, their suggestions, their instructions, their directions and their meanings, is an altogether more complex and challenging endeavour for the adult, but one which should be an accepted protocol, an understood way of being.

## Conclusion

Piaget (1969) identified two kinds of cognitive patterning, specifically *figurative* (linked with early perception) and *operative* (linked with action). This chapter has focused on the *figurative* patterns, which Athey (2007) considered to be represented in children's two- and three-dimensional representations.

This chapter has shown a correspondence between how Henry was using the things around him to pursue his dynamic thought patterns, his action schemas (dynamic vertical, dynamic back and forth, and containing and enveloping) and his corresponding mark making. A perceptual correspondence to *form* in mark making using a variety of materials and tools synchronic with similar *forms* of dynamic actions was demonstrated. To presume symbolic meaning from marks in the absence of speech is inappropriate, but evidence of similarity in *form*, a parallel between marks made and dynamic actions observed, is apt. Figurative representation has a foundation in dynamic exploration which both Athey (2007) and Meade and Cubey (2008) observed in their work.

The opportunity for adults to connect to children's *forms* of thinking, both dynamic and figurative, is something to be seized, for, as Dunsmuir and Blatchford (2004: 479) recognised, 'capturing a child's interest and enjoyment may be the key to promoting writing development, and educators need to be aware of the desirability of providing tasks that pupils perceive as purposeful and valuable'. Although their study sought to explore factors influencing children's attainment and progress in writing between the ages of 4 and 7 years, the fundamental message of *connection* is clear. Dunsmuir and Blatchford's (2004) recognition of the importance of relating to what the child is interested in and, in reference to Henry, what he was concerned with conceptually – his thinking interests – was significant for professional adults working with young children. What would be of purpose and value for Henry would be an environment of possibilities and an involvement which matched his dynamic and figurative *forms of thought*.

## Reflection

Three specific questions emerged from this chapter:

- What aspects of thinking, learning and development do young children reveal in their schematic behaviour?
- How can adults intervene to support young children as they pursue their schemas?
- What are the implications of schema identification on the learning experiences of young children?

As the children play, evidence of their thinking patterns appears and the importance of the role of the adult in supporting and nourishing these *forms of thought* becomes ever more apparent. As shared times with the children revealed, it became increasingly significant for adults to attune and respond to children in a way which matched their particular thinking concerns.

Seen through the lens of schematic theory, those working with young children can reflect upon and shape their practice in an effort to provide a cognitive *match* in learning encounters. It allows accompaniment in learning to be a relevant and pertinent occasion which affords children the respect they deserve.

Think once more about Henry's use of the tambourine and consider the following questions:

- Do you take account of the spontaneous *form* of children's thought and the environmental content children may use?
- Do children in your setting with particular schemas select certain things to play with? Do they appear to be sensitised to particular environmental content?
- What additional experiences can be provided to nourish children's dynamic vertical schema?

## Further Reading

Coates, E. and Coates, A. (2006) Young children talking and drawing. *International Journal of Early Years Education*, 14(3): 221–241.

Donaldson, M. (1978) *Children's Minds*. London: HarperCollins.

Kellogg, R. (1969) *Analyzing Children's Art*. Mountain View, CA: Mayfield Publishing Co.

Meade, A. and Cubey, P. (2008) *Thinking Children: Learning about Schemas* (2nd edition). Wellington: New Zealand Council for Educational Research and Institute for Early Childhood Studies, Wellington College of Education/Victoria University of Wellington.

# PART 3
# DEVELOPMENTAL JOURNEYS: TRACING DEVELOPMENTS IN CHILDREN'S THINKING FROM MOTOR TO SYMBOLIC BEHAVIOURS

In this part of the book we cover a number of children's developmental journeys through their schemas. Richly detailed observations depict the movement from motor to symbolic thinking, including evidence of the children's understanding of functional dependency relationships and the effects of their actions on objects. The observations are discussed to reveal their significance in terms of schemas and of other aspects of young children's development. We show how children's behaviour can be interpreted both from a schematic perspective and from a holistically developmental perspective. Examples show how observations can map on to other assessments of children's development and how they can also articulate with and support parents' perspectives of their children's development.

*Note*: The observations were made by Frances and the 'I' refers to her.

# PART 3

# DEVELOPMENTAL JOURNEYS: TRACING DEVELOPMENT IN CHILDREN'S THINKING FROM MOTOR TO SYMBOLIC BEHAVIOURS

# CHAPTER 7

# CONTAINING AND ENVELOPING SCHEMA

This chapter explores the playful pursuits of four young children in an early years setting. It reveals what they were telling us about their thinking, learning and development when they played. The observations of the children, aged from eight months to 17 months, are discussed schematically and trace developments in the Children's thinking from motor to symbolic behaviours. The observations also tell another story, that of the holistic thinking of young children, revealed as they play, for as Goldschmied and Jackson (2004: 99) reminded us:

> Watching a baby as she explores, it is fascinating to see the zest with which she chooses objects that attract her, the precision she shows in bringing them to her mouth and the quality of concentration as she makes contact with the play material. We see her intent observation, her ability to choose and return to a favoured item, her ability to select and experiment.

During these observations, the children were engrossed in activities of great personal consequence. For them, the unfolding stories depict moments of intense individual activity.

The material of the play was merely that which was reachable: miscellaneous items, sometimes used unpredictably or occasionally items of dubious suitability, but nevertheless personally identified for use in play. These apparently commonplace things belie the astonishing *forms of thinking* displayed in their use. Intricate behaviours depicting these *forms of thinking* were noted through alert yet sensitive observation.

The observations, which were taken over a 12-month period, were interpreted schematically (Athey 2007) and within the context of the Early Years Foundation Stage (DfE 2012). The chapter begins with a set of schema-oriented observations. This is followed by an 'unpacking' which answers the 'so what?' questions that many people have once they have observed schemas.

## The observations tell a schema story...

*...About dynamic containing and enveloping*

- Motor level
- Symbolic level
- Functional dependency relationships

## The observations tell another story...

*...About areas of learning and development*

Prime Areas

- Personal, Social and Emotional Development
- Physical Development
- Communication and Language

Specific Areas

- Literacy
- Mathematics
- Understanding the World
- Expressive Arts and Design (DfE 2012: 5)

## Containing and Enveloping Schema: Motor Level Observations

*Annie (0.8) selects the basket and explores it busily. She spends time examining it, turning it over, putting her hand inside and using her mouth. As her hand roams around inside the basket, she follows it with her gaze.*

Figure 7.1  Exploring the basket

Figure 7.2  Hand inside

Figure 7.3  Tissue box as a container

Figure 7.4  Lid inside tissue box

*Annie (0.11) sees the tissue box and picks it up. She notices the hole at the top of the box and looks inside. She picks up a metal lid and posts it through the hole in the top of the box. Annie then pushes her hand inside the box. She takes her hand out, tips the box upside down and shakes it until the lid falls out.*

Corbetta and Snapp-Childs (2009) confirmed that through sensory exploration young children secure knowledge of the physical characteristics of objects in the environment, which can be evoked at a later date. These are powerful discoveries. According to Athey (2007: 200), 'experience provid[es] the content of representation ... the "stuff" or "content" of mind'. Annie was able to bring such experiences to later environmental encounters.

When Annie (0.8) explored the basket inside and out, she was involved in what Corbetta and Snapp-Childs (2009) refer to as *haptic investigations*. While she was physically exploring the objects I imagined her to be thinking, 'What is this and what can I do with it?' 'It's lumpy and bumpy', 'It's prickly in my mouth', 'I can hold it in two hands', 'If I turn it over, I can see the bottom', 'The bottom is not like the sides', 'I can fit my hand inside', 'I'll have to put it on the floor if I want to put both hands in', and so on.

When Annie (0.11) inspected the tissue box and noticed the hole in the top, she may have been drawing on her experience with the basket. When she dropped the lid inside the box, she had already experienced insideness, as when she put her hand into the basket at eight months old. She repeated this action in her attempt to get the lid out of the box. Meltzoff and Moore (1998: 224) observed that 'detecting regularities, forming expectations and even making predictions about future states of affairs' resonate. In tipping the box upside down and shaking it until the lid falls out, she may have formed an expectation that up-ending the box will make the lid will fall out, particularly if it is shaken.

Piaget and Inhelder (1969: 11) observed that it is not until the fifth stage of the sensori-motor period, at about 11 or 12 months, that children 'search for new means by differentiation from schemes already known', which was observed as 'more complete acts of practical intelligence' (1969: 10) as Annie co-ordinated means and ends. She knew the lid was inside the box even though it was now out of sight. She wanted to get the lid out so she poked her hand inside the box to pick it out. When this was unsuccessful, she employed another means – she shook the box.

Athey (2007) clarified that a child of Annie's age would not be able to imagine this sequence of events because, as Piaget (1950: 121) testified, sensori-motor co-ordinations consisted of 'successive perceptions and overt movements ... without fusion'. Piaget likened sensori-motor intelligence to 'a slow motion film, in which all the pictures are seen in succession' (Piaget 1950), whereas Willattes (1984: 133) maintained that '9-month old infants were able to co-ordinate two separate actions into an effective sequence'. This could be seen with Annie, who reached for the lid inside the box, up-ended the box, shook it and retrieved the lid. She did so through active experimentation and not, we suggest, through thought alone.

**Figure 7.5 Inside the mirror box**

*Annie spends time putting objects (lids, toy animals, blocks, wooden balls, banana, herself) inside containers (yoghurt pots, tissue boxes, baskets, snack bowl, mirror box).*

*Annie (0.10) is playing at the water trough, she put both hands under the water. She pulls a yoghurt pot towards her and puts both hands inside the tub. Later, Annie (1.1) is playing at the treasure basket. She picks up the small ball and holds it in one hand. She picks up an egg cup and tries to fit the ball inside the egg cup.*

*Annie (1.6) crawls over to the floor sand pit. She clambers in and sits down. She picks up a spade and fills a tub. She empties the tub of sand and refills. She fills and empties the tub three times, then crawls out of the sand pit.*

CONTAINING AND ENVELOPING SCHEMA  99

**Figure 7.6** Annie (1.8) covers her palms …

**Figure 7.7** … then paints the backs

**Figure 7.8** Hand into the paint pot

**Figure 7.9** Hand covered

*Annie (1.8) is sitting at the painting table. She dips the paint brush into the paint and paints the palm of her hand. She turns her hand over and paints the back. Annie tries to fit her hand into the paint pot then holds it up in the air.*

Annie was engrossed in vital exploration. Her investigations were essential, practical endeavours which underpin later understandings. She noticed, identified, resolved and made discoveries. These practical engagements are acknowledged to be fundamental. Indeed, Piaget (1959: 283) asserted that they constitute 'the foundation of symbolism and representation'. Bruner (1966: 16) confirmed this, suggesting that they provided 'the necessary and sufficient condition for progress'. Bruner's 'condition' serves as a warning to practitioners of the imperative for young children to have these kinds of explorative, investigative opportunities. Bruner's 'condition' was a stipulation, a prerequisite, which alluded to the nature of the environment in which young children should find themselves.

## What do the observations reveal?

Annie's (1.10) containing and enveloping schema was evidenced by a series of motor level actions, including hands inside baskets, lids posted, lids tipped out, banana emptied out, banana slices dropped back into snack bowls, hands under water, hands into yoghurt pot, ball into egg cup, covering hands in paint, hands into paint pot and climbing inside spaces. These 'patterns in children's actions' (Meade and Cubey 2008: 3), which Flavell (1963) recognised have an underlying sameness, 'can be used intentionally through the emergence of the process of assimilation and accommodation' (Donaldson 1978: 134). Annie was able to assimilate information from her environment (content and company) and incorporate this into her existing schema (containing and enveloping). She then accommodated her existing schema to fit these external influences. Howard (1987: 133) acknowledged 'that this is the means by which a child's cognitive structures develop'.

The observations also revealed the holistic nature of Annie's thinking as she immersed herself in the learning environment. Nutbrown (2006: 117) reminded us that 'when children are thinking, talking and applying their existing knowledge, [they] attend to the task in hand. Children do not analyse their knowledge in terms of subjects.' Annie pursued her schema of containing and enveloping which allowed for a range of ideas to be explored.

## The observations tell a schema story…

### …About containing and enveloping

- Selecting containers from the treasure basket
- Hands inside basket
- Looking at hole in box
- Posting lid inside box
- Reaching inside box for lid
- Dropping banana into bowl
- Annie inside mirror box
- Gazing inside basket

- Hands under water
- Hands into yoghurt pots and paint pots
- Ball into egg cup
- Hands covered with paint

### ...About dynamic vertical

- Shaking box to get lid out
- Up-ending basket

### ...About circular rotation

- Basket rotated
- Selecting round lid to post

### ...About going through a boundary

- Fingers through hoop

## The observations tell another story...

### ...About characteristics of effective learning

- Showing high levels of energy, fascination (DfE 2012: 6)
- Finding new ways to do things (DfE 2012: 7)
- Finding ways to solve problems (DfE 2012: 7)

Annie was offered an environment of choice. She explored her surroundings and the resources within it. She made particular selections (basket, box, different containers) and investigated their possibilities. She was coming to know what she preferred at this time, demonstrated in how she used the things around her. She was developing a confidence to search for, inspect and examine objects of interest around her. She persisted for periods of time (inspecting the hole in the tissue box, posting, attempts to retrieve the lid) and persevered until tasks were completed (the lid shakes out of the box). She displayed high levels of involvement when she absorbed herself in tasks which she herself directed. Laevers' (1976) description of involvement in learning, expressed by total focus and intense mental activity, was suggested in Annie's actions with the basket and box.

She was busy following through her own particular interests here, with content she appeared to find appropriate and applicable. To enable this level of involvement to be maintained, the provision of intriguing environmental content for young children is an enduring responsibility for practitioners in the early years. Practitioners should be conscientiously accountable for such provision and embrace it fully.

## ...About physical development

- Reaches out for, touches and begins to hold objects
- Explores objects with mouth, often picking up an object and holding it to the mouth (DfE 2012: 22)

Annie was surrounded with resources that offered possibilities. She was observed using her senses to investigate objects around her. She was purposeful and made choices in attempting to change position, move towards and away from things, selecting and rejecting objects and setting herself new challenges.

Selleck (2001: 90) acknowledged the extent to which 'children's preoccupations' should influence adults in the learning environment. She asserted that to be 'out of synch with an infant's moods and meanings' can impact upon the quality of a child's play and learning. It was through meticulous watching that we may come to know children more thoroughly. This level of acquaintance, established through painstaking observation, echoes Arnold's (2003) understanding of children's physical development. She asserted that it was 'not simply an outlet for excess energy, but lays the foundation for thought' (Arnold 2003: 40).

Neisser (1976: 57) observed that 'the perceiver engages in an act that involves information from the environment as well as his own cognitive mechanisms. He is changed from the information he picks up'. This resonated with Arnold's (2003) comment about the place of action underpinning thought. Through her physical action, Annie's mental activity could be interpreted. What she selected from things around her and how she used them suggested her *form of thinking*.

The everyday experiences to which Annie was exposed may be assimilated to her containing and enveloping schema. There was, however, a particular sensitivity and receptiveness to matching environmental stimuli. Cheng and Holyoak's (1985: 135) 'context-sensitive' structure relates to Athey's (2007: 92) 'schemas ... sensitized to similar things in the environment'. Annie's selection of containers (basket, tissue box, mirror box) and containing objects (lid, banana, hands, herself) suggested a certain inclination. She appeared to spot specific things around her which enabled her to follow her *form of thought* (of containing and enveloping).

## ...About communication and language

- Communicate needs in a variety of ways, including crying, gurgling, babbling and squealing
- Makes own sounds in response when talked to by familiar adults (DfE 2012: 19)

Annie concentrated on things which captured her interest (gazing at the hole in the box, putting her hand inside the basket, sitting inside the mirror box).

Although her thinking was not articulated audibly and not recorded figuratively here, Annie's activities appeared to convey her thoughts, with important considerations fluently expressed in action. To give young children plenty of time to relax into environments, offering gentle support and tranquil encouragement when needed, is vital. When Annie was working in the treasure basket, there was a pervading serenity and quietness. To give young children time to become, and be, engrossed, without interruption, is an affordance which is sometimes difficult for adults to accept. The temptation to impose and intrude upon children's necessary private thinkings is to be resisted on occasion. Knowing when these occasions arise requires a perceptive and insightful professional understanding on the part of the practitioner. Goldschmied and Jackson's (2004: 107) characterisation of the adult role when working with babies 'to provide security by [an] attentive, but not active, presence' is challenging because it proposes an alternative comprehension of commitment and involvement, one of cautious, considered and timely connection.

Annie was communicating with the accompanying adult. They were physically close in sitting near each other around the treasure basket. They made eye contact, the adult smiled, she sometimes placed different objects within reach of Annie, or occasionally offered Annie something different to explore. The adult was quietly present. She played alongside Annie, picking up objects, touching them, not talking but watching and listening. Annie and the adult work alongside each other. Annie was aware of the adult but appeared happily engrossed.

Bruner (1997: 63–64) suggested that the mind had 'inherent subjectivity', which he clarified in that 'for all its privacy, mind generates a product that is public ... there is adaptation to the natural and social worlds through appropriate actions'. Although Annie was involved in an individual endeavour, she was not isolated and separate. She was mentally active in trying things out (the space inside the basket), was solving problems (shaking the box to release the lid), but did so in a social context. She revealed her private thinkings in her public actions. Annie's partners in learning may witness this, understand this, interpret this and respond. Alternatively, they may not, as to do so appropriately requires a highly skilled, professional understanding, confidence and competence.

As Annie co-ordinates hand and eye movements, she was engaging in significant motor activities which could be brought forward to support later representations. Shore (1997: 51) highlighted the significance of these first physical (and social) encounters for babies and very young children as having 'dramatic impacts on the architecture of their brains'. Friedman (2006) understood this when he noted a link between appropriate stimulus in the early years and dramatic brain development. In this respect, as Annie used an increasing range of objects, resources and materials, her skills in manipulating these develop. The journey from reaching and grasping, towards mark making... via dough and clay, paint and glue, sand and water, threading and baking... using brushes, sponges, rollers, knives, sticks, scoops, sieves... was under way.

## ...About understanding the world

- Looks around a room with interest; visually scans the environment for novel, interesting objects and events
- Smiles with pleasure at recognisable playthings
- Becomes absorbed in combining objects, e.g. banging two objects or placing objects into containers (DfE 2012: 39)

Annie was investigative and explorative and employed her senses to make meaning from her experiences. She appeared to contemplate objects carefully and inspected them during her work with the treasure basket. Annie appeared determined to solve problems through her action on objects (when the lid could not be retrieved by reaching inside, she shook the box upside down so that it would fall out). It cannot be said that she was displaying true functional dependency, which Athey (1990: 70) defined as 'the effects of action on objects or material', as this, Athey confirmed, is an indicator of impending conservation.

Piaget's (1950: 59) observation that 'at this pre-operatory level the reactions are centred on perceptual or imagined configurations', with perception defined as 'a knowledge we have of objects or of their movements by direct and immediate contact', resonated with Annie's actions in trying to release the lid from the box. She cannot be said to be an imminent conserver, as her problem-solving approach was more trial and error. She did not identify an immediate resolution before embarking on her actions. Annie tried one thing (groping inside the box); it failed. She then tried another tactic (up-ending and tipping), with success this time. If she had been a conserver, she would have understood that in order for the lid to be released, the box needed to be tipped and shaken. She would have been able to mentally orientate her mind around the problem before embarking on any action, an ability which Piaget and Inhelder (1969: 99) suggested was absent until the age of 7 or 8.

Athey (1990: 70), however, recognised the importance of practical undertakings such as Annie's which, she suggested, support later internalised operations. She confirmed that 'sensory and perceptual information accompanying motor actions led to true operations that can be carried out in the mind'. Annie needed time to explore, play and seek meaning in her experiences (DfE 2012). She needed time to think things through and solve practical problems in an exciting and enjoyable environment. Piaget (1950) confirmed that these early explorations and investigations, in which Annie was involved, could be seen as essential, concrete foundations for later mental activity. When Annie is older and faced with a problem to solve, she may not need to be immediately physically dynamic, as she may be able to recall these early actions and think problems through.

In the basket and box play, Annie has worked alongside the adult happily. She did not appear distressed or try to crawl away. She was beginning to form attachments to significant others and responding to adult attention. The response may not be overt and explicit but one of quiet contentment. For Annie to continue with her activities in the presence of another person was a positive response from her.

Bornstein, Haynes, Legler, O'Reilly and Painter (1997: 202) found that children's reactions in the learning environment were more positive 'when the stranger/experimenter acted like mother'. This was echoed in Malmberg, Stein, West, Lewis, Barnes, Leach and Sylva's (2007) work, which suggested that the sensitivity of the mother impacts upon the mood of the infant in that change in infants' moods was related to change in mothers' sensitivity. Annie was starting 'to build relationships with special people' (DCSF 2008: 32) and appeared comfortable with the adult present as she seemed happy to continue with her activities in her presence.

Erikson's (1963: 249) proposal that a relationship 'which combines sensitive care of the baby's individual needs and a firm sense of personal trustworthiness' was important for adults working with young children. The adult was not Annie's mother but was calm, gentle and considerate when working with her. This was vital to enable Annie to feel contented, at ease, secure and relaxed, and therefore more inclined to absorb herself in her work.

Scientific concepts related to materials and their properties were being developed as a result of Annie's exploration of insideness. Her investigations with a variety of containers (rough baskets, shiny lids, smooth boxes, hard bowls) helped develop her experiences of similarities and differences in materials. She was coming to know about cause and effect in that her actions can have an effect on objects and materials (shaking can release stuck lids). When Annie selected objects from around her to inspect, she was also developing ideas about grouping and classifying materials according to their properties in that she chose items that were containers, and then appeared to find things to contain.

The Department for Education document *Statutory Framework for the Early Years Foundation Stage* (DfE 2012: 7) recognises that 'finding ways to solve problems, finding new ways to do things, making links and noticing patterns, making predictions and testing and developing ideas are *Characteristics of Effective Learning*' (italics added). Annie was observed solving problems as she explored things around her. She could not get the lid out of the tissue box at the first attempt, so tried something different (shaking). Whether she had made a connection with past experiences in her previous practical investigations of insideness cannot be confirmed but the repeated form of her actions was clear to see. She had an understanding 'that things exist, even when out of sight' (the hidden lid) (DfE 2012: 32) and was 'showing curiosity about objects' in her sensory exploration of the basket, and bananas at snack time (DfE 2012: 6).

Piaget and Inhelder (1956: 10) recognised that when an object was 'passed from one hand to the other, turned over in all directions, touched at the same time as it is looked at', there was a development of a 'perceptual constancy of shape and size'. Annie was coming to know through her investigations with the basket and tissue box that some objects were the same size and shape even when they were turned around and were upside down.

Concepts of estimation and capacity were being developed as a result of Annie's exploration of things inside. She was investigating what fits, in putting the lid in the box, her hands in the basket and herself in the mirror box. In selecting to inspect objects that appeared to contain, Annie was developing an understanding of classification and comparison in that some objects were containers and could fit things inside and some were not and so could not.

## ...About expressive arts and design

- Explores and experiments with a range of media through sensory exploration and using whole body (DfE 2012: 43)
- Expresses self through physical action and sound (DfE 2012: 45)

Boyce (1935), in her account of an educational experiment at an infant's school between 1933 and 1936, found that it was unfeasible to detach sensory experiences from a child's own preferences, their own inclinations, their own personal, practice choices. There is soul in Boyce's meaning. Creativity is seen as the personal expression of a unique spirit, the essence of an individual made known.

Moyles (1989) recognised the affective nature of creativity but included the conceptual. She saw creativity as a 'personal expression and interpretation of emotions, thoughts and ideas' (1989: 70). She went on to emphasise that creativity 'is a process which outweighs any product particularly' (1989: 70). Moyles' 'process' suggested a certain dynamism which should not be confused with action. Moyles' 'creative process' seemed more aligned with journeying. At times the journey was halted or impeded, but at other times it proceeded without delay. This ebb and flow was acknowledged by Malaguzzi's (1998) characterisation of creativity as having the ability to come in and out of view:

> Creativity? It is always difficult to notice when it is dressed in everyday clothing and has the ability to appear and disappear suddenly. Our task, regarding creativity, is to help children climb their own mountains, as high as possible.
> (Malaguzzi 1998: 77)

Creativity therefore seems to be about adventure and inventiveness, excitement and poignancy, struggles and accomplishments. It is about enabling and reciprocal relationships. It is about professional adults who infuse their practice with opportunity and a knowing understanding of who and what they observe. It is about children who feel free to share the most intimate matters of personal significance.

Brierley (1994: 67) understood creativity as 'the capacity to respond emotionally and intellectually to sensory experience', which Selbie and Wickett (2010) alluded to in their consideration of playful approaches. They stated that 'whenever and wherever play is encouraged, babies and young children will be learning through exploration, at a practical level but also in self-discovery' (Selbie and Wickett 2010: 76).

Brierley (1994) and Selbie and Wickett (2010) went further than a consideration of an essentially practical engagement with content, a sensory exploration of the learning environment. They inferred something more complex in acknowledging the place for emotional response and a personal coming to know. There was a reflectiveness about this, a suggestion of looking inward to what actually stirs our way of being. Forman and Fosnot's (1982: 190) acknowledgement that 'one can be mentally active yet physically passive' suggested that, although there may be times when babies and young children appear unmoving, even dormant and not fervently in action, their industry may be hidden. A mental busyness is obscured from view yet made visible through creative expression.

## Containing and Enveloping Schema: Further Motor Level Observations

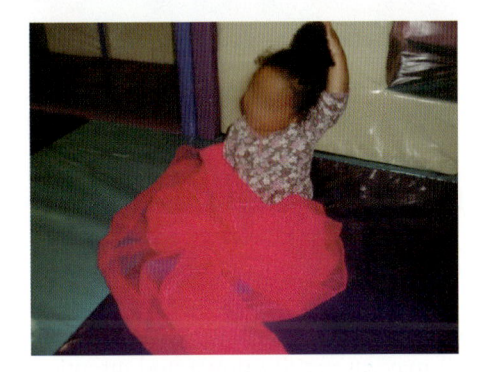

Figure 7.10  **Florence covers her legs**

Figure 7.11  **Patrick covers his head**

*Florence (1.6) covered her legs with a net and then with sand. Patrick (1.11) used the net to envelop his head and Nell (2.4) busied herself on several occasions covering hands and arms with glue, paint, glitter and felt pen.*

Athey (2007: 190) accepted that societies have conventional 'norms and mores'. She acknowledged however, that children's schematic pursuits did not absolve them from appropriate and accepted behaviour. The norms (accepted

**Figure 7.12** Covering hands with glue

**Figure 7.13** Covering with paint

**Figure 7.14** Covering with glitter

**Figure 7.15** Covering my arm

**Figure 7.16** Covering with felt pen

behaviours) of this society (the Children's Centre) may be challenged by children immersed in the pursuit of their schema. In using a variety of media (glitter, glue, paints and felt pen) to cover herself, Nell may attract the unwanted attention of a constraining adult, who may not be aware of the underlying schematic form in her behaviour. According to Athey (2007: 129), 'schematic explanations of such behaviours [are] more interesting and reassuring than thinking of such behaviours as random'.

Meade and Cubey's (2008: 152) idea of the 'novice adult' presented an opportunity for those working with young children to become apprentices to schematic theory. Bruce (2005: 71) supported this in stating that 'the study of schemas helps early childhood practitioners to develop a vocabulary of observation'. A knowledge of schema theory can be enlightening. It allows for previously unfathomable behaviours to be understood for the conceptual exploits they actually are. It permits an optimistic interpretation of children's behaviour. For adults working with young children, Bruce's (2005) 'vocabulary' – an eloquent knowledgeable discourse about children's capabilities as thinkers – should be a professional prerequisite.

Although Tommy (1.6) spent time getting inside cars and tunnels, he also (perhaps less unacceptably) squeezed himself into the dolls' house and sink unit. Patrick (1.11) joined in, in his pursuit of 'containing and enveloping', in emptying the container box and putting it on his head. The underlying repeated *form of thinking*, that of containment and envelopment, is obvious to the trained eye.

Figure 7.17  Inside the car

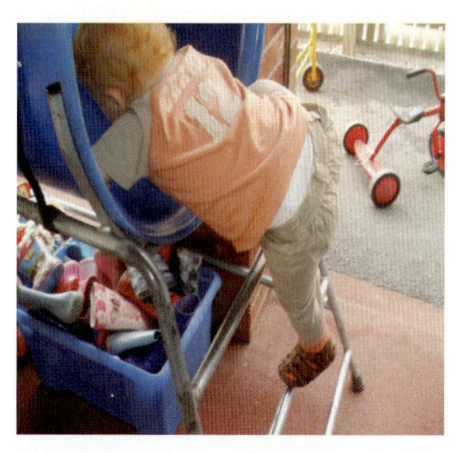

Figure 7.18  Inside the tunnel

Figure 7.19  **Covering with container box**

Figure 7.20  **Tommy inside the doll's house**

*Tommy (1.6) put toy cars inside the teapot. He took the bowl out of the sink. He got the toy cars out of the teapot and dropped them into the hole. The cars fall down inside the sink unit. When the teapot is empty, he drops the teapot through the hole as well. Tommy then goes under the sink unit and retrieves the toy cars and teapot.*

**Figure 7.21  Objects inside teapot**

**Figure 7.22  Teapot inside sink unit**

**Figure 7.23  Making an enclosure**

*Later, he makes an enclosure with the fence panels and puts random objects inside (giraffe, van, car).*

It seemed that it was not the possibility of journey play, pushing vehicles around the mat that was important. Nor was it the prospect of making roaring noises during an investigation into the contents of the zoo box. What was significant for Tommy appeared to be that the objects were containable and that he could contain them.

It was snack time but Nell did not appear to be interested in eating her Shreddies. She was busy working on some important investigations. Nell (1.8) was pursuing her dominant schema of 'containing and enveloping'.

*She tips the bowl out on the high chair tray. Nell picks up handfuls of Shreddies and drops them under the table on to her knee. She perseveres with this task until all the Shreddies have disappeared from the table. The Shreddies were inside the pinny.*

Nell had used accessible objects around her (Shreddies) to pursue her schema of containment. She had put them inside an available container (the pinny).

# CONTAINING AND ENVELOPING SCHEMA

**Figure 7.24** Tipping out at snack time

**Figure 7.25** Dropping Shreddies

**Figure 7.26** Pinny full of Shreddies

It seemed that, for Nell, this was a purposeful, conceptual endeavour. For adults in a busy Children's Centre, trying to facilitate the smooth running of snack time, it was not perhaps an activity to be encouraged. Nor perhaps was Patrick with the container box on his head or Tommy inside the sink unit and doll's house. However, it was important to acknowledge the underlying thinking of the children here. A suggestion to Nell, for example, of other equally appealing, attuned activities was perhaps called for, and inviting her to explore something else after snack time would have been appropriate.

As Nutbrown (2006: 20) identified, 'children will not be easily interrupted in their doing and thinking', which was evident with Nell's occupation with the Shreddies. She would perhaps have used other content in her schematic investigation if it had been available at the time. Arnold's (2003: 148) recommendation to have 'open-ended resources freely available [and] the freedom to explore materials in [their] own way' is important. This allows for children with different schematic concerns to use objects around them in a way which is stimulating to their *form of thought*. Arnold does, however, caution adults working with young children to be vigilant (in observation) and responsive to particular thinking needs in the way the environment is offered and in the way interactions within it proceed.

*Annie (1.6) posted shapes into the shape sorter and tipped them out when it was full. Florence (1.6) also used a variety of containers to fill and empty.*

**Figure 7.27** Posting shapes

**Figure 7.28** Tipping out

**Figure 7.29** Florence (1.6) Empties buckets

**Figure 7.30** Emptying yoghurt pots

*Tommy (1.6) used the tin buckets to put the dolls inside and carried them around. He did not play with the dolls but what appeared important was that they could be contained. Tommy selected the dolls and fitted them inside the buckets.*

**Figure 7.31** Filling buckets

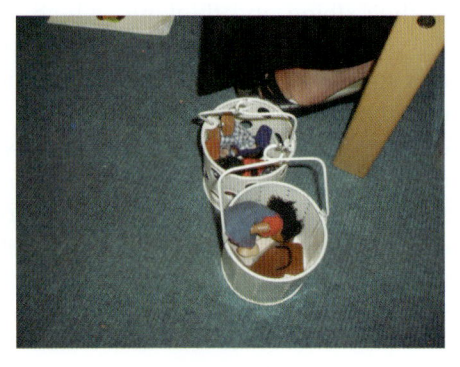

**Figure 7.32** Tommy's buckets are full

CONTAINING AND ENVELOPING SCHEMA   113

**Figure 7.33**  Florence (1.10 ) in the tunnel

**Figure 7.34**  Toys inside the boot

*Florence sat inside the tunnel and Nell did not appear to want to play with the toys – she enclosed them inside the boot of the car.*

Florence, Annie and Tommy's containing and enveloping behaviour, observed in a variety of motor level actions, included putting things in, emptying out, refilling and covering. These experiences provided valuable practical foundations upon which higher order concepts could develop.

*Florence (1.4) was finding out about what would fit in and what would fit through. She was using the wooden pegs to investigate insideness and exploring 'what will go in here?'*

*She pushed the pegs into the holes she found in the mechanism of the stair frame. She then got the tissue box and tried to post the pegs inside. She turned the pegs around so that they fitted through the hole in the top of the box.*

Through a functional dependency relationship, Florence appeared to understand that in order for the pegs to fit through the hole in the top of the tissue

**Figure 7.35**  Pegs into gaps

**Figure 7.36**  Pegs into tissue box

**Figure 7.37** Pegs falling out

**Figure 7.38** Pegs through holes

box, she needed to rotate them around. After posting all the pegs inside the box, she tipped the box upside down and shook it until they all fell out. Her action (shaking) had an effect (pegs drop out). She took the pegs then poked them through the holes into the tin pot.

Table 7.1 identifies specific concepts and relates these to Florence's actions. It highlights what Florence actually did and makes links between these actions and particular concepts in suggesting what Florence might have been thinking while involved in her work.

Nell (2.1) was also busy fitting objects inside containers. Alongside this, she was exploring going through (spade through porthole), as was Florence

Table 7.1  **What Florence might have been thinking**

| Concept | What Florence did | An interpretation of what Florence might have been thinking |
|---|---|---|
| Matching | Florence turned the peg around so that it fitted lengthways into the tissue box. | 'If I turn the peg the long way around, it will fit into the hole in the box.' |
| Estimation | She rotated the peg to fit through the hole. | 'The long pegs will fit through the long hole in the top of the box.' |
| Size | She poked pegs into the holes in the side of the tin cup. | 'The hole in the tin cup will fit a peg through.' |
| One-to-one correspondence | She poked one peg through each hole. | 'One peg will fit through one hole.' |
| Capacity | She put all the pegs into the tissue box. | 'The tissue box is nearly full now.' |

**Figure 7.39** Stones inside beaker

**Figure 7.40** Spade through porthole

(pegs through holes). Their understanding of what fits through was one of Athey's (2007) action schemas of 'going through a boundary'. Nutbrown (2011) clarified that although dominant schemas were recognised, other schemas were part of children's repertoires.

The containing and enveloping behaviour of Florence and Nell had been observed through a series of motor level actions. These included putting assorted objects (sand, stones, pegs, Shreddies) inside a range of containers (plastic beaker, tin cup, tissue box, pinny) and covering things (legs, hands and arms) with a variety of materials (glue, glitter, sand, paint, felt and net).

An exploration of insideness had been observed at different levels of increasing complexity. At 8 months Annie had turned the basket over and around and put her hand inside. Piaget (1954: 151) confirmed that she 'locates objects in relation to [her] own body and as a function of [her] acts of prehension, [she] does not locate them in relation to each other'. This represents an egocentrism which inhibited a shift from the subjective to the objective in terms of perception of space.

Piaget (1952a/b: 165) would perhaps question whether there was intent in confirming that 'even when the child grasps an object in order to suck or look at it, one cannot infer that there is a conscious purpose'. He thought this was suggestive of what seems a lesser intelligence. He stated that it was not until the child 'sets out to obtain a certain result, independent of the means he is going to employ, [that] more complete acts of practical intelligence' could be observed, and that the child was then 'on the threshold of intelligence' (Piaget and Inhelder 1969: 10). Piaget and Inhelder appeared to reduce these nascent explorations to an intelligence of activity which they infer did not belong in a discussion of an intelligent act. Annie's founding investigations seemed to be portrayed as a 'becoming intelligence', an intelligence in the making. Although her exploits with the basket and other objects at this time lacked representation and were confined to her perceptual field, they inferred a vigorous competence and aptitude. The significance of early timely enquiries, upon which later conceptual thought is reliant, is to be acknowledged.

Annie's exploration of insideness (aged 11 months) demonstrated an advance in thinking in that she posted lids into boxes, turned the box upside down and shook it until the lid fell out and she had retrieved it. She had become capable of searching for disappeared objects. She realised that the object (lid) had a permanence even when masked by a screen, in this case the sides of the tissue box. She tipped the lid out knowing that it was there.

Annie's posting, hiding and tipping evidenced an exploration of 'spatial interrelations of objects: the relation of *contents to container*'. Although Piaget suggested that this only appeared at the beginning of the second year, it was seen in Annie's actions earlier than that (Piaget 1954: 192). Up-ending the box to retrieve the lid she had put into the box was evidence of reversible operation.

Florence's (1.4) play with the pegs and tissue box revealed a progression in accomplishment in terms of reversal. Through her manipulation of the peg and her adjustment of it to fit through the gap in the tissue box, Florence was developing an understanding of 'spatial interrelations among objects' (Piaget 1954: 196) which was distinct from Annie (0.11), who rotated an object by itself and not in relation to other objects. Although Florence did not appear to realise that the narrowness of the gap in the box dictated the orientation of the peg in terms of its fit, valuable experience of spatial relationships among objects was being developed.

Piaget (1954: 200) recognised that this 'is a matter of apprenticeship and in no way give[s] rise to images detached from the action'. Her success in posting the peg into the box was a matter of trial and error and not thought alone. Although Florence was experiencing the relationships of objects with each other through her actions, she did not seem to be able to anticipate yet the nature of these relationships. She did not yet understand that solid objects (pegs) cannot penetrate solid surfaces (lid of box) unless the solid object was rotated to align with a gap.

In addition, when Florence and Nell had been observed putting things through gaps and holes (going through a boundary), there was a co-ordination with 'containing and enveloping' at a motor level. Piaget and Inhelder (1967: 454) observed that 'in the course of such an experiment, the child learns something of the way his [sic] actions are co-ordinated and how one determines another'. 'Containing' behaviour necessarily involved a container and containables. There may have been a rim on a cup, a lip on a jug, an edge to a beaker, a frame on a box. As children put things inside containers, the idea of 'going through a surround or boundary' is being developed. The putting inside involves moving objects from outside an enclosure to inside an enclosure. The object becomes surrounded (by the cardboard of the tissue box, by the plastic of the pinny, by the blue cylinder of the tunnel, by the yellow plastic of the teapot walls), having passed through a boundary (the edge of the tissue box hole, the piping on the pinny, the rim of the tunnel, the lip of the teapot).

*Florence was playing at the sand tray. She filled and emptied buckets and moulds and covered the plate with sand. She patted the sand down, then poked holes into it with her finger.*

*At snack time, Tommy prodded his toast and crackers, making holes in them.*

He did not seem to be concerned with eating his food at these times but appeared occupied with more important enquiries. Tommy was pursuing his dominant schema of 'containing and enveloping'.

Piaget and Inhelder (1956: 104) described three types of surroundings which defined different spaces. A one-dimensional surrounding defined a line and could be seen where a point was situated 'between' two other

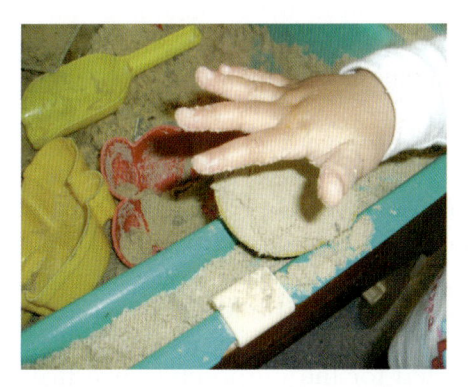

**Figure 7.41** Florence (1.4) Covers the plate

**Figure 7.42** Poking holes in sand

**Figure 7.43** Tommy (1.6) Poking holes in toast

**Figure 7.44** Making holes in crackers

points. A two-dimensional surrounding defined a surface and could be seen where a point was located 'inside or outside a closed figure', for example in a drawing of a face. It was the three-dimensional enclosure, which defined a space and was 'the relationship of a point, whether inside or outside a closed box', which was resonant here.

Several observations where children explored what Piaget and Inhelder (1956) described as a three-dimensional space (sand, stones, pegs, Shreddies placed inside a range of containers, plastic beakers, tin cups, tissue boxes, pinnies) were observed. The spaces were defined by an assortment of surroundings.

When Florence poked holes into the sand and Tommy prodded holes into his toast, they were active in exploring containing and enveloping but not, on this occasion, by 'containing' objects or 'enveloping' items. Instead, they were making enclosures with what was to hand, specifically toast or sand. When they removed their fingers from the toast and sand, they left an impression, which was not Piaget and Inhelder's (1956) closed box, designating a three-dimensional enclosure, but was undoubtedly a containing space defined by boundaries. Florence made a containing space – a small hole – with walls of sand. Tommy made a containing space – a tiny hole – with a surrounding made of bread.

Adults unacquainted with schematic theory may view Tommy's play at snack time with the toast as disruptive and inopportune. Athey's (2007: 144) perception of the behaviour, however, would be more optimistic, acknowledging that if children's behaviours are understood from a schematic perspective, then 'interpretations are positive ... instead of attributing naughtiness'. Tommy's snack time play, although unwelcome in the reality of practice, could be recognised schematically as an exploration of containing spaces, and therefore accepted for the purposeful, investigation it was. A gentle invitation to Tommy, suggesting an alternative (more acceptable?) pursuit, may have been required, which discouraged, yet was still supportive in suggesting an acceptable alternative. This response was from an accepting, courteous and considerate adult, a knowing adult who was hopeful of sustaining the child's interest in a fitting environment.

## Containing and Enveloping Schema: Observations

Table 7.2 identifies specific actions observed as the children went about their pursuits in the day care setting. It lists these incidences of behaviour and suggests links to particular curriculum areas outlined in the *Statutory Framework for the Early Years Foundation Stage* (DfE 2012).

**Table 7.2**

| Observed behaviour | Links to EYFS curriculum area (DfE 2012) |
|---|---|
| • Legs, arms, heads, covered with net, sand, boxes, glue, glitter, paint.<br>• Climbing inside cars, tunnels.<br>• Making enclosures with fence panels.<br>• Animals, vehicles, Shreddies contained.<br>• Teapots, cars, posted through holes.<br>• Ambulances swapped for smaller vehicles to post into tubes. | • Showing particular interests. (DfE 2012: 6)<br>• Developing ideas of grouping, sequences, cause and effect. (DfE 2012: 7)<br>• Enjoys filling and emptying containers. (DfE 2012: 35)<br>• Enjoys playing with small-world models such as a farm, a garage, or a train track. (DfE 2012: 39)<br>• Realises tools can be used for a purpose. (DfE 2012: 44)<br>• Shows control in holding and using jugs to pour, hammers, books and mark-making tools. (DfE 2012: 23)<br>• Explores and experiments with a range of media through sensory exploration, and using whole body. (DfE 2012: 43)<br>• Persisting with activity when challenges occur. Showing a belief that more effort or a different approach will pay off. (DfE 2012: 6) |

# Containing and Enveloping Schema: Functional Dependency Relationships

Nell was outside playing with the vehicles. She picked up the big ambulance and tried to fit it inside the cardboard tube (the inside of a roll of carpet). The ambulance would not fit. She discarded the ambulance, got a small car and posted it into the tube. She watched it roll out at the other end. Through a functional dependency relationship, Nell appeared to understand that in order for a vehicle to fit into the cardboard tube, it needed to be an appropriately small size.

*Nell (1.9) fills the yellow cup with sand. She 'drinks' from the cup. She puts the cup in the microwave and waits. She takes the cup out, swills it around and pokes her finger inside. 'Baby' and puts the doll inside the pram. Nell picks up the teapot and 'drinks', 'gall gone'. She gets a plate and spoon and 'feeds' the doll in the pram.*

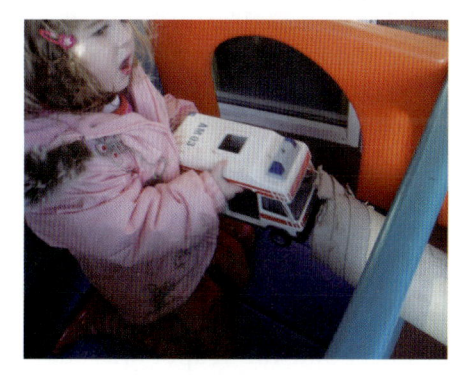

**Figure 7.45** Nell tries to fit the ambulance inside the cardboard tube

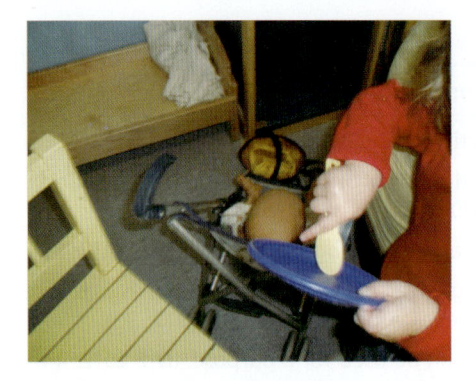

**Figure 7.46** Nell (1.9) feeds the baby

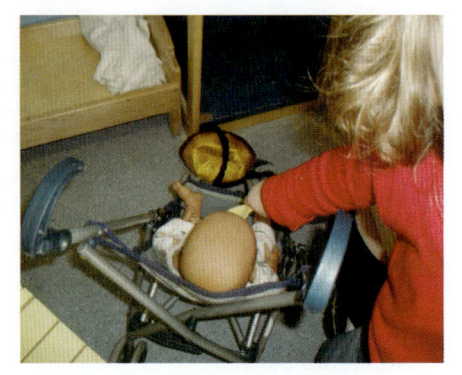

**Figure 7.47** Food into the baby's mouth

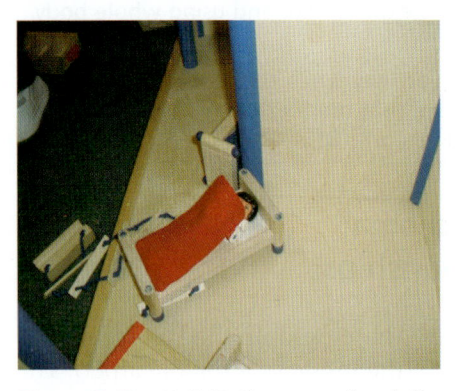

**Figure 7.48** Nell (2.8) covers the doll

**Figure 7.49** Nell (2.8) 'Bowbies'

Nell accompanied her actions with appropriate language: 'baby' and, when she finished drinking from the teapot, 'gall gone'. Piaget's (1959: 39) observation of egocentric speech, where 'young children strive continuously to share their thoughts with those around them, have in fact no verbal continence,' resonated in that Nell was intent on escorting her actions with relevant talk.

Nell's speech was a soliloquy: she spoke alone, was not in conversation and did not intended an exchange. She accompanied her actions with relevant schematic speech, 'gall gone'. Nell appeared to articulate an understanding of full and empty. She seemed to know that in her play of 'drinking' the tea from the teapot, through a functional dependency relationship, at one point the teapot was full but when she had drunk it, the teapot was empty – the tea was 'gall gone'. In order for the teapot to be empty, the tea must be drunk.

Nell's later play with the dolls appeared to demonstrate cognitive advance. She took the clothes off the big doll and put them inside the sink. She washed them and put them on the radiator. She placed the doll inside the cot and covered it with a blanket.

Nell said:

'I'm just taking the baby's clothes off'

'She's going to bowbies now'

'Baby, I'm going to get a pillow for you'

'Let's put this cover on you'

'A pillow'

In this observation, Nell revealed her schematic explorations in several ways. Her use of the things around her (material as a cover, sink, cots), her actions (dolls clothes into sink, blanket over doll) and in her speech ('cover on you') suggested a schema of containing and enveloping. Nell was exploring 'fit' (the dolls inside the cots) and covering or enveloping (material as blankets). Through these actions she was also experiencing a range of other concepts, as listed in Table 7.3.

Smidt (2006) queried whether this action could be classified as truly symbolic. In putting the doll inside the cot, was the child was actually putting a baby to bed or was she simply exploring insideness in placing an object into a container? The observation of Nell and the dolls could be interpreted as symbolic as she attached appropriate language to her play with the dolls without a scaffolding adult present.

Table 7.3 **What Nell might have been thinking**

| Concept | What Nell did | An interpretation of what Nell might have been thinking |
| --- | --- | --- |
| Size | Nell put the small doll in the small cot in the dolls' house. She put the big doll in the cot inside the house. | 'The big doll won't fit in the cot in the dolls' house, it's too big. Only the small doll will fit in there.' |
| Length | Nell put the dolls in the beds with their heads at the top. | 'The dolls will fit in the cots if they are lying down this long way. They'll poke out if they lie across the beds.' |
| Position | Nell put the dolls in the cots with the heads at the top of the cots and their feet pointing to the bottom. | 'The dolls' head should be at the top where the pillow is.' |
| One-to-one correspondence | Nell put one doll in one bed and one in the other. | 'One doll will fit in one cot and needs one pillow.' |

Piaget (1959: 18) would have described the type of speech used by Nell in the observation with the doll as a collective monologue: an example of egocentric speech where the speaker 'is not speaking to anyone [but] talks aloud to himself [sic] in front of others'. Nell accompanied her actions with speech not intended to convey information to a hearer but simply to complement her action. Piaget (1959: 279) drew a distinction between the generally accepted meaning of egocentrism – 'that of conscious self-preoccupation, which precludes a feeling for the community' – and egocentrism, which described a difficulty in understanding differences in perspectives between people. Piaget and Inhelder (1969: 118) later clarified the discrepancy in referring to this alternative sense as an 'epistemological meaning'.

Nell's language, 'Baby, I'm going to get a pillow for you', 'Let's put this cover on you', appeared to dispute these definitions and suggested an orientation of mind: a projection of her thinking to that from the perspective of the baby's. It seemed that Nell recognised that the baby would be cold without a blanket and uncomfortable without a pillow. Through a functional dependency relationship, she gathered the items to rectify the dilemma, knowing that in order for the baby to be warm and comfortable certain items needed to be assembled (blanket, pillow). These opportunities, where children are able to 'observe the effects of action on objects or material' (Athey 1990: 70), are important practical explorations which later lead to operations that can be performed mentally.

Nell's actions appeared to contest Piaget's characterisation of egocentrism as she seemed not to be consciously preoccupied only with herself, but seemed to display empathy for the 'baby'. Her actions and speech implied a cognitive advance in that she appeared to be able to view from another perspective (that of the 'baby') and therefore contested Piaget and Inhelder's (1969: 118) definition of having 'difficulty in understanding differences in points of view between the speakers and therefore in decentration'.

Piaget (1959: 279), however, made an important clarification in that egocentrism and a feeling for others were not mutually exclusive. He related an observation of a 6-year-old boy who stated that balloons go up into the air 'because they love the air'. Piaget confirmed that the boy was egocentric as 'he sees the balloon as being like himself and endows it with purpose. ... [He] projects his inner qualities into the thing'. Piaget would therefore perhaps offer an interpretation of Nell's thinking as egocentric in that she appeared to have bestowed upon the doll her own experiences, in bringing forward and imitating routines from her own bedtime habits. In the light of this, evidence from the observation suggested that she had not been able to detach herself (the subject) from the baby (the object) and appeared to have projected herself and her experiences upon it.

Nell illustrated Wood's (1988: 26) definition of the egocentric nature of young children's thinking as that which reflected 'their own thinking, activity and point of view' and in no way addressed Piaget's (1959: 282) requirement that a decrease in egocentrism is an ability 'to detach subject from object [and] to cease to look upon one's own point of view as the only possible one, to co-ordinate it with that of others'.

Donaldson's (1978: 142) clarification that to be able to decentre was the ability 'to move freely from one point of view to another – and back again' was relevant, however, as there did seem to be a certain repositioning of Nell's thinking from that of herself (subject) to that of the 'baby' (object) in the awareness she demonstrated in action and language of what the 'baby' may need.

Nell was involved in important practical investigations that provided a valuable foundation for later operations which are carried out mentally. When she 'washed' the 'baby's' clothes and put them on the radiator to dry, at a sensori-motor level she was experiencing the beginnings of reversibility in that the dolls' clothes were dry, are wet when washed in the sink but will be dry again after time spent on the radiator. Piaget and Inhelder (1969: 20) stated that reversibility was 'the source of future "operations" of thought', highlighting the essential place of these motor level experiences in providing the foundation upon which operations can be carried out in the mind.

Vygotsky's (1978: 89) claim that 'good learning' was only that which is 'in advance of development', and was facilitated by the sensitive intervention of the guiding adult, resonated with Rogoff's (1990: 39) metaphor of the 'apprentice'. Rogoff viewed children as 'active learners [apprentices] in a community of people who support, challenge and guide novices as they increasingly participate in skilled, valued sociocultural activity'. Vygotsky (1978: 87) highlighted the significance of adult intervention in young children's learning and extended this to include knowledgeable peers. He emphasised the prospective nature of children's thinking in the creation of the zone of proximal development.

Isaacs (1930) appeared to share Vygotsky's (1978) view in her questioning of Piaget. She criticised Piaget for negatively characterising young children's thinking and learning as being in deficit and as a direct consequence of their stage of development. Isaacs (1930: 58) revealed 'direct *positive* evidence against Piaget's *negative* evidence' of young children's interests and interactions with the environment. Piaget (1959) disagreed with Isaacs when he reflected on her work at the Malting House. Isaac's observations and findings at the school in the 1920s recognised the imperative of meeting 'the spontaneous inquiries of the children ... and to give them the means of following these inquiries out in sustained and progressive action'.

He conceded that Isaacs' approach, which encouraged interaction and co-operation with peers and adults, could produce socialised speech, which, according to Piaget, marked an advance in children's speech from the egocentric categories.

Isaacs' observations in the 1920s appeared to be closely linked with those of Athey in the 1990s. Isaacs (1930: 80) recognised the imperative of meeting 'the spontaneous inquiries of the children … and to give them the means of following these inquiries out in sustained and progressive action'. This approach was reflected in Athey's (2007: 200) schema observations. She asserted that practitioners need to ensure that the 'content of experience "feeds" the forms of thought'. Athey's 'forms of thought' and, arguably, Isaacs' 'spontaneous inquiries of the child' both essentially have the child and the child's concerns at the heart of the learning environment.

There was a missed opportunity for the adult to engage with and respond to Nell's play with the 'baby'. Although Nell seemed to be accompanying her own play with a commentary that fleshed out and supported her actions, this could have been nurtured in an effort to extend the play. An understanding of Nell's schematic preoccupations could have led to a dialogue which reflected the conceptual rather than the associative. Talking about the 'baby's' name, the colour of its eyes, whether it sleeps all night or likes milk could have been avoided and instead a more attuned conversation aimed at strengthening Nell's investigation of covering and fitting, containing and enveloping could have taken place. The movement towards association with an audience shifts the speech from monologue to socialised speech. In entering into dialogue with the hearer, there is adapted information which, where the child actually makes the hearer listen, actually contrives to influence the hearer.

Piaget (1959) identified the child's attempt to communicate thought. Although an opportunity was missed in the observation with Nell, Tommy's connection with the hearer in the observation below revealed a cognitive advance. There was no evidence in earlier observations of Tommy (in the car and tunnel, filling buckets with objects, making enclosures for giraffes and cars, posting cars into the sink, poking holes into toast) of an attempt to communicate his thoughts to an audience. Here, however, a dialogue unfolded.

*Tommy (1.11) tips the yellow jug up into the blue cup, 'shshshsh'. He 'fills' the jug under the tap in the play house and continues to 'fill' the blue cup. Tommy opens the cupboard door in the play house, gets out a pear and puts it inside the pan. He puts the pan inside the microwave, then inside the oven and then into the sink.*

Tommy was pursuing his dominant schema of containing and enveloping in action here. He filled and emptied containers (jugs, cups, pans) and put objects (pans, pears) inside containers (microwave oven, pan, cupboard, sink). The pattern of his thinking was insideness, which could be seen as he continued his play in the sand (where the farm animals were available). He did not involve himself with the farm animals as one might conventionally

# CONTAINING AND ENVELOPING SCHEMA 125

**Figure 7.50** Tommy (1.11) filling the blue cup

**Figure 7.51** Pear inside pan for 'tea'

**Figure 7.52** Tommy looks inside

**Figure 7.53** Tommy scoops up the sand

expect, perhaps making oinking noises with the pigs, galloping the horses around or sailing the ducks on the water. He took the containers he was using (pan, blue cup, yellow jug) into the sand and filled them with farm animals and sand.

*Tommy (2.0) was in the sand again. He used the black plastic container to scoop up the sand. He filled the plastic container with sand and tipped it over the police car.*

    Adult:    *You've covered the car with sand.*

    Tommy:    *On* [pointing to the police car. Tommy puts the plastic container over the police car.]

**Figure 7.54** Covering the car with sand

**Figure 7.55** Container covers car

Adult: *The police car has disappeared. Where has it gone? Is it inside the stable?*

Tommy: *I know* [He lifts the plastic container off the car and pushes the police car into the stable.] *Nee nor, nee nor.*

*Tommy gets the police car out of the stable and covers it with the container again. He then lifts the container off the police car and says 'Look, car'. He tips the plastic container up on end and fills the top with sand.*

Moyles (2010: 20) suggested that play and playfulness can be categorised into three major concepts, of which one is 'pure play'.

> Pure play is under the control of the child(ren). It is initiated and led by the child(ren) and sustained and developed by them for their purposes. It represents activities and responses chosen and owned by the child(ren) and used at their own discretion. It is highly creative, open-ended and imaginative.

**Figure 7.56** Car inside the stable

**Figure 7.57** Container top full of sand

Tommy was thoroughly absorbed in his play in the sand. He was pursuing his containing and enveloping schema in action and accompanied his investigations with speech. Tommy was focused and his underlying *pattern of thought* persisted throughout. He filled and emptied containers in the sand (inside and on top of black plastic box, stable), covered objects with sand (police car) and fitted things inside (car inside stable, box on top of car). He repeated the investigations of fitting, enclosing, covering, filling and emptying.

He gathered things he needed from around the room. The black plastic box was with the junk model resources, the police car was in the vehicle box and the stable was with the small world items. This did not deter Tommy. He needed them for his play. He moved around the room collecting items which to the uninitiated could appear to be a diverse jumble but, for Tommy, allowed important explorations to proceed. There was nothing to fit, enclose, fill or empty in the sand tray that day but there was now. Tommy had orchestrated it to be so. He may have assembled an eclectic assortment of objects and may use them unconventionally but for Tommy these resources were vital as they could be filled, fitted into, enclosed and covered and, what is more, Tommy could do the filling, fitting, enclosing and covering.

If the adult observing this unfolding episode did not understand Goouch and Lambirth's (2010: 57) demand for empathy and emotional connection with children as players, did not have a 'genuine interest in their play and acute sensitivity', then not only could Tommy's purposeful, conceptual explorations be missed, but his self-esteem, contentment, happiness, confidence, self-reliance and trust in others could be undermined if his important enquiries and explorations are misconstrued.

Anning (2010: 30) confirmed that 'deep and meaningful learning evidenced in children's self-initiated and socio-dramatic play' could be the basis for 'reflection and planning'. Meaningful learning is important and necessitates adults to be sufficiently attuned to what they observe. The adult who works with children is not one who has compassion, honesty, sincerity and understanding, but is one who *is* compassionate, *is* sincere, *is* understanding, *is* warm and feeling and *is* intent on nurturing relationships in the learning environment with children, who take the time they need. This goes beyond knowing about how important these qualities are in relationships with children and is about living out these qualities in encounters with children.

Filippini and Vecchi (1996: 128), whose depiction of the child as 'unique and the protagonist of his or her own growth [who] yearns to create ties with others and to communicate', clearly understood the position of adult and child in the learning environment – that of influential adult and precarious child. Goouch and Lambirth (2010: 55) supported this, warning that:

> to accompany children in their play is a sophisticated role that can be achieved only by those who know and understand children, who allow the sometimes complex intentions of children at play to take precedence and who will demonstrate respect for such intentionality.

Both Filippini and Vecchi, and Goouch and Lambirth allude to an accomplishment which may not be a conscious reality for all those who work with children; it separates the practical from the philosophical. A willingness to acquiesce is not understood passively but is a desire to accept and embrace the position of accomplice. It is a moral which goes beyond the rhetoric of respecting and valuing the child. To respect and value the child suggests that this is something adults working with children *do*, rather than something they should instinctively feel.

The adult accompanying Tommy accepted Filippini and Vecchi's (1996) 'protagonist' and embraced Tommy's leading role, as well as Goouch and Lambirth's (2010) 'precedence', in her manner of accompaniment. She escorted Tommy in his pursuit of his containing and enveloping schema with appropriate language (covered with sand, inside the stable). She accompanied his schematic action (scooping and filling the plastic box, covering the car with sand, covering the car with the plastic box, putting the car inside the stable, covering the box with sand) with language which links meaning and *form of thought*. The opportunity for this kind of attuned match of action and language must not be missed (Athey 2007; Nutbrown 2011).

The observation of Tommy in the sand suggested a cognitive competence in terms of his use of speech and in his understanding of cause-and-effect relationships. In saying 'I know', he responded to the adult's question. Piaget (1959: 20) categorised this kind of speech as 'adapted information [where] the child actually makes his hearer listen, and contrives to influence him, i.e. to tell him something'. Tommy was intent on conveying to the adult his thoughts, in particular his understanding of where the police car was hidden. In revealing the car, concealed from view by the box, he demonstrated his understanding of functional dependency relationships, in that in order for the adult to be able to see the car, he needed to lift the box.

This observation of Tommy in the sand, where he exchanged thoughts with the adult, also revealed that he had become capable of searching for disappeared objects. He realised that the object (car) had a permanence even when it had vanished from view. He lifted the box to reveal the police car, knowing that it was there. In hiding, then retrieving objects, Tommy was exploring reversible operation. Smidt (2006; 69) proposed that this use of speech, as an 'external symbolic means, … assists internal problem solving' in that children talk aloud as they solve problems or describe their actions. Here Tommy responded to the adult's query by exposing the concealed police car. Tommy was beginning to internalise his thinking in that the thought required for problem-solving was being established. In saying 'I know', he anticipated the action which solved the problem.

Saying 'nee nor, nee nor' while pushing the police car along into the stable was a behaviour which Piaget and Inhelder (1969) suggested was evidence of the appearance of the semiotic function. The 'verbal evocation of events that are not occurring at the time' is seen here as Tommy recalled the sound of a police siren and represented it in his play (Piaget and Inhelder 1969: 53).

The 'signified' something [a moving, chasing, noisy police car] represented by means of a 'signifier', serves a representative purpose [the verbalisation of the police car siren, 'nee nor, nee, nor'].

Tommy's speech was becoming gradually more socialised in trying to involve and influence those around him. His motive for communication shifted towards the need to be understood. Brierley (1994: 47) recognised that 'there is one necessary condition for a child's poised brain to learn speech: he must have continuous and lengthy lessons from a competent speaker'. Nutbrown (2006) clarifies what Brierley's 'competent speaker' should look like in the learning environment: she recognises that adults are more able to connect with children in their learning if they pay attention to what children 'are already paying attention to, have demonstrated interest in through their actions, speech and graphic representations' (2006: 121). In so doing, the association between adult and child could be a more meaningful involvement.

Brierley (1994: 54) confirmed that 'sometimes silence is the best help and too much well-meant interference with explanations can destroy the silent sensory pleasures of looking, feeling, smelling and listening'. Brierley's 'interference', even if 'well meant', must be avoided if a genuine bond with children is to be realised. There is no place for interference in children's learning. Interference is an intrusion which thwarts purposeful enterprise. Brierley's 'well-meant' is a luxury adults in the learning environment cannot afford as it is a disservice to children and should be averted by Meade and Cubey's (2008) adult, who is motivated by an informed understanding and genuine desire to tune into the thinking concerns of the child, by identifying and feeding their *forms of thought*.

Parker-Rees (2010: 69) acknowledged that 'absorbed engagement [is] kept afloat by a sea of cultural support'. And in continuing his metaphorical description of relationships, he states that adults in the learning environment should not inadvertently sink children's engagement with inopportune interruptions and inappropriate, irrelevant resources, but endeavour to avoid turbulent waters with calming interventions typified by finely tuned, precise accompaniment.

## The observations tell a schema story...

### ...About containing and enveloping

- Stable, sink, pan, cot, pram, cups, plastic box as containers
- Pears, dolls, water, police cars, contained
- 'Baby', police car covered
- Sand, plastic box as covers
- Plastic box as container
- 'Let's put this cover on you'
- 'On' [Tommy covers the police car with the plastic box]
- Sand in holes on top of box

## The observations tell another story...
### ...About characteristics of effective learning

- Showing curiosity about objects, events and people
- Using senses to explore the world around them
- Engaging in open-ended activity
- Showing particular interests
- Pretending objects are things from their experience
- Representing their experiences in play (DfE 2012: 6)

### ...About personal, social and emotional development

- Builds relationships with special people
- Interacts with others and explores new situations when supported by familiar person
- Shows interest in the activities of others and responds differently to children and adult (DfE 2012: 8)

### ...About communication and language

- Has a strong exploratory impulse
- Concentrates intently on an object or activity of own choosing for short periods (DfE 2012: 15)
- Developing the ability to follow others' body language, including pointing and gesture
- Responds to the different things said when in a familiar context with a special person
- Understanding of single words in context is developing
- Understands simple sentences (DfE 2012: 17)
- Uses language as a powerful means of widening contacts, sharing feelings, experiences and thoughts
- Holds a conversation, jumping from topic to topic (DfE 2012: 20)

### ...About mathematics

- Beginning to organise and categorise objects (DfE 2012: 32)
- Attempts, sometimes successfully, to fit shapes into spaces
- Uses blocks to create their own simple structures and arrangements
- Enjoys filling and emptying containers
- Notices simple shapes and patterns in pictures
- Beginning to categorise objects according to properties such as shape or size (DfE 2012: 35)

### ...About understanding the world

- Becomes absorbed in combining objects, e.g. banging two objects or placing objects into containers

# CONTAINING AND ENVELOPING SCHEMA

- Knows things are used in different ways
- Explores objects by linking together different approaches: shaking, hitting, looking, feeling, tasting, mouthing, pulling, turning and poking
- Remembers where objects belong
- Matches parts of objects that fit together
- Enjoys playing with small-world models such as a farm, a garage, or a train track
- Notices detailed features of objects in their environment (DfE 2012: 39)

## ...About expressive arts and design

- Explores and experiments with a range of media through sensory exploration, and using whole body
- Move their whole bodies to sounds they enjoy
- Beginning to construct, stacking blocks vertically and horizontally, making enclosures and creating spaces
- Joins construction pieces together to build and balance
- Realises tools can be used for a purpose (DfE 2012: 43–44)

**Figure 7.58** Tommy (2.3) fills the truck with blocks

**Figure 7.59** Tipping the blocks out

**Figure 7.60** Putting more blocks inside

**Figure 7.61** Even more blocks will fit

*Tommy (2.3) fills the truck with blocks and pushes it along 'brummm'. He tips the blocks out and puts more blocks in.* [A block keeps falling out.] *The adult says 'Is the truck full yet?' Tommy switches the block around to stop the one falling out and says 'It's full now'.*

Later that day Tommy (2.3) went back outside to play with the truck again.

*Tommy (2.3) is playing with the truck and the fire engine in the sand tray. He fills the truck with sand, tips it up and covers the fire engine.*

*Tommy says 'guk' (stuck) 'gone'*

*Tommy says to the adult 'ache it' (shake it)*

*He pushes his hand under the sand. 'Guk' (stuck)*

*He puts the truck under the sand. 'Gar tuck now' (car stuck now)*

*He gets a little car and covers it with sand. 'Guk it over'*

*Adult says 'Cover it over?'*

*Tommy says 'Yeh'*

Anning (2010: 31) warned that in order for adults to become partners in children's play, 'negotiating entry into play episodes' is a requirement. The adult's negotiation here was built upon many months of observation and gradual familiarisation. It was more a reunion; there was no awkward tension. The child was at ease and the two slipped into a comfortable exchange. Brierley (1994: 53) reminds us that 'for teaching and learning, related knowledge is powerful to understanding and is remembered'. Here the adult had observed patterns in Tommy's behaviour and was ready. At first this readiness was a quiet 'seeing what happens' kind of attention.

Tommy could be seen trying to fit, enclose and cover. He symbolically represented the noise of the car 'brummm' and used other language to accompany his actions. This was evidence of Piaget's (1959: 20) 'adapted information' Tommy engaged in a dialogue with the adult and attempted to influence her: 'guk' (stuck), 'ache it' (shake it). Through a functional dependency relationship, he realised that the fire engine was covered with sand – it had 'gone' – and in order for it to be uncovered it must be picked up and shaken to remove the sand. He was busy communicating his thoughts, which had an underlying pattern of containing and enveloping, in action and speech.

We can talk of socialised speech here in that Tommy responded to a question which was pertinent to the action and, moreover, recalled his *form of thinking*: 'Is the truck full yet?' Tommy did not continue with his symbolic representations 'brummm' while pushing the block, oblivious to the interjection, but appeared to consider what he had heard. He then provided an answer to the question which involved thought in action.

Tommy switched the block around in the truck to stop the troublesome one falling out. His answer responded appropriately to the question heard. He solved the problem of fit, through action, and concluded the episode with an appropriate statement: 'It's full now'. The common pattern of his thinking – that of containing and enveloping – is observed in action and language.

As a result of his explorations, Tommy was developing his understanding of 'spatial interrelations among objects' (Piaget 1954: 196), which signified an advance from investigations that allow for 'spatial interrelations of objects (1954: 192). Tommy was not simply filling and emptying the truck of blocks in relation to himself as the filler and emptier but, significantly, adjusted how the blocks fitted into the truck by manoeuvring them around each other. Piaget's (1959: 282) requirement that for a decrease in egocentrism to be apparent an ability 'to detach subject from object' is necessary was suggested in Tommy's actions. He appeared to orientate his thinking from the purely subjective towards a more objective perspective. In modifying the fit of the blocks in the truck, he appeared to detach himself (the subject) from the blocks (the object) through his adjusting, changing, amending actions.

## The observations tell a schema story…

### …About containing and enveloping

- Fits blocks inside truck
- Says 'full now'
- Tips truck up
- Manoeuvres blocks inside truck to stop them falling out

## The observations tell another story…

### …About characteristics of effective learning

- Showing curiosity about objects, events and people
- Using senses to explore the world around them
- Engaging in open-ended activity
- Showing particular interests
- Pretending objects are things from their experience
- Representing their experiences in play (DfE 2012: 6)

### …About personal, social and emotional development

- Builds relationships with special people
- Interacts with others and explores new situations when supported by familiar person
- Shows interest in the activities of others and responds differently to children and adults (DfE 2012: 8)

*...About physical development*

- Shows increasing control over objects
- Handles tools, objects, construction and malleable materials safely and with increasing control (DfE 2012: 15)

*...About mathematics*

- Shows an interest in shape and space by playing with shapes or making arrangements with objects (DfE 2012: 36)

*...About understanding the world*

- Developing ideas of grouping, sequences, cause and effect (DfE 2012: 7)
- Notices detailed features of objects in their environment (DfE 2012:39)

*...About expressive arts and design*

- Uses various construction materials
- Selects appropriate resources and adapts work where necessary (DfE 2012: 44)

## Conclusion

This chapter has shown how the playfulness of young children can reveal a more thorough and insightful understanding of their astonishing capacities as thinkers. In order for young children to feel free to investigate and pursue their own interests through play, there are responsibilities to be embraced by those working with them. A responsibility to protect children is not a duty that attempts to shield and guard, but is more one of advocacy. An active protection requires a campaigner who wants to defend what is appropriate in terms of practice with young children. For Tommy, Nell, Florence and Annie, their campaigner should be someone with whom they feel comfortable, relaxed and easy, someone they can trust and depend upon, someone who has come to know them, who takes time to be with them, who is concerned with their concerns and who continually seeks to make a meaningful difference to their lives.

Article 12 of the United Nations Convention on the Rights of the Child reminds us that children have the right to be heard and the right to convey their views in matters of importance to them (United Nations 1989). If children have the right to be heard, then those who care for and work with young children have a responsibility to hear. If children have the right to convey their views, then there is a responsibility to receive and respond to these views. If children have a right to express views that are significant to them, then there is a responsibility for adults to put aside their self-interests and to share the interests of the child. Doing this makes the chance of a real connection and release of startling potential more likely.

## Reflection

Think about Annie's actions revealed in this chapter.

- Consider ways in which a child's significant adult in the setting might support their continuous patterns of thinking revealed as they play.
- Consider opportunities in which a child's significant adult might share insights into individual children's thinking concerns and schemas with other practitioners, parents and carers.
- What extension activities and experiences could be offered to children who display a containing and enveloping schema? How could you add to the resources already available in your setting to nourish this pattern of behaviour?

## Further Reading

Nutbrown, C. (ed.) (1996) *Respectful Educators – Capable Learners: Children's Rights and Early Education*. London: Paul Chapman Publishing.

Piaget, J. and Inhelder, B. (1969) *The Psychology of the Child*. London: Routledge and Kegan Paul.

# CHAPTER 8

# GOING THROUGH A BOUNDARY SCHEMA

This chapter has at its heart a set of observations of two children who are focusing on *'going through a boundary'* activity. They were interpreted schematically (Athey 2007) and within the context of the Early Years Foundation Stage (DfE 2012). The observations, taken over a 12-month period, are then discussed to reveal their significance in terms of schemas and of other aspects of young children's development. The chapter begins with a set of schema-oriented observations. This is followed by an 'unpacking' which answers the 'so what?' questions that many people have once they have observed schemas.

## The observations tell a schema story...

### ...About going through a boundary

- Motor level
- Symbolic level
- Functional dependency relationships

## The observations tell another story...

### ...About areas of learning and development

Prime Areas

- Personal, Social and Emotional Development
- Physical Development
- Communication and Language

Specific Areas

- Literacy
- Mathematics

- Understanding the World
- Expressive Arts and Design (DfE 2012: 5)

The observations in this section are discussed schematically and holistically and expose the musings of Annie and Greg as they involved themselves in explorations and discoveries. The observations revealed aspects of thinking as these young children played. Annie was 8 months old and Greg 23 months old when Frances met them in the day care setting of a Children's Centre.

*Annie (0.8) selects the small green hoop. She holds it with one hand and pokes her other hand through the middle.*

**Figure 8.1  Through the hoop**

## Going through a Boundary Schema: Motor Level Observations

*Annie (0.10) chooses a CD from the basket and prods a finger through the hole in the middle. She swaps hands, stares at the hole in the middle and pushes another finger through.*

**Figure 8.2  Poking fingers**

**Figure 8.3  Gazing at the CD**

*She selects the metal whisk and pokes her fingers through the gaps in the metal. She reaches into the treasure basket, selects a wicker ball and pushes her fingers through the gaps. She spends time looking at her hand holding the shaker.*

**Figure 8.4** Metal whisk

**Figure 8.5** Fingers through holes in ball

**Figure 8.6** Hand through gap in shaker

Athey (2007) described many motor level examples of 'going through a boundary' behaviour, where children experimented by pushing one thing through another. Annie (0.8) pushed her hand through the green hoop, poked her finger through the hole in the middle of the CD and through the gaps in the whisk. She pressed her fingers into the wicker ball and held the shaker by putting her fingers through the handle. Annie was exploring how one thing (fingers, hands) could go through another (green hoop, hole in CD, shaker handle). She was furthering her knowledge of 'going through' in these practical occupations.

Alongside these incidences of 'going through', Annie could be seen exploring insideness through her use of containers (yoghurt pots, tissue boxes, baskets, snack bowl, mirror box) and objects to contain (lids, toy animals, blocks, wooden balls, banana, herself). In pursuing her schema of containing and enveloping, of putting things inside, Annie was learning about the relationship of 'going'.

Athey (2007: 153) observed that 'co-ordinations of schemas can only be illustrated and described rather than measured' and from these early observations of Annie, explorations of the schemas enveloping and containing and 'going through', could be seen. These valuable investigations establish a richness of experience which support later understandings, as Piaget and Inhelder (1956) argued in their recognition of the association between the construction of shape and action displacements. Annie's knowledge and understanding of shape is founded upon physical and mental activity.

Through these motor level explorations (hands through hoops, fingers through holes, hands through handles) Annie was, we suggest, building up *systems of thought*. Gardner's (1984: 64) idea that 'one or more basic information-processing operations or mechanisms ... deal with specific kinds of input' was echoed by Nutbrown (2011: 67) who observed that schemas were the 'structures' within which children learn about new ideas.

Through Annie's exploration of 'going through' (and containing and enveloping) she was experiencing a range of ideas, including shape, size, rotation and space. By co-ordinating schemas, Annie was able to assimilate different and new content into her existing schemas. Meade and Cubey (2008: 155) confirmed this in their observation that children 'make connections between schemas to form new ideas (concepts)' through early practical encounters.

Elkind (2007: 107) also recognised the importance of action in learning: 'children will engage in all important intellectual activity on their own for long periods of time if given the materials and freedom to do so'. Elkind did not dwell on the merely practical but emphasised the place of mental activity in learning. He went on to state that 'the infant's mastery is organised and purposeful, even if it is not obvious to us'. Elkind's proficient and prospective view is accompanied with censure. To be able to respond to the capabilities of the young child is a competence which, he suggested, is not universally possessed.

The correlations, associations and relationships in children's thinking, revealed in their play, cannot be understood unless those observing have a conceptual awareness of what is seen. To be able to discern children's *forms of thinking* as they play is a required insight which allows for a more appropriate accompaniment in learning, an accompaniment which adjusts and modifies in the light of what is seen and heard.

*Greg (2.4) picks up the tambourine and spends time looking through the hole in the middle. He does not play the instrument but holds it up to his eye and gazes through the hole at things around the room.*

Figure 8.7  **Through the tambourine**

**140** UNDERSTANDING SCHEMAS AND YOUNG CHILDREN

*Greg (2.7) picks up the chime bar and looks through the hole in the middle, like a telescope. He spends time gazing through the hole in the chime bar at different things around the room.*

**Figure 8.8** Through the chime bar

*Greg places the tambourine over his head. He lifts the tambourine up with both hands above his head. He slips the tambourine back over his head, resting it on his shoulders.*

**Figure 8.9** Tambourine over head

*Greg (2.6) squeezes through the gap between the cupboard and the wall of the house.*

**Figure 8.10** Squeezing through

*Greg (2.4) pulls the handle of the suitcase up. He pushes it back down inside the suitcase. He repeats this pulling and pushing action.*

**Figure 8.11** Lifting up and pushing down the handle

*Greg (2.4) takes the shopping basket out of the house and fills it with items to hand. He takes the basket over to the house and posts it through the window of the house. The basket falls on to the floor inside the house. Greg climbs through the window of the house.*

**Figure 8.12** Basket through the window

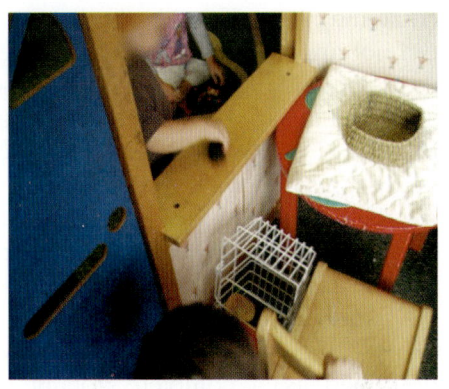

**Figure 8.13** Basket on the floor

*Greg (2.8) selects the trowel from the sand trough and takes sand to the window. He presses the sand on to the window frame with the trowel.*

**Figure 8.14** Sand at the window

Greg's 'going through' (in some cases, 'looking through') behaviour was evidenced by a series of motor level actions, including pushing the shopping basket through the window, looking through the tambourine, squeezing through gaps to get inside places, using sand like putty on the window and looking down the chime bar. These all represented his prevailing *form of thinking*, that of 'going through' (or 'looking through'), which Athey (2007) noted were topological notions of space and which Piaget and Inhelder (1969) recognised as constituting a broad foundational basis for later concepts of space. The tambourine, the chime bar and the house with the window had similar characteristics, as they all had a single hole, unaffected by changes in size.

Greg moved from outside the house to inside through the boundary of the window and then through the gap between the house and the cupboard. There was evidence of co-ordinated schemas in the observations, with Greg containing himself inside the house after climbing through the window. He did not appear concerned with the gap between the wall of the house and the cupboard. Athey (2007: 148) discussed 'discontinuity in the boundary,' which, in this case, enabled Greg to move from inside the boundary (house) to outside. A child with a dominant containing and enveloping schema may be disconcerted with a 'discontinuity' in the boundary and be intent on closing the gap so as to be fully contained.

Greg used his dynamic 'vertical trajectory' schema to make the suitcase handle go through the boundary of the suitcase top. Greg pulled to make the handle come out and pushed to make it go back in, a practical engagement with the concept of reversibility which Piaget and Inhelder (1969: 159) described as 'a complete, totally balanced system of compensations in which each transformation is balanced by the possibility of an inverse or a reciprocal'. Athey (2007: 54) clarified, stating that reversibility was a characteristic of operational thought; it is 'essential for conservation. For the stable mathematical operation of *addition*, the mental action of grouping together must be able to be cancelled out by reversing the process ... *subtraction* cancels *addition*'.

In the light of this, Greg's use of the suitcase handle was of interest in that he could extend it to its fullest point and retract it to see less and less, until it disappeared. Greg was experiencing, on a practical level, addition and subtraction of length through a functional dependency relationship. The handle 'going through the boundary' of the suitcase lid was functionally dependent on him pushing or pulling it up or down, which Athey (1990: 70) described as the 'effects of action on objects' and from which 'the sensory and perceptual information accompanying these motor actions lead[s] to true operations that can be carried out in the mind'. If this is the case, eventually Greg will know that operations can sometimes be reversed without the need for action. Greg's schematic behaviour, evidenced in a series of motor-level actions, through which he explored functional dependency relationships, is the foundation from which thought and operations carried out in the mind will emerge.

The observations of Greg with the chime bar did not suggest that there had been a move towards an understanding of reversibility. The observation with the chime bar did not suggest that he had 'freed himself of the individual's perception ... from the egocentric viewpoint' (Piaget 1947: 164), that he was able to mentally reposition himself from the 'immediate here and now' of sensori-motor experience (Gleitman, Friedman and Reisberg 1999: 548).

Donaldson acknowledges the mental 'situatedness' of the egocentric child to which Piaget refers. A subjective place which cannot see an objective other. This view seems pertinent here. Greg did not demonstrate a decentred point of view but a fixed point. He simply looked through the chime bar and did not accompany this action with language.

If Greg, in using the chime bar as a telescope, had said 'I am looking through my telescope', and had gone on to draw, for example, a boat with pirates and telescopes and described 'there are the pirates', articulating what the pirates could see (treasure, islands, other boats, land ahoy), this would have denoted a level of decentration. Greg would not have been able to do this unless he had the cognitive ability to decentre. In just looking down the chime bar and without the presence of language, evidence of his decentred perspective was not apparent.

## Going through a Boundary Schema: Symbolic Level Observations

*Greg (2.7) peeps through the bars in the climbing frame and says 'Hello'. The adult says 'I can see you through those bars'.*

**Figure 8.15** **Looking through the slats**

When Greg peeped through the climbing frame bars and said 'hello', to which the adult responded 'I can see you through those bars', Greg had attempted to engage the adult in conversation. He had demonstrated a shift from the personalised notion of monologue towards the more socialised aspect of dialogue in his initiation of conversation. The adult's response provided a match with Greg's observed prevailing *forms of thought* in saying 'through the bars'. Nutbrown (2011: 70) reminds us that 'children have the opportunity to obtain meaning from this kind of verbal match ... if adults use appropriate descriptive language when working with children, language of *form* as well as appropriate *content* descriptions'. The adult did not depart on a mismatched tangent, discussing how cold it was and that it was a good job he had his coat on (it was very cold that day) or wonderings about where his friends were as he was on his own on the climbing frame, or taking the opportunity to discuss the merits of the wooden slats or plastic handle of the frame. No, Greg did not have to make what Athey (2007: 152) described as a 'polite departure' in terms of personal conceptual relevance because the adult had an understanding of what Greg was busy with.

Coming to know schemas and identifying them in practice is significant but understanding their relevance for learning and being able to respond at a conceptual level to these threads of thinking, which tie perceived indiscriminate behaviours together, is a continuing professional challenge. Loreman (2009: 119) acknowledged that 'we need to provide [children] with opportunity, with authentic environments, and scaffolds on which they can build their own understandings of the world'. The authenticity that Loreman described relates to Nutbrown's (2011: 142) 'processes of learning ... *how* children learn [being] as important as the content of their learning – *what* they learn' in that authenticity is indeed about a physical environment full of opportunity, a realistic space for wonder, excitement, challenge and fun, and much more. Authentic encounters are faithful and genuine, they are legitimate and true. Authentic encounters are times when adults and children come together and share common ground. They can be simple moments where there is unspoken understanding or a time to settle and stay, to inhabit a space together to see what unfolds.

Meade and Cubey (2008: 156) understood the importance of conceptual accompaniment in proposing that 'teachers should be helping children move up through schema and other progressions. At the higher levels of schema development, this has to involve discussion'. However, to share time with a child in an effort to come to know what is important to that child, and to be able therefore to respond to that child, suggests an approach to working with young children that goes beyond professional expertise and towards a moral ethic.

Gallard's discussion about perspectives and views of the child acknowledged this complexity of working with young children:

> When we stereotype children we are not taking account of what is happening in both the interior world and exterior world for that unique child, in their specific situation, for just that moment in time ... (Gallard 2010: 42–43)

Gallard continues in recognising a psychological perspective in noting that 'if we begin to look at a child not for who they are (i.e. genetic inheritance and birth) but how they are (or how we, although all human, come to be so individual and different to each other) and what they could be, or their "individual" potential' (2010: 43).

Gallard recognised the exceptional child, the particularised nature of the individual, the distinctive concerns which make a child distinct. The need to

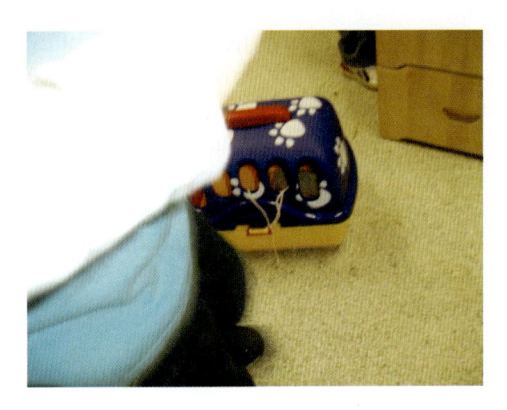

**Figure 8.16** Holes in the box

cultivate the thinking of the child with appropriate content is identified, yet something deeper is suggested. To come to know a child is to see more clearly each child's spirit, their essence, their character, their personhood.

*Greg (3.1) is playing outside and goes over to another child who is playing nearby. Greg says, 'Open your mouth and let's see'. 'What can you see inside there, Greg?' Greg replies, 'A tooth, a tooth is in there'.*

*Greg goes and gets a toy dog. 'He's got a headache', 'He's got marks on his face', 'He's going in the basket now'.*

*Greg puts the toy dog in the basket and says 'He's got marks on his face down there' (pointing to his own face).*

*The adult says 'I can hear barking coming from inside the box', Greg picks up pieces of 'dog food' (buttons) and pokes them through the holes in the box. He looks at the dog through the bars.*

Greg's 'going through' ('looking through') behaviour was further evidenced by a series of actions accompanied by speech. Through a functional dependency relationship, Greg understood that in order for him to be able to see inside the child's mouth, the child would have to open it. In co-ordinating his schema of containing and enveloping, of putting things inside, Greg was learning about the relationship of going through in his action of looking inside a mouth. Anticipating the next move, the adult intervened and suggested an alternative pursuit before Greg could move his finger from outside to inside through the boundary of the child's lips!

Greg's play with the toy dog and the carrying basket revealed his co-ordinated schematic explorations. His particular choice of things around him (a basket with slats to see through), his actions (dog inside basket, food inside basket) and in his speech ('in the basket') suggested a schema of containing and enveloping. Greg was learning about the relationship of going through in his actions of putting things inside (dog inside through the boundary of the basket door, buttons inside through the boundary of the basket slats).

In simply looking through the slats of the basket and without the presence of language, there is no evidence of a decentred perspective. This action demonstrated a fixed perspective. However, in responding to the adult's comment 'I can hear barking coming from inside the box' by poking buttons (dog food?) through the slats into the basket where the dog was, this suggested a level of decentration. Greg's actions implied that he had the cognitive ability to decentre. Athey (2007: 169) accepted that 'intention and meaning were clearer when utterances were made in context. As speech use and comprehension increased, ambiguities decreased'. If Greg had accompanied the action of pushing buttons through the slats into the basket with appropriate language, 'he's hungry, he always barks when he's hungry, he is happy when he's had his dinner', a more secure insight into Greg's understanding could be reached. This understanding is not a matter of knowing that food pacifies hunger but, for the adult, the significantly more complex discernment of cognitive ability. Greg may be able to decentre, demonstrated through his action, but this is inferred; with accompanying speech, a more secure awareness would be assured.

In this context, when Greg puts the dog in the basket and says, 'He's got marks on his face down there' but points to his own face, this again implied an advance in cognitive ability. He appeared to be able to migrate his thinking from himself (the subject and the mark on his own face) to the dog (the object and the mark on his furry face). The language was explicit here and suggestive of cognitive advance, but the action was implicit. Although it would be tempting to suggest that Greg had put the dog into the basket to take it to the vet, knowing that this would make the dog better, the opportunity of continuing the conversation to possibly establish this, or otherwise, was missed.

In the use of the things around him (baskets, open mouths, buttons, chime bars, climbing frames, tambourines, suitcases), his actions (dog inside basket, buttons through slats, looking through slats, peering down chime bars, gazing through tambourine holes, lifting up and pushing down handles) and in his speech ('a tooth's in there', 'he's going in the basket now') suggested co-ordinated schematic behaviour. Evidence of containing and enveloping, dynamic vertical and going through a boundary were apparent. Through these schemas, Greg experienced several higher order concepts.

Table 8.1 identifies specific concepts and relates these to Greg's actions. It highlights what Greg actually did and makes links between these actions and particular concepts in suggesting what Greg might have been thinking while involved in his work.

The *Statutory Framework for the Early Years Foundation Stage* (DfE 2012) recognises the individuality of young children and recommends that practitioners recognise and respect this in their approach to practice. In paying attention to children through meticulous observation, a holistic and schematic picture of children's thinking, learning and development can emerge. This schematic interpretation of children's behaviour, alongside existing policy milestones, helps secure our understanding of children as they play.

In the light of this, the observations of Annie and Greg were interpreted schematically (Athey 2007) and within the context of the *Statutory Framework for the Early Years Foundation Stage* (DfE 2012) (see Table 8.2).

Table 8.1  What Greg might have been thinking

| Concept | What Greg did | An interpretation of what Greg might have been thinking |
|---|---|---|
| Size | Greg held the tambourine above his head then pulled it down over his head and rested it on his shoulders. | 'My head fits through the hole in the tambourine.' |
| | Greg squeezed through the gap between the house and the cupboard. | 'The gap between the house and the cupboard is wide enough for me to fit through.' |
| | Greg looked down the hole in the chime bar and looked through the middle of the tambourine. | 'The hole in the chime bar is small but the hole in the tambourine is big.' |
| | Greg pushed the basket through the window in the house. | 'The basket fits through the window of the house.' |
| | Greg climbed through the window in the house. | 'I fit through the window of the house.' |
| Shape | Greg lifted the chime bar up to his eye and looked down the hole. | 'The chime bar is round and long.' |
| | Greg held the tambourine with two hands and put it over his head. | 'The tambourine is round.' |
| Position | 'He's going in the basket now.' | 'The dog is going inside the basket.' |
| | 'A tooth, a tooth is in there.' | 'Inside that mouth are teeth. If I poke my finger in, I can feel them.' |
| Force | Greg pulled the handle of the suitcase up and pushed it back down. | 'If I pull the handle of the suitcase, it comes up and if I push it, it goes down.' |
| Speed | He repeated the pulling and pushing movements. | 'If I pull the handle of the suitcase quickly, it comes up fast. If I push the handle of the suitcase slowly, it goes back down slowly.' |
| Height | He watched how he made the handle go up and down. | 'I can make the suitcase handle come half way up or right up to the top.' |
| | Greg climbed through the window. | 'I need to climb up high to reach the window in the house.' |
| | Greg played on the climbing frame. | 'I'm up here at the top of the climbing frame. It's very high and I can see through the slats.' |
| Equivalence | Greg put the toy dog in the basket. | 'Only one dog fits in one basket.' |
| | He put the tambourine over his head. | 'Only my head fits through the tambourine at once.' |

## Going through a Boundary Schema: Observations

Table 8.2

| Boundary schema | Links to EYFS curriculum area (DfE 2012) |
|---|---|
| • Fingers through CD hole, hands through hoops, fingers through wicker ball, hand through handle, fingers through whisk.<br>• Shopping basket through window, Greg through the window.<br>• Moving through gaps.<br>• Looking through holes in tambourines, chime bars, wooden slats, basket slats.<br>• Buttons pushed through gaps. | • Showing particular interests. (DfE 2012: 6)<br>• Manipulate materials to achieve a planned effect. (DfE 2012: 44)<br>• Attempt to fit shapes into spaces. (DfE 2012: 35)<br>• Developing ideas of grouping, sequences, cause and effect. (DfE 2012: 7)<br>• Understands that different media can be combined to create new effects. (DfE 2012: 44)<br>• Use gestures sometimes with limited talk. (DfE 2012: 20)<br>• Use language as a powerful means of widening contacts, sharing feelings, experiences and thoughts. (DfE 2012: 20)<br>• Be willing to 'have a go'. (DfE 2012: 6)<br>• Taking a risk, engaging in new experiences and learning by trial and error. (DfE 2012: 6)<br>• Uses senses to explore the world around them. (DfE 2012: 6)<br>• Pretending objects are things from their experience. (DfE 2012: 6) |

## Conclusion

This chapter has discussed how young children form new ideas in the physical and mental busyness of their play. In these early explorations, important discoveries are being made about themselves, the things around them and the people they meet. The consequences of these early experiences can be far-reaching and draw attention to the responsibility and accountability of those working with young children.

The chapter illustrated how a schema, specifically going through a boundary, may be explored at different developmental levels. Motor level actions, symbolic representations and functional dependency relationships were discussed, as children pursued their *forms of thought*. Co-ordinations of schemas, where children bring together different *forms of thinking*, were also observed, and these allow children to explore the environment in different and complex ways.

> John was walking to school with his father. 'If there's woodwork today... if there's the woodwork things... if there is I'm gonna, I'm gonna do my plane. I'm gonna finish the nailing and put on the wings – then I think I can paint it.' John's father asked, 'Have you got much to do to it?' 'Could be a morning's work there.' (Nutbrown 2011: 37)

The complexity of children's thinking should shape their working environment. As children come into our settings, they should be faced with things around them which generate in them a sense of wonder and possibility. They should meet with practitioners who have a preparedness to respond to individual needs, to particularised important instincts. The 'John' in Nutbrown's observation, it is hoped, would be able to work with a practitioner who understood the significance of his 'morning's work', and was determined for him to continue and not be deterred by that day's distractions, enabling John to take the time he needs, providing him with the space and equipment he needs to complete his self-initiated enterprise.

Practitioners who are disposed to fall into step with young children and help them to move along in their learning need a level of sensitivity which may feel out of reach, but it is an obligation that should be accepted and embraced.

This chapter explored the importance of early sensory explorations which help young children secure their knowledge of the physical characteristics of objects in the environment. These rich early experiences may be evoked at a later date as children bring forward previous incidences in subsequent activities and representations. Bruner (1966), Piaget (1959) and Athey (2007) all acknowledged the place of cultivating environments and the practical engagement that is necessary within such environments.

Splendid encounters brought about by perceptive, insightful observation and tender, enabling interventions were revealed. Young children's concealed thoughts, made known in action and talk, were observed. These occasions portrayed moments of significant personal meaning.

## Reflection

Consider the following questions in the context of your setting.

- A knowledge and understanding of schemas allows us to view children's behaviour in a different way. To what extent can you use this knowledge and understanding as a tool for observation?

- Consider the ways in which the schematic pursuits of the youngest children can be nourished and supported on their learning journeys.

- To what extent do the curriculum policies used in your setting allow children's personal interests and schemas to be followed, and followed through by accompanying adults?

## Further Reading

Athey, C. (2007) *Extending Thought in Young Children* (2nd edition). London: Paul Chapman Publishing.

Goldschmied, E. and Jackson, S. (2004) *People under Three* (2nd edition). London: Routledge.

# CHAPTER 9

# DYNAMIC VERTICAL SCHEMA

This chapter has at its heart a set of observations of five children aged from eight months to 17 months who are focusing on vertical activity. The observations, taken over a 12-month period, are then discussed to reveal their significance in terms of schemas and of other aspects of young children's development. It begins with a set of schema-oriented observations. This is followed by an 'unpacking' which answers the 'so what?' questions which many people have once they have observed schemas.

## The observations tell a schema story…

### …About dynamic vertical

- Motor level
- Symbolic level
- Functional dependency relationships

## The observations tell another story…

### …About areas of learning and development

Prime Areas

- Personal, Social and Emotional Development
- Physical Development
- Communication and Language

Specific Areas

- Literacy
- Mathematics

- Understanding the World
- Expressive Arts and Design (DfE 2012: 5)

This chapter reveals what children were telling us about their thinking, learning and development when they played. Patrick was 18 months old and Greg was 23 months old when I met them. They attended the day care setting of a Children's Centre on a sessional basis. The observations in this chapter are discussed schematically and trace developments in children's thinking from motor to symbolic representations. The observations also tell another story, that of the holistic thinking of young children revealed as they played. During these observations the children were absorbed in activities of great significance. For them, the unfolding stories depict moments of profound personal engagement.

The substance of the play was simply objects to hand, things around, jumbled mixtures of items, sometimes of questionable suitability (or objects used unconventionally) but available, accessible and personally chosen. The use of seemingly ordinary items contrasted with the extraordinary displays of forms of thinking revealed in their use. Often, finely nuanced behaviours depicted forms of thought, which were captured through careful observation.

## Dynamic Vertical Schema: Motor Level Observations

**Figure 9.1  Up the wooden slide**

**Figure 9.2  Up the pink slide**

**Figure 9.3  He pushed the car up the slide**

*Patrick (1.6) clambers up the big wooden slide to the top then moves on to the small pink slide and does the same. He pushes the toy car up the slide and watches as it rolls down again.*

*He enjoys action songs and joins in with 'Peter hammers with one hammer', banging one fist up and down on the other. In another song, he holds his arms in the air, bends his knees and bounces up and down.*

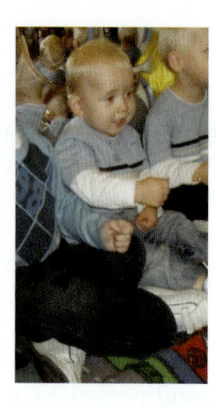

**Figure 9.4** Fists up and down

**Figure 9.5** Lifted his legs up dancing

*At snack time, he thumps his spoon up and down on his tray, puts a spoon on his head and drops pieces of pear on to the floor. When he is playing with the parachute, he holds it with both hands and shakes it up and down.*

**Figure 9.6** Xylophone up-ended

*Patrick (1.8) appeared to be exploring verticality with the things available to him. He did not appear to want to play the xylophone but stood it up on end. It seemed that it was not the musical possibility which interested him but the dynamic vertical characteristic which intrigued him.*

*When Patrick is outside, he stands on top of the wooden crocodile and watches the other children from this vantage point.*

**Figure 9.7** On top of the crocodile

*Patrick spends time scrambling up the net into the climbing frame then easing himself back down again. When he plays with the rope ladder, he cannot be found underneath it but likes to climb right to the top. He goes up and down the slide acquiring vertical trajectory motor experiences.*

**Figure 9.8** Climbed up

**Figure 9.9** Eased himself down

**Figure 9.10** At the top

**Figure 9.11** Slid to the bottom

Climbing up, sliding down, climbing down, up-ending the xylophone, moving his fists up and down, bouncing his legs, dropping his pear, putting his spoon on his head, standing on top of crocodile all represented Patrick's prevailing form of thinking. His dynamic vertical schema, evidenced in a variety of actions, was observed.

*Greg (1.11) pushes the handle of the suitcase down and then pulls it back up. He repeats this action with the handle. He gets the beaters and bangs the drum.*

**Figure 9.12** Push and pull the handle

**Figure 9.13** Beaters up and down

**Figure 9.14** Choosing the helicopter...

**Figure 9.15** ...and the aeroplane

**Figure 9.16** Pushing the plane up the slide

*Greg chooses aeroplanes and helicopters from around the room. He pushes the aeroplane up the slide of the garage and watches it fall back down. He holds the red aeroplane up in the air.*

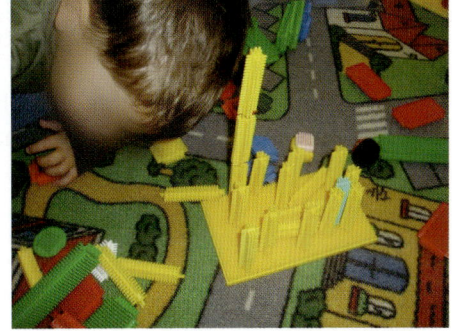

**Figure 9.17** Making tall structures

**Figure 9.18** Making more tall structures

*Greg chooses long pieces of Stickle Brick and joins them together to make tall structures.*

**Figure 9.19** Making piles

**Figure 9.20** Making more piles with plates

Nutbrown and Page (2008: 72) showed how easy it can be for practitioners unwittingly to thwart children's important schematic investigations when they 'mistakenly intervene or dissuade children from following their pattern of interest which seeks only to upset and frustrate them as they are interrupted in their play'. Acquiring a knowledge of schemas enables practitioners to view the play they observe differently. It allows an alternative interpretation of what children disclose as they play. This alternative schematic interpretation should not be viewed as a substitute but as a complementary way of coming to know children's thinking revealed as they play more fully, more richly.

A schematic interpretation of children's behaviour works with existing policy in deepening our understanding of children's *forms of thinking* as they play. The *Statutory Framework for the Early Years Foundation Stage* (DfE 2012) recognises the individuality of children and urges practitioners to accommodate this uniqueness in their response. Through careful observation, a holistic and schematic picture of children can emerge. This view of children's thinking, learning and development is observed only by highly skilled practitioners who can discern what is seen.

Current English government policy states that:

> Children are born ready, able and eager to learn. They actively reach out to interact with other people, and in the world around them. Development is not an automatic process, however. It depends on each unique child having opportunities to interact in positive relationships and enabling environments. (DfE 2012: 2)

In the light of this, the observations of Greg were interpreted schematically (Athey 2007) and within the context of the Early Years Foundation Stage (DfE 2012).

## The observations tell a schema story...

### ...About dynamic vertical

- Suitcase handle pulled up and pushed down
- Drum beaters lifted up and banged down
- Pushing aeroplanes up a slide
- Piling up plates
- Lifting toy helicopters and aeroplanes into the air

## The observations tell another story...

### ...About characteristics of effective learning

- Finding out and exploring
- Showing curiosity about objects, events and people
- Using senses to explore the world around them
- Maintaining focus on their activity for a period of time
- Showing high levels of energy and fascination showing particular interests (DfE 2012: 6)

### ...About personal, social and emotional development

- Seeks out others to share experiences
- Shows affection and concern for people who are special to them
- Uses a familiar adult as a secure base from which to explore independently in new environments (DfE 2012: 8–9)

### ...About physical development

- Shows increasing control over an object in pushing, patting, throwing, catching or kicking it
- Uses simple tools to effect changes to materials
- Handles tools, objects, construction and malleable materials safely and with increasing control (DfE 2012: 24)

### ...About communication and language

- Has a strong exploratory impulse
- Concentrates intently on an object or activity of own choosing for short periods (DfE 2012: 15)
- Uses language as a powerful means of widening contacts, sharing feelings, experiences and thoughts (DfE 2012: 20)

### ...About mathematics

- Beginning to organise and categorise objects (DfE 2012: 32)
- Attempts, sometimes successfully, to fit shapes into spaces
- Uses blocks to create their own simple structures and arrangements
- Enjoys filling and emptying containers
- Beginning to categorise objects according to properties such as shape or size (DfE 2012: 35)
- Shows an interest in shape and space by playing with shapes or making arrangements with objects
- Shows awareness of similarities of shapes in the environment
- Shows interest in shape by sustained construction activity
- Shows interest in shapes in the environment
- Uses shapes appropriately for tasks (DfE 2012: 36)

### ...About understanding the world

- Developing ideas of grouping, sequences, cause and effect (DfE 2012: 7)
- Enjoys playing with small-world models such as a farm, a garage, or a train track
- Notices detailed features of objects in their environment (DfE 2012: 39)

### ...About expressive arts and design

- Uses various construction materials
- Beginning to construct, stacking blocks vertically and horizontally, making enclosures and creating spaces
- Joins construction pieces together to build and balance
- Realises tools can be used for a purpose (DfE 2012: 44)

These motor level examples of trajectory behaviour in the vertical plane were significant as foundation experiences for later symbolic representations, co-ordinations and thought. Isaacs (1930) recognised the value of these early real, practical experiences, which Bilton (1998) acknowledged in confirming that it was through the child's own investigations and explorations that they found out about the world around them.

Gardner (1997) accepted the implication of environment in suggesting that the precise realities of the environment exert a significant impact on what the being becomes. These environmental particulars to which Gardner referred suggest both the physical and social characteristics of environment. There is an inference of manipulation here in that the being or person is influenced and shaped by what and, perhaps more significantly, whom, they encounter.

Nutbrown (2011: 114) clarified that 'play is a central component of children's experiences and a key means by which they learn'. In the light of this, play must be considered as one of Gardner's (1997: 9) 'particular facts'. However, Gardner's 'particular facts' represent a challenge in terms of environment. There is an exacting and meticulous implication describing professional understanding, an approach to practice that is painstaking in its attention to detail, both in terms of what is offered to children and what is understood to have been received.

Montessori (1988: 202) understood this in warning that 'no one acting on the child from the outside can cause him to concentrate'. To be captivated by their environment and absorbed in it is a motivation that cannot be imposed. It is an intrinsic enthusiasm which professional adults working with young children should not only respond to, but also anticipate. It is through careful observation that adults working with young children can come to know, and more fully understand, what children are actually thinking about when they play.

*Patrick and Tommy play alongside each other in the sand tray. Tommy (2.0) covers the police car with sand as he pursues his form of thinking of containing and enveloping. Patrick (2.4), however, stands up, repeatedly sprinkles sand on to the floor, watching it drip through his fingers.*

Figure 9.21  **Sprinkling sand on to the floor**

Patrick and Tommy displayed different dominant schematic behaviours in their actions, which were evident in their use of the sand in the floor tray. Tommy covered; Patrick sprinkled from a height. The *content* for Tommy was sand and his *form of thinking* was containing and enveloping. For Patrick, again, the *content* was sand, but his *form of thinking* was vertical trajectory. They used the same content to pursue their different *forms of thinking*. Both schemas were explored at a motor level as there was no obvious symbolic representation.

*Patrick is playing with the big blocks. He piles them up into a tower. He gets the hat from the builder's box and stacks the blocks up on end into another tower.*

**Figure 9.22** Towers with blocks

**Figure 9.23** Another tower

Although Patrick did not accompany his play with the blocks with language, nor did he talk to the child with him, he could be pursuing his dynamic vertical schema at a symbolic level in his choice of wearing the builder's hat while piling up the blocks. It is tempting to think of Patrick 'the builder' being involved in the construction of tall towers but this would be supposition. If he had complemented his actions with language, 'tall towers', 'buildings', 'roof', 'walls', then a more secure understanding of his symbolic thinking would have been possible. What was clear in the observations of Patrick was Athey's (2007: 113) 'commonalities and continuities ("cognitive constants") in spontaneous thought and behaviour'. Patrick's dynamic vertical schema was evidenced by a series of motor level actions which included making piles, heaping things on top of things and stacking. These continuous actions had a common thread weaving through them. Patrick used a wide range of objects in a distinctive way as he pursued his dynamic vertical schema.

## Dynamic Vertical Schema: Symbolic Level Observations

**Figure 9.24** Shark in the water

*Patrick (2.6) is playing outside at the water trough. He puts the shark on top of the red boat and fills the boat with water. He lifts the shark up above his head and says 'I see something down there'. The adult asks, 'Is that shark diving into the water?' Patrick replies 'Diving into the water' and drops the shark into the water.*

*Patrick goes to the see-saw, climbs on and pushes himself up and down singing 'See saw Marjory Daw'.*

**Figure 9.25** Painting outside

*Outside again, Patrick (2.1) is playing with a bucket of water and paint brush. He paints the side of the tee-pee up and down: 'I painting'. Then he goes inside it. He climbs on the bench inside and pokes his head out of the window. He says 'I painting' and the adult responds, 'Yes, painting up and down'.*

Patrick's dynamic vertical schema was demonstrated by a series of actions which included lifting objects up (shark, paint brush), climbing up (on to a seat inside the tee-pee), pushing down (see-saw, paint brush, hands under water), and dropping objects (shark into the water). He used a variety of things around him in a particular up-and-down way. What was important to Patrick was to find things easily to hand around him with which he could explore up and down movements, that is, the pursuit of his dynamic vertical schema. It was not the shark swimming in the water or the task of painting the tee-pee which appeared important, but that Patrick was able to lift the shark up and drop it down, could stand on top of the seat, could make himself higher, and could move an object up and down. He was able to select things offered and use them in a way which was meaningful to him.

At the water trough, he did not spend time repeatedly filling and emptying the teapot, tipping the water out and watching it pour back into the trough. He did not submerge his hands or press the shark down under the water and push it along as though swimming. He did not sit underneath the tee-pee and use the water from the bucket to cover the floor. He used the things around him in a specific and focused way.

Gardner (1997: 9) suggested that 'humans come equipped not only with keen sensory systems and sense-making capacities, but also with strong proclivities to focus on certain experiences, to draw certain inferences, and to pass through certain cognitive, affective, and physiological stages'. Gardner's 'proclivities' resonated with Neisser's (1976: 56) description of a schema as 'a pattern of action as well as a pattern for action'. Patrick's 'proclivities' were inclinations towards things which he could move up and down. His dynamic vertical schema – his 'pattern of action' – evidenced in his use of content, revealed this form of thought.

Meltzoff and Moore (1998: 229) reinforced Neisser's (1976: 56) notion of 'pattern for action', which moves on from understanding schematic behaviour as that which simply absorbs content into existing cognitive structures. They suggested that schemas 'serve as "discovery procedures" for developing more comprehensive and flexible concepts'. Patrick did not simply absorb content into his existing schema of dynamic vertical trajectory. He was not involved in a purely assimilatory process, but in an accommodatory one. Patrick's pattern of thinking, his schema, functioned as a dynamic blueprint through which higher order conceptual understandings could come to be known.

When Patrick was inside the tee-pee and said 'I painting', and when he saw the adult with him, there was evidence of a movement towards socialised speech. Piaget (1959) observed the transition from monologue towards speech that attempted to convey thought, seen here in Patrick's effort to engage the observer, the hearer. The adult response, 'Yes, painting up and down', was an accompaniment which matched the nature of his action; it reflected his dynamic vertical schema depicted in his up and down use of the paint brush.

Patrick was just over two years old when he painted the tee-pee. He demonstrated a behaviour pattern that Piaget (1969: 53) described as appearing during a child's second year and that is characteristic of the appearance of the semiotic function, specifically 'deferred imitation'. As he painted the tee-pee with water from the pot using a big paint brush, Piaget's account of a representation 'in a physical act but not yet in thought' (1969: 55) could be suggested. Patrick used appropriate language 'I painting' in the presence of the object (the pot and brush). It was not a representation in thought but a representation of a previously seen event, which he may have been imitating;

perhaps it was his mum or dad painting their house which he chose to represent in his actions and language in the tee-pee.

Vygotsky (1978) appeared to support this in his discussion about a child playing with a doll, repeating what they have seen their mother do. He suggested that:

> There is very little of the imaginary. It is an imaginary situation, but it is only comprehensible in the light of a real situation that has just occurred. Play is more nearly recollection of something that has actually happened than imagination. It is more memory in action than novel imaginary situation. (Vygotsky 1978: 103)

Patrick's painting therefore could be seen as an evoked memory of a previously witnessed event. An incident observed, even shared, which he called to mind in his play.

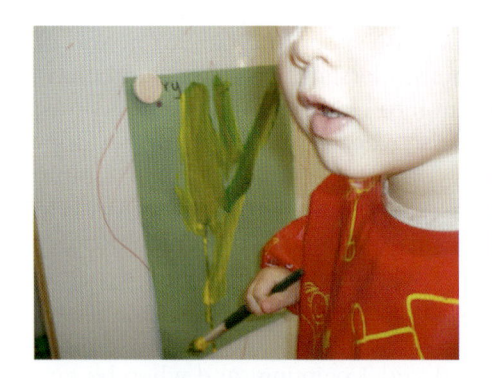

**Figure 9.26** He painted lines

**Figure 9.27** Paint pot tower

**Figure 9.28** Enveloping hands

**Figure 9.29** Hands covered

*Patrick is working at the painting easel. He mixes a colour and makes marks on the paper, starting at the top of the paper and going downwards with his paint brush. He takes the paint pots to the table and stands them on top of each other. 'I've got two paint pots' (he has two pots at the time). 'It's high, it's big.'*

*Patrick gets the paint brush and begins to cover his hand with paint.*

    Patrick:  I paint my hand.

    Adult:    All covered in green paint.

    Patrick:  It's all diggy. (sticky)

    Adult:    Sticky hands.

Gauvain (2001: 63) recognised that 'children's experiences in the family, with peers and in the community directly affect cognitive development through the opportunities, support and constraints they exert on children's learning and thinking'. A negative interpretation of Patrick's behaviour with the paint and paint pots could bring about Gauvain's 'constraints' if understood as unruly rebelliousness. Athey (2007) placated this interpretation when she suggested that, viewed through a schematic lens, seemingly unfathomable behaviour could be understood more favourably.

Patrick's use of the paint and paint pots must be understood for the purposeful endeavour it actually was. Patrick was decisive in his use of the resources that were available. He was securing an aspect of knowledge and understanding of the world (DCSF 2008a) explored in his exploit with the paint pots. The conflicting needs of practitioner and child, however, were clear to be seen: purposeful intent versus acceptable behaviour. It was important, on this occasion, to suggest alternative pursuits for Patrick, to avoid a chaotic mess in the painting area. Initially, however, it was also important to tolerate his seemingly unacceptable behaviour as a learning schema, although only a knowledgeable, understanding adult would realise this.

Montessori (1988) advised that children should be understood for the astonishing thinkers they are. She argued that children are 'endowed with great creative energies, which are, of their nature, so fragile as to need a loving and intelligent defence' (1988: 26). The fragility to which Montessori referred described the precarious position in which children can find themselves in learning environments. She recognised the astounding potential of children and inferred the ease with which these capabilities could be crushed. To have suggested that a 'loving and intelligent defence' was needed is a consideration fraught with responsibility. To be able to defend a child's action in the learning environment demands knowledge, understanding and the ability to articulate what appropriate practice should be like. It describes the kind of adult who is required to work with young children. This person is not just someone who is able to defend a child, but is also someone who is prepared to do so. This is a subtle but significant difference. This adult knows the child in their care, wants the best for that child, understands the thinking of that child and is ready to centre the child and their needs before their own. To do so is not to accept an inferior position in the learning environment, but to occupy a place which prioritises the child. It is a delicate relocation which has nothing to do with geography and everything to do with relationships and respect.

Montessori (1988: 120) continued to reflect upon the characteristics of adults who work with young children, and confirmed the complexity of relationships in the learning environment. She advised that self-reflection was imperative and suggested an altogether more challenging responsibility for the adult in the training of children's 'character' and in preparing their 'spirit'. These requirements go far beyond a theoretical understanding. Adults were, as she said, 'to help life'. This is a clear pointer to the preciousness of the child and the responsibilities of the adult to be knowledgeable and, more importantly, to have a reverence for the child. A reverence in this context means esteem and high regard – essential prerequisites upon which practice should be founded.

As Patrick played with the paint pots he appeared to be co-ordinating different thought patterns. His investigations involved more than one schema. In using the paint to cover his hand ('I paint my hand'), an exploration of dynamic containing and enveloping could be seen. Alongside this, when he piled the paint pots on top of each other saying 'It's high, it's big', his dynamic vertical thought patterns were evident. The co-ordination of these two schemas – those of containing and enveloping and dynamic vertical – allowed for a range of ideas to be explored. Meade and Cubey (2008: 155) observed this in their work: children 'make connections between schemas to form new ideas (concepts)'. The observation of Patrick with the paint pots clearly revealed the holistic nature of his thinking.

## The observations tell a schema story…

### …About containing and enveloping

- Painting hands with paint
- 'I paint my hands'

### …About dynamic vertical

- Paint pots in a pile
- 'It's high, it's big'

Patrick was investigating a range of ideas through his schematic pursuits. Through his actions, speech and representations, which depicted his *forms of thinking*, he was experiencing several areas of learning and development described in the Early Years Foundation Stage (DfE 2012), which complements the schematic view of Patrick's thinking and enriches our understanding of him.

## The observations tell another story…

### …About characteristics of effective learning

- Showing curiosity about objects
- Using senses to explore the world around them
- Showing particular interests (DfE 2012: 6)

### …About personal, social and emotional development

- Seeks out others to share experiences
- Uses a familiar adult as a secure base from which to explore independently in new environments (DfE 2012: 8–9)

### …About physical development

- Shows increasing control over an object
- Uses simple tools to effect changes to materials
- Handles tools, objects, construction and malleable materials safely and with increasing control (DfE 2012: 24)

### …About communication and language

- Has a strong exploratory impulse
- Concentrates intently on an object or activity of own choosing for short periods (DfE 2012: 15)
- Uses language as a powerful means of widening contacts, sharing feelings, experiences and thoughts (DfE 2012: 20)

### …About mathematics

- Begins to organise and categorise objects (DfE 2012: 32)
- Begins to categorise objects according to properties such as shape or size
- Begins to use the language of size (DfE 2012: 35)
- Shows an interest in shape and space by playing with shapes or making arrangements with objects (DfE 2012: 36)

### ...About understanding the world

- Developing ideas of grouping, sequences, cause and effect (DfE 2012: 7)
- Notices detailed features of objects in their environment (DfE 2012: 39)

### ...About expressive arts and design

- Uses various construction materials
- Beginning to construct, stacking blocks vertically and horizontally, making enclosures and creating spaces
- Joins construction pieces together to build and balance
- Manipulates materials to achieve a planned effect
- Constructs with a purpose in mind, using a variety of resources
- Uses simple tools and techniques competently and appropriately
- Selects appropriate resources and adapts work where necessary (DfE 2012: 44)

## Dynamic Vertical Schema: Functional Dependency Relationships

Athey (2007: 184) observed children connecting objects, describing their actions, connecting more, making things bigger and longer through an exploration of functional dependency and noted, therefore, that 'early schemas [were] co-ordinated into new, higher-order concepts'. These vital early practical explorations, where Patrick was involved in motor level schematic activities, provided an essential basis for future tasks carried out symbolically and in thought.

Vygotsky (1978: 50) specified that 'the child's thinking depends first of all on his [sic] memory'. This supports Athey's (2007) later confirmation of the importance of early practical encounters with objects and events for young children's developing conceptual understandings. Vygotsky went on to clarify that 'for the young child, to think means to recall' (1978: 51). In this, Vygotsky understood the need for children to have concrete experiences which they could later evoke. He maintained that early real and tangible activities were the foundation upon which children's conceptual thinking emerged and that this was dependent upon their memory.

Children call to mind previous experiences and replay them in their play, but Vygotsky's assertion that this was dependent upon memory serves as a salutary warning. Children's reliance on memories are therefore, to an extent, reliant upon those who are in a position to provide and support these.

Gauvain (2001: 41) recognised the place of experience in the development of children's thinking, stating that 'experience with other people is instrumental in the formation and developmental course of human intelligence'. In this, Gauvain clarified the place of the child as an individual thinker within a collective environment, where the opportunity for the social construction of knowledge was possible. She acknowledged the indispensable contributory influence of experience. In fact, she clarified as formative the relational aspect of cognitive development. Grieshaber and McArdle's (2010: 40) assertion that the 'condition made available to them by the teacher' influenced the prospect of achievement for children in the learning environment confirmed Gauvain's place of experience.

Grieshaber and McArdle's (2010: 40) conditions are many and certainly include innovative and imaginative environmental incentives. However, a condition of greater significance is the kind of adult the child meets in the learning environment. The individual thinker, the child, is reliant upon encountering adults in the learning environment who are able to identify each individual child's individuality.

Erikson (1972: 691) talked of a '*leeway of mastery* in a set of developments or circumstances'. He specified that the German language had a word for it, *Spielraum*, which suggested '*free movement* within *prescribed limits*'. A literal translation is that space of, or space for, play – what the rules of the game allow. Patrick was observed over a period of months pursuing his dynamic vertical schema. He was often seen busily engaged with a range of objects and occupied with them in a particular way. These occupations were often seemingly conventional – lifting objects (shark, paint brush), climbing up (on to a seat inside tee-pee), pushing down (see-saw, paint brush, hands under water), dropping objects (shark into the water) – but seen altogether, a common schematic thread was apparent.

This allowed the seemingly unconventional occupations – xylophone up-ended, pear dropped, paint pots piled up, spoon on head – to be understood. Erikson's (1972: 691) '*free movement* within *prescribed limits*' is relevant in terms of acceptability and appropriateness from a practitioner perspective. There should be freedom and autonomy for the child to follow their own particular motivations, yet there should also be 'prescribed limits' which may comprise sensitive distractions and suggestions from practitioners who are eager to nurture but not suppress.

Erikson (1972: 691) went on to comment that 'where the freedom is gone, or the limits [are set], play ends'. The expertise required to explicate and realise this in practice is considerable. Adults have an emancipatory role in releasing young children to feel free and unbounded in the learning environment so that they may embrace opportunity unreservedly. To be able to liberate, yet constrain, children is a balance so subtle, so slight, that it requires a perceptive and temperate approach to intervention:

> I caught him [the thief] with an unseen hook and an invisible line which is long enough to let him wander to the ends of the world and still to bring him back with a twitch upon the thread. (Chesterton 1911, cited in Waugh 1945: 206)

The significance, of course, is implication. It is a skill and professional understanding of considerable consequence, for to cherish, nurture and enrich the extraordinary young children we meet in learning environments is an obligation to be willingly embraced.

## Conclusion

This chapter has shown how young children's actions and talk depict the vitality of their minds. It considered the natural investigative and explorative tendencies of young children and showed how these provided an insight into their *forms of thought*. The observations illustrated schematic behaviours and, in addition, offered an insight into the holistic learning and development of young children.

The discussion here illustrated how a dynamic vertical schema may be explored at different developmental levels. Motor level actions, symbolic representations and functional dependency relationships were discussed. For young children, the opportunity to immerse themselves in an enriching environment, to busy themselves with the things around them in ways which are appropriate to them, and to meet adults there who are responsive to their own particular requirements should be an experience felt by all.

## Reflection

Think about Patrick and Tommy's repeated patterns of behaviour in general, and their play in the sand tray together in particular, where Patrick is seen standing up sprinking sand through his fingers and Tommy is seen sitting, covering cars with sand. Consider ways in which children's different schematic interests might be supported in your setting with open-ended resources which allow for diverse use.

- Does the provision you offer support children's varying and exploratory endeavours? To what extent does it offer a range of opportunities, inside and out, for children to pursue particular thinking concerns?

- Examine how you work with children as they play. Do you take time to attune to what children may be thinking about in their actions, talk, makings and marks? Do you accompany children in their learning in a conceptual rather than associative way?

## Further Reading

Athey, C. (2007) *Extending Thought in Young Children* (2nd edition). London: Paul Chapman Publishing.
Piaget, J. (1959) *The Language and Thought of the Child*. London: Routledge and Kegan Paul.
Piaget, J. and Inhelder, B. (1969) *The Psychology of the Child*. London: Routledge and Kegan Paul.

# CHAPTER 10

# STORIES FROM HOME

This chapter focuses on communication between home and settings. The importance of taking time to talk with parents and carers about their child's learning and development is recognised. In sharing detailed observations, the significance in terms of schemas and other aspects of their child's development is revealed. Instances of schema behaviour in the home are discussed during these conversations, as the opportunity to dwell upon their child's developing thinking is enjoyed.

The chapter includes:

- Shared schema stories from the home and setting
- Children's comments about their own activities
- Examples of formats for sharing information between home and school

## Stories from Home

> Nothing gets under a parent's skin more quickly and more permanently than the illumination of his or her own child's behaviour. The effect of participation can be profound. (Athey 2007: 209)

This chapter draws together observations made by parents of their child playing in the home setting. Annie, Tommy, Patrick, Nell and Henry attended the day care setting of a Children's Centre on a sessional basis where Frances had met their parents and talked with them on several occasions. These conversations were an important, continuing dialogue, but in addition, it was important to capture what the children were doing when they played at home, for as Athey (2007: 209) stated, 'parents and professionals can help children separately or they can work together to the great benefit of the children'. Nutbrown (2011: 26) confirmed this in stating: 'When parents, teachers and other early childhood educators work in partnership to share their observations on the children they live and work with, the possibility of continuity in children's learning and development is enhanced.'

'Schema conversations' evolved where moments with parents were seized and important happenings shared. Things were noticed, never too tiny to disregard or too inconsequential to mention, but as significant instances drawn together, which formed, and continued to form, a picture of their child's rich and deep thinking. These ongoing fleeting meetings were supplemented with additional times when there was opportunity to gather and linger. The photographs taken of their child in the setting provided a powerful focus for conversation and the opportunity to share unhurried times about their child was of great significance.

Although the study was about the children and the observations taken in the setting were the foundation of the work, the focused conversations with the parents provided additional, complementary details which were illustrative of the children's schematic endeavours at home.

In his discussion about facilitating learning, Wells (1987: 101) suggested that:

> ...the aim must be the *collaborative* construction of meaning, with negotiation to ensure that meanings are mutually understood. ... What better way of knowing where [children] are than by *listening* to what they have to say, by attending, in the tasks that they engage in, to the meanings that they make.

The images and narratives, shared with the parents, proved to be important initiators in coming to know their child in a different way. Talking about the photographs and narratives, and what they depicted about the holistic thinking, learning and development of their child, appeared to confirm to the parents just what an astounding soul they knew their child to be. As one parent testified, 'he has amazed me with his learning capabilities and speed'.

Introducing a schematic perspective for interpretation, however, was revelatory. Their child, so familiar, whose behaviour was so recognisable, a child so well understood, initially became unfamiliar, unusual and whose behaviour seemed often unfathomable.

Clough and Nutbrown's (2007: 49) suggestion for researchers 'to see their topic with *new* and *different lenses*, in order to look beyond and transform their own current knowledge ... to allow for an alternative way of seeing' was particularly appropriate, in that during the conversations another view of their child came into focus. Athey (2007: 129) acknowledged in her observations that 'parents found schematic explanations more interesting and reassuring than thinking of such behaviours as random. Such discussions sharpened adult perceptions in that related examples were then observed.' As the conversations continued, the parents became increasingly open and relaxed, and parents described, with almost a sense of relief, examples of their child's antics at home which had seemed haphazardly roguish but, viewed from a schematic perspective, now became deliberate and meaningful. These dialogues strengthened and enriched knowledge about their child as more and more stories from the setting and home were shared. Wells' (1987) notion of 'collaborative construction', so vital in the relationship between adult and child in a learning context, is pertinent also in conversations between practitioner and parent, to enable a more rounded, detailed understanding of their child's thinking concerns to come to be known.

Nutbrown (2011: 165) is clear that parents and professional educators 'both have important and distinctive roles, so an attitude is needed where these roles are recognised and respected [to the benefit of the children]'. This is challenging because a shift in perceived responsibilities towards an egalitarian relationship where contributions are understood as distinct, complementary, equal and knowledgeable by both parents and practitioners alike is required. Meade and Cubey (2008: 154) confirmed this, stating that it was important 'that teachers and parents share information about children's learning and recognise they share the educational role'.

The approach to involving parents in the study reported in this book was to develop a recording and exchanging format which encouraged parents to look at their child when they were playing from a schematic perspective and capture incidences of this play to share. Photographs of their child, accompanied with short captions summarising examples of behaviour as their child played in the setting, were compiled. They were pictorial diaries, stories from the setting, to inspire 'stories from home.'

## Stories from Home about Tommy

### In the setting, Tommy is exploring things going inside…

*Containing and enveloping*

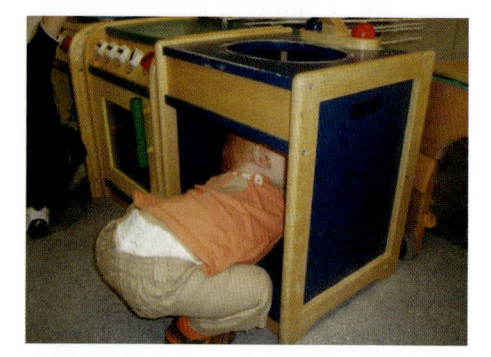

**Figure 10.1**

**Figure 10.2**

- Tommy (1.7) fills the blue bowl with shapes (encloses the shapes inside a container). He puts the blue bowl inside the climbing frame (encloses the bowl inside a frame).

- Tommy opens the sink cupboard and climbs inside (encloses himself in a container).

## Stories from home…

- 'Tommy keeps putting his cars in vases and the television speaker. He has his own hiding places. He likes to help putting the washing in the washer with me. He gets out the washing powder to give me.'

## In the setting, Tommy is exploring things going inside…

*Enclosing and enveloping*

**Figure 10.3**

**Figure 10.4**

- Tommy (1.8) likes to play with the train. He puts the play people inside the carriages and pushes the train along.

## Stories from home…

- 'Tommy is a very quick and clever boy. I think this is because of his brother and sister being older. We often visit the fire station and look at the engines. He has amazed me with his learning capabilities and speed.'

In the setting, Tommy's 'containing and enveloping' behaviour was evidenced by a series of motor level actions, including shapes into bowls, bowls into climbing frames, toy cars dropped into sink, Tommy under the sink collecting toys, toy cars dropped inside again. At home, this *form of thinking* continued, with Tommy putting cars into vases and speakers, having special hiding places, and helping put the washing into the washer. Although there was a thematic consistency in the parent's story about the cars, this was extended to include the anecdote about the washing. This was significant in that Tommy's mum had included an example of Tommy's play which displayed his underlying form of thinking. This had been shared many times during conversations in the setting and which was recognised and responded to at home. Smidt (2011: 30) noted that:

> Children are part of a culture, a context and a community and this is where they play and learn ... and they do this through interactions with others in their community and contexts – with their siblings and peers, with their parents and grandparents, with their teachers and other significant people.

There is a collective responsibility here, a relational context which Smidt (2011) recognised. The 'significant people' in Tommy's life came to understand his thinking concerns, his motives in play, the complexity of his behaviour which reveal the depth of his unique ingenuity. Interactions can intensify understanding if their nature is reciprocal. In a relationship of shared worth, balance enables there to be a mutual insight.

## Stories from Home about Patrick

### In the setting, Patrick is exploring things going up and down...

*Dynamic vertical* (August 2006)

Figure 10.5                                   Figure 10.6

- Patrick puts the car at the top of the ramp and lets the car roll down.
- Patrick pushes the car down the slide inside the garage.

## Stories from home...

- 'Patrick has a garage at home and loves to push the cars and the little men down the slides. He will also spend ages locking them in a little carport with doors.'
- 'He has a fire-engine with an extendable ladder and climbs the little man up and down the ladder.'

## In the setting, Patrick is exploring things going up and down... and back and forth...

*Dynamic vertical* (October 2006)

Figure 10.7

Figure 10.8

- Patrick pushes the car along and likes to push the scooter and bikes along as well.
- Patrick climbs up the slide.

## Stories from home...

- 'Whenever Patrick goes to any park he always climbs up the slides. He prefers this to sliding down.'
- 'When Patrick was learning to walk he would push his toy box along or the "tool station" or even my dining chairs. He still moves things around now.'
- 'Patrick has always been a big climber. Cots, washing machines, anything that looks like a "step higher". He always climbs into things as well. I often find him sat in a toy box or a plastic basket that we keep cars in.'

## In the setting, Patrick is exploring how high things can get...

*Dynamic vertical* (April 2007)

**Figure 10.9**

**Figure 10.10**

- Patrick held up two paint pots and said 'two paints'.
- He piled up the paint pots into a tower and said 'it's high, it's big'.

## Stories from home...

- 'Patrick loves to make towers with his building blocks. He likes to get my tins out of the kitchen cupboard and stack them up (supervised by me). He says "I'm making a tower with your shopping." Patrick has for the last few months been asking about everything.'
- 'Patrick plays made up games with his brother. They pretend the settee is a rescue boat and the floor is the water. They pretend to fall off the boat shouting "get me out of the water". Patrick makes his nan play with him, "play rescue boats nanny".'

In the setting, Patrick's dynamic vertical schema was evidenced by a series of motor level actions, including pushing cars up ramps, crawling up slides, climbing down rope ladders, rolling cars down slides, piling up paint pots. His dynamic vertical schema had been apparent in the language he used to accompany his actions: 'it's high, it's big' (paint pot tower). At home, this *form of thinking* continued in pushing cars and toys down slides, climbing toys up the extendable fire engine ladder, climbing up the slide at the park, climbing up anything that looks 'a step higher'.

Patrick's mum acknowledged that he had always been 'a big climber', substantiating the observations seen at the setting. It was interesting to note Patrick's mum's departure from using associative examples of behaviour to the inclusion of seemingly random acts, yet which expressively depicted Patrick's *form of thinking*. His dynamic vertical schema was evidenced in his actions (piling tins up into a tower, leaping off the settee on to the carpet) and language ('I'm making a tower with your shopping' and 'rescue me from the water'). Arnold (2003: 7) accepted the importance of sharing understandings about the child (in her observations) in acknowledging that 'the family are interested in getting to know him as well as helping him to get to know them'.

When Patrick got the tins of food out of the cupboard and built a tower, which his mum was keen to point out 'was supervised by me' (from a safety point of view it was later revealed), this concealed an exchange of profound and complex implication. Patrick knew that getting the tins out of the cupboard to build with was accepted; he had done it many times before. To Patrick, it was an important opportunity to extend his fascination with making things high and higher. Through his schema of dynamic vertical, a fascination of movement in the vertical plane, he was able to explore concepts of height, addition, shape, size and position, supported by a knowledgeable adult.

However, Patrick's mum did not appear to realise the significance of her contribution in categorising it as merely 'supervision'. Patrick's action was evidence of a secure sense of self-esteem and confidence, which his parents had nurtured in affirming his creative, investigative tendencies with tranquil acceptance and support. This was not about an acceptance of unruly, unmanageable behaviour, but wanting their child to feel free to follow his instincts. And, as Patrick's mum said, 'supervised by me' suggested an understanding of boundaries of behaviour. This seemingly mundane event, this ordinary time together, revealed a confident Patrick ('I'm building a tower with your shopping'), who was secure in the knowledge that his mum would not reprimand him for using the things which were to hand (tins). To him, they were perfectly acceptable and useful items to play with, but more importantly, his mum felt the same. She may have considered herself to be in a supervisory role, but her acknowledgment of his actions, conveyed through quiet affirmation, was respectful of her child and the business of his play. In the conversations at the setting, as Patrick's schematic pursuits became clearer from the observations at home and in the setting, incidences with the tins could take on a new meaning. As Athey (2007: 217) asserted, 'parents and teachers can and must work together to further the educational process in individual children'.

## Stories from Home about Nell

### In the setting, Nell is exploring things going inside…

*Enclosing and enveloping* (August 2006)

- Nell filled the buckets. She enclosed things inside.
- She put the bucket full of shapes inside the car boot. She enclosed the bucket inside the boot.
- Nell climbed inside the tunnel.

**Figure 10.11**          **Figure 10.12**

## Stories from home…

- 'When Nell is having crisps, she likes to empty the crisps into a bowl.'
- 'She took the clean washing out of the washing basket and climbed into the basket!'

## In the setting, Nell is exploring putting things inside…

*Enclosing and enveloping* (November 2006)

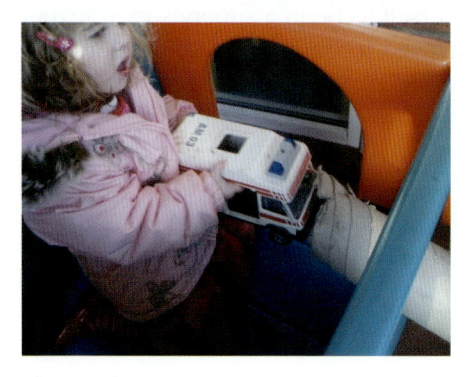

**Figure 10.13**          **Figure 10.14**

- Nell likes to put lots of different things inside other things.
- She tried to put the big ambulance inside the cardboard tube.
- She put the toys inside the boot of the big car.

## Stories from home…

- 'Nell likes to pour liquids from one container to another.'
- 'She likes to have her sweets or crisps in bowls, not the packet. She pours them into bowls herself.'

In the setting, Nell's containing and enveloping schema was evidenced by a series of motor level actions (covering hands and arms with paint and glitter, sand tipped through port holes, stones into beakers) and in her speech use ('cover over you'). At home, this continued in pouring liquids from one container to another, tipping sweets and crisps into bowls and climbing inside the washing basket. It is significant that Nell's mum shared an account of her behaviour (getting into the washing basket) which she considered unusual. This emerged during conversation and can be gleaned from the way she has written the account.

As a result of the conversations and when photographs were shared and incidences discussed, these unusual behaviours were understood as less curious and peculiar. Palmer (2006: 223) confirmed the importance of a strong sense of collaboration between parents and practitioners in recognising that 'when communication is good, everyone benefits – especially the children'. Conversations with Nell's mum brought enlightenment, in that aspects of her child's behaviour, which had seemed at first bizarre, were increasingly understood as important, purposeful intentions.

Although Empson and Nabuzoka's (2004) discussion was in the context of children's atypical behaviour, the essence of their message is pertinent in acknowledging the place of equivalence between children and professional adults in the relationships formed in learning environments:

> Children function not only within the family environment but increasingly, as they grow up, in the context of school, neighbourhood and the wider world. The reciprocal interactions between the child and others in these different contexts will influence and be influenced by the developmental status of the child.
> (Empson and Nabuzoka 2004: 143–144)

This equivalence was expressed in antiphonal exchanges – knowledgeable interactions enriched by understanding – and was founded upon a coming to know the child through sensitive observation. These observations inform adult intentions when working with children, who, in turn, make known their intentions to be received. The professional challenge here requires adults who are prepared to spend time getting to know children properly, actually, and who are willing to keep doing so, in an evolving and strengthening connection. It also requires children who feel contented and at ease, who are able to be themselves, happy and ready to enter into liaisons with significant others. To borrow Rogoff's (1990: 39) metaphor of 'apprentice', to bring about these comfortable yet vibrant relationships is an accomplishment of great skill and expertise and is not easily or hurriedly achieved.

## Stories from Home about Annie

**Figure 10.15**

**Figure 10.16**

### Annie is exploring insideness…

#### Containing and enveloping

Annie was playing with the wooden sorting tower. She tipped it upside down. All the shapes fell on to the floor. She picked up the wooden stick and tried to poke it into the hole in the middle. She put the stick down and poked her finger into the hole.

### Stories from home…

**Figure 10.17** 'Annie took the straws out of the plastic tub'

**Figure 10.18** 'Then started to put the straws back into the tub'

Figure 10.19  'Annie tips the straws out of the tub all over the floor'

Figure 10.20  'She starts to put the straws back into the tub'

Figure 10.21  'Annie picks up the cup and tries to put a straw inside'

Figure 10.22  'She puts the yellow straw into her mouth then puts it into the cup'

At the setting, Annie had been busy exploring insideness, evidenced in a range of motor level actions, including putting hands inside baskets, posting lids, tipping out, and climbing into spaces. Through her containing and enveloping schema, Annie was experimenting with fitting things inside objects. These valuable actions were important foundations upon which later concepts of capacity, volume and space are built. At home, Annie's prevailing *form of thought* was clear in her work with the straws. Picking straws out of the tub, putting straws back in, tipping straws out, and posting them back, then repeating this pattern with a different container (pink cup), were evidence of her containing and enveloping schema, her exploration of insideness and fit.

At the setting, Annie had also been busy testing how one thing (fingers, hands) could go through another (green hoop, hole in CD, shaker handle). There were many examples of motor level, 'going through a boundary' behaviours, which included pushing her hand through hoops, poking fingers through holes in CDs and through gaps in whisks, pressing fingers into wicker balls and putting fingers through handles. These consistent patterns of behaviour, Annie's predominant *forms of thought*, were to be expected at home and were vividly captured in her mum's photographs. They are powerful images of a child's enduring thinking concerns. In bringing them to conversations at the setting, the adults involved with Annie were able to intensify their understanding of what was important for Annie conceptually, and therefore were in a position to be able to respond more appropriately. As Erikson (1963: 222) stated, 'the playing child advances forward to new stages of mastery'. Although Annie was not yet able to verbalise her thinking, she eloquently articulated this in her actions.

## Stories from Home about Henry

Henry's mum and dad captured examples of his play at home in a diary. They wrote their observations and comments and brought it into the setting to share. They would leave it for Frances who would write a reply. The diary covers a 10-month period in Henry's life and complements the conversations his parents and Frances had at the setting. Extracts from the dairy are included here.

> Henry likes to have his cars lined up in an orderly fashion. He gets irritated if he can't line them up perfectly.
>
> Henry likes to jump off the couch on to the big bean bag. He always lines the bean bag up before he starts his routine.
>
> He likes to fill things up like emptying the pegs out of the bag and putting them back in. He likes filling the container up with bird seed.
>
> When he played with the fireman he said, 'Fireman down the ladder'.
>
> He still likes to line everything up.
>
> He likes to build things and put things inside.
>
> We play a lot of games with Henry. The commentaries tend to be very one-sided, with Henry correcting us when we don't match his own high standards!
>
> He likes to play cards, like Bob the Builder snap, but lines them up and calls it 'a big, long snake'.

Observations of Henry saw him combining schemas in his play, which Nutbrown (2011: 30) confirmed 'mark [an] important progression in learning at all stages where combinations and co-ordinations of schemas develop into higher-order concepts'. Henry's containing and enveloping behaviour was evidenced by a series of motor level actions, including putting spoons inside cups, knives inside teapots, spades and scoops in buckets, raisins into milk, stones into bottles and mixed objects (elephant, horse and policeman) inside the stable together. This absorption with fitting and insideness could be seen at home where these patterns in his thinking continued (bird seed into containers, filling and emptying the peg bag, 'he likes to put things inside').

At home, Henry lined cars up and used Bob the Builder cards to make a line, 'a big, long snake'. This corresponded with his desire to further his knowledge of movement in the horizontal plane in his motor actions of displacement observed in the setting. He moved a range of objects (toy animals, soft shapes, small wooden blocks) and made piles with them. He collected different items to hand (spoons, teapots, forks, cups, trains) and stacked them on tables. He often chose to play with cars, trucks, vans and lorries, appearing to concentrate his choice of objects to those which moved horizontally.

His dynamic back and forth schema was evidenced in action (lining objects up, moving objects around and making stacks, choosing objects which moved) and in speech ('a big, long snake'). The underlying pattern of horizontal movement was unmistakable in his apparently random actions and unconventional use of the objects to hand. Meltzoff and Moore (1998: 229) suggested that 'initial mental structures ... serve as "discovery procedures" for developing more comprehensive and flexible concepts'. Seen altogether, Henry's actions and speech describe considered and deliberate thought. His schemas allowed higher order concepts (e.g. length, speed, force) to be experienced through these early practical investigations.

The co-ordination continued with his exploration of movement in the vertical plane. At the setting, Henry had extended his understanding of vertical movement in spending time climbing and crawling up steps, walking, running or slithering down slides, building towers, throwing objects on to the floor ('I'm making a bouncy castle I'm jump on'). At home, the pattern continued (jumping off the couch, 'fireman down the ladder'). These important stabilities in his thinking, evidenced in his action and speech and visible at the setting and in the home, confirmed the formidable nature of Henry's capabilities. In his play, Henry described the detail of his thinking. The descriptions were not always verbal and were only accessible to those prepared to see and hear, yet a fluent expression of Henry's capacity as a thinker they undoubtedly were.

When Athey (2007: 209) observed that 'all the adults watched and listened with ever-increasing interest to what the children were saying and doing', she understood the considerable power of children's thinking, evidenced in their repeated behaviours. Her 'ever-increasing' inferred how coming to know children, by spending time with them, through observations, through conversations with other knowledgeable adults, through sharing moments captured, could prove to be revelatory. The astounding capabilities of children are seen as less and less of a surprise, if ever this were the case.

## Conclusion

This chapter has considered the vital relationship between home and setting in supporting the learning and development of young children. Whalley (2001: 4) acknowledged 'the key role which parents play as their child's first educators', which Dex and Joshi (2005: 98) extended to include a broader network of support in referring to the role of grandparents. Wells (1987: 68) also recognised the significance of secure relationships between the home and setting in stating that:

> ...continuity between home and school is important for social and emotional reasons. ... [E]ntry into school should not be thought of as a beginning, but as a transition to a more broadly based community and to a wider range of opportunities for meaning making and mastery. The teacher's responsibility is to discover what they are and to help each child to extend and develop them.

The sense of community to which Wells referred is an inclusive moral which invites participation and involvement. To achieve and maintain successful collaborations between the home and setting is complex yet vital. The learning and development of young children is enhanced when all those who have the child's best interests at heart come together. When practitioners and parents meet and share understandings, more powerful and deeper understandings can emerge. As Athey (2007: 217) found in her work:

> There was a unanimous opinion, shared by both parents and professionals involved in the Project, that parents and teachers can and must work together to further the educational process in individual children.

This chapter has reflected upon observations made by parents which emerged following conversations with the practitioner. During these conversations, important moments of their child's time in the setting had been shared. These times together had enabled the parents to have a new and different understanding of their child and in turn allowed me (Frances) to have privileged access to happenings at home. These occasions enriched our understandings of the child and appear to be the essence of continuity and community to which Wells (1987) referred: continuity in common understanding, and community in terms of mutual devotion to the well-being of the child.

Returning to the overarching research question which asked *how young children are pursuing their schemas*, this chapter has examined young children's schematic pursuits in their home settings. Observations of Annie, Tommy, Patrick, Nell and Henry made by their parents as they played at home, and opportunities to share important incidences of the children's learning in the day care setting made for a shared understanding of these young children's learning. Photographs of the children taken in the setting enriched these 'schema conversations' with the parents, which allowed for a richer picture of their child's thinking to form.

The 'stories from home' enhanced our portrait of the children since they captured *forms of thinking* that underpinned and ran through their play. Annie, Tommy, Patrick, Nell and Henry could all be seen involved in patterns of behaviour similar to those observed in the day care setting.

The parents became more familiar with something that *was* already so familiar, their child's play, but now they were able to view it from a schematic perspective. The ways in which these adults supported their children's schemas became clearer. As the parents and Frances shared the 'stories from home', a greater understanding of particular, sometimes unusual, actions was cemented, and ways of responding to their child that matched their *forms of thought* as they played were discussed.

The implications of schema identification on the learning experiences of young children therefore include ones of empowerment. To be able to look at children's behaviour from a schematic perspective allows for a more complete understanding of children's actions, speech and representations. The parents appeared to be genuinely enthused in spotting particular patterns of behaviour when their child played at home, which they were happy to talk about and share.

The opportunity to talk with parents about their child's learning and development, and to take time to reflect upon this together, is a vital, relational prospect which can only benefit the child. If the significant adults in a child's life can come together in collaboration, and with respect for each other's expertise regarding the child, then the benefits of this for practitioner, adult and child can be boundless.

## Reflection

Consider the professional relationship you have with the parents and carers of the children in your setting.

- How might your setting develop further opportunities for dialogue, where parents, carers and practitioners come together to share their particular expertise?

- To what extent does your setting support parents and carers in coming to know about schemas?

- Consider ways in which parents may be supported to work with their child in the home setting in response to a developing knowledge and understanding of schemas.

## Further Reading

Arnold, C. (2010) *Understanding Schemas and Emotion in Early Childhood*. London: Paul Chapman Publishing.
Rinaldi, C. (2006) *In Dialogue with Reggio Emilia*. London: Routledge.

# EPILOGUE

This book has reported a study of the schemas of babies and toddlers and asked *how they pursued their schemas in an early years setting*. It has investigated aspects of thinking, learning and development that were revealed in children's representational behaviours. The study also explored how adults could intervene to support young children as they pursued their schemas and considered what the implication of identifying schemas could be in practice on the learning experiences of young children.

The nature of relationships between adults and young children in the learning environment must emphasise nurturing, sensitive, responsive adults who situate the child at the heart of learning. In order to match children's *forms of thinking* – their schemas – and to be able to accompany them in their learning in a relevant and meaningful way, Bartlett's (1932: 85) assertion is pertinent:

> It is not merely a question of relating the newly presented material to old acquirements of knowledge, ... it depends upon the active bias, or special reaction tendencies, that are awakened in the observer by the new material, and it is these tendencies which then set the new into relation to the old.

Bartlett (1932) understood the active nature of children's minds and the necessary place of relevant experiences which may be assimilated to cognitive structures. Athey's (2007: 50) definition of schema as 'a pattern of repeatable behaviour into which experiences are assimilated and that are gradually co-ordinated' therefore supports Bartlett's clarification of knowledge acquisition. Bartlett and Athey articulate the personal active endeavour of the learner, in that knowledge acquisition is not a passive integration but an active process of cognitive disturbance.

There is an understanding here of the uniqueness of the child and their precise, distinct thinking idiosyncrasies. If the experiences a child encounters are to nourish their *forms of thought*, and if the adult is to be a meaningful accomplice in this process, one who actually takes account of a child's cognitive structures and allows this to shape intervention, then more attuned accompaniment is possible. Those who work alongside children need to be mindful of these personal cognitive features of mind, so that time spent together in learning environments can be attendances of conceptual relevance.

There is a correspondence with their subsequent mark making, *how children use the things around them to pursue their schemas*, both in action and in subsequent mark making. The observations in this book have shown that there is a connection between *form* revealed in dynamic actions and *form* observed in subsequent mark making, using a variety of tools and materials (Athey 2007; Meade and Cubey 2008). A richness of experience and opportunity in the early years, therefore, in the company of adults who are able to respond to the individual needs and interests of young children, is the preferred environment for these fervent young thinkers. When children have time to explore and investigate, make decisions, take risks, choose, organise and follow things through, their potential can be released. It is important to cultivate this potential and enable children, through the experiences they encounter and the people they meet, to blossom and grow.

*A range of schemas may be explored at different developmental levels.* The foundation for future representations, which enriching sensory experiences can provide, was articulated through a series of observations of young children's investigations. Motor level actions, symbolic representations and functional dependency relationships were revealed as children absorbed themselves in their play, pursuing their *forms of thought*. These observations described the holistic nature of children's thinking, evident in actions, speech and representations, and were evidence of the astonishing competencies of the young child.

The responsibility for adults who work with children in learning environments not only to accept the profound nature of young children's thinking, but to herald this in their practice, was acknowledged. The right of a child to be heard, to express their views and describe what is of consequence to them, through their actions, in their talk and in the things they made, featured as an essential discussion. Alongside this, the person the child may hope to meet in their learning was made known. An implicit philosophy of respect, which weaved through the work as an unspoken, yet understood imperative, described this adult as one who is receptive and responsive to the needs of the other, the child.

In seeking to address the importance of the relationship between the home and setting, *it is important to acknowledge the shared nature of understanding and the harmonising potential of parents and practitioners coming together to talk about their child*. This connection allows a deeper and more enriched knowledge about children's holistic thinking, learning and development to be more fully realised. The potential of these shared times together, where insights could be divulged and understandings further secured, was invaluable in building an image of the child which accurately described their exceptional qualities.

Wells (1987) and Athey (2007) understood the essential place of parents in their child's care, learning and development in acknowledging the significance of collaborative relationships. Parents and practitioners coming together to share their own expertise and insights about the child is an involvement and engagement which the authors identified as vital if an authentic picture of the child is to be formed. This book has identified examples of shared times where significant adults converged to discover more about the child who was their shared focus, creating chances to get to know a child better by talking about what had been seen. This simple premise, however, belies the considerable significance of talking together, in that these times proved to be wonderful enabling opportunities for reciprocal enlightenment.

*When early years practitioners, who have the learning, development and care of children at heart, come together with parents to share pedagogical understandings, the prospect of delightful details emerging which add to and enrich the unfolding picture of the child can be shared.* Children spend time in different places, doing different things, with different people, so when there is a coming together with the shared purpose of interest in and support of the child, a happy collision of deeply rewarding consequence can be the result. Warm relationships can evolve where all feel able to contribute what they know about the child to deepen their understandings.

Holliday, Harrison and McLeod (2009) recognised the formidable capabilities of young children in asserting that they should be given uninhibited opportunities to express their thoughts. They foreground the contribution children make so that their thoughts, concerns and feelings count, indeed must be heard. It is a prospective view which describes a powerful child and locates that child in the prime position. It understands the peripheral influences of place and relationships but distils the focus to converge on the child. *Conversations with parents can allow relationships to develop so that, through a schematic lens, the learning and development of a child so well-known can be more fully and richly understood.*

This book has shown *how adults can intervene to support young children as they pursue their schemas*. Through conversations with parents about observations taken of their child in the setting and brought from home, a new and different way of understanding particular representational behaviours was described. *In these shared times, where children's behaviour was reinterpreted from a schematic perspective, an alternative appreciation of familiar endeavours was made possible.* The implication of this new way of looking, which sought to reconsider something so well-known, celebrates Clough and Nutbrown's (2007: 48) clarification of 'radical looking', which attempted to 'make the familiar strange'. To interpret children's behaviour schematically suggests a different and complementary understanding and enables intervention in learning to be more securely attuned to the thinking concerns of the child. The implication for practice is in the way this alternative understanding may shape how adults accompany children in their learning.

When practitioners are able to see the conceptual in young children's repeated behaviours, it supplements the detail which children reveal about their thinking in the things they do. It has been shown that the children in this study were able to bring all that was needed, in any given moment, to whatever they may be involved with at the time. Through these investigations, clear insights into what is important for the child and what is being experienced are visible. These children demonstrated their thinking through their representations, which adults may or may not fully understand. The implication for practice is that adults should watch attentively and seek to reflect on and learn from their observations in concert with parents and the child.

In this book, we encountered Annie, Florence, Tommy, Nell, Patrick, Henry and Greg, who were all under two years old when Frances first met them. Her careful observations of these young children, taking time and gradually building up a picture of their unfolding interests, have informed our understanding of their learning. *The observations, made over many months, revealed the children's schematic* forms of thinking *and the development of these in motor and symbolic behaviours.* In addition, the holistic nature of thinking was revealed in representational behaviours, as they went about their business in an early years setting.

Arnold (2003), Bruce (2005), Athey (2007), Meade and Cubey (2008) and Nutbrown (2011) have taken account of children's schematic pursuits in their observations of children in different environments, focusing mainly on children over three. In the light of current curriculum policy focusing on the youngest children (DfE 2012), the Early Years Foundation Stage acknowledges the remarkable competency of young children's thinking and challenges practitioners to take account of this. The *Statutory Framework for the Early Years Foundation Stage* (DfE 2012) acknowledges that children's own thinking concerns, their unique qualities and characteristics, are of fundamental importance and should be at the heart of planning for learning. The entitlement of children, therefore, to a curriculum that celebrates powerful young thinkers resonates throughout key policy documents of recent years which recognise the implications of this in terms of response.

The DfE (2011) report, *The Early Years: Foundations for Life, Health and Learning – An Independent Report on the Early Years Foundation Stage,* features familiar, expected themes which must not be considered as mere rhetoric. The confirmation of things of such fundamental importance for the early years, which are essentially present again in the Tickell Review (2011), cannot be over-emphasised. Many of the key issues which appear in the Tickell Review are resonant with aspects of practice which have been part of the early childhood tradition and understood by practitioners steeped in the field for many years. The Nutbrown Review, *Foundations for Quality* (Nutbrown 2012), argued for high-quality provision with well-qualified practitioners as being key to that quality:

> It is vitally important that babies and young children have rich and varied opportunities to play both indoors and outside, and I regard it as a fundamental part of their early education and care. It is worth making clear in qualifications that an understanding of the importance of play in children's lives and learning – both guided exploratory play through a well-planned environment, and play which allows children to explore their world for themselves – is part of fully understanding child development and fostering independent and enquiring minds. It is necessary, therefore, that adults understand their roles in providing for play, including when they should participate to extend and support learning, and when they should observe and not interfere. (Nutbrown 2012: 20, para 2.10)

The role of parents and carers as partners in their children's learning is recognised as essential, with the guidance and support children receive in settings as complementary and building upon home experiences. *Understanding the importance of parents' active involvement in children's learning with clear and shared theoretical understandings about learning is crucial to young children's development, and the different and complementary roles parents and professional educators have needs to be recognised.* In coming together to talk, parents and practitioners can strengthen their own understanding of the child's learning through schemas which allows for interventions to be more closely matched to the thinking concerns of the child.

*Children pursue their schemas in an early years setting and in so doing reveal aspects of thinking, learning and development evident in children's representational behaviours.* Professional early years practitioners who pay careful attention to children's patterns of learning, their thinking concerns, through finely detailed observation, are able to develop their approach to working with young children, which is acutely attuned to their particular interests.

To acknowledge the rich legacy of the early years pioneers and to embrace contemporary contributors who continue to enhance our understanding of this vital time have a significant influence on how professional adults may work with young children. Noticing what matters to children, and letting them know this, is an approach to practice in the early years which understands the entitlements and respect these young souls deserve. For as Nutbrown (2011: 177) has reminded us:

> Children's hearts, minds and bodies are valuable and precious. Young children must receive the respect and recognition they deserve as capable thinkers and learners in all aspects of their learning and development.

Throughout this book we have seen how looking at young children's learning through a schematic lens can illuminate behaviours that might seem inconsequential, showing them to be consistent threads of learning woven by capable learners.

# BIBLIOGRAPHY

Abbott, J. (1999) The search for expertise: the importance of the early years. In L. Abbott and H. Moylett (eds), *Early Education Transformed*. London: Falmer.

Abbott, L. and Langston, A. (2005) Ethical research with very young children. In A. Farrell (ed.), *Ethical Research with Children*. Maidenhead: Open University Press.

Agar, M. (1991) The right brain strikes back. In N. Fielding and R. Lee (eds), *Using Computers in Qualitative Research*. Thousand Oaks, CA: Sage.

Alderson, P. (2000) *Young Children's Rights*. London: Jessica Kingsley.

Alldred, P. (1998) Ethnography and discourse analysis: dilemmas in representing the voices of children. In J. Ribbens and R. Edwards (eds), *Feminist Dilemmas in Qualitative Research: Public Knowledge and Private Lives*. London: Sage, pp. 147–170.

Anderson, R., Reynolds, R., Schallert, D. and Goetz, E. (1977) Frameworks for comprehending discourse. *American Educational Research Journal*, 14(4): 367–381.

Angelides, P. and Michaelidou, A. (2009) The deafening silence: discussing children's drawings for understanding and addressing marginalization. *Journal of Early Childhood Research*, 7: 27–45.

Angrosino, M. and Mays de Perez, K. (2003) Rethinking observation: from method to context. In N. Denzin and Y. Lincoln (eds), *Collecting and Interpreting Qualitative Materials*. Thousand Oaks, CA; London: Sage.

Anning, A. (2003) Pathways to the Graphicacy Club: the crossroad of home and pre-school. *Journal of Early Childhood Literacy*, 3: 5–35.

Anning, A. (2010) *Developing Multi-professional Teamwork for Integrated Services: Research, Policy and Practice*. Maidenhead: Open University Press.

Archard, D. (1993) The wrongs of children's rights. In D. Archard, *Children, Rights and Childhood*. London: Routledge, pp. 88–93.

Arnold, C. (2003) *Observing Harry*. Buckingham: Open University Press.

Arnold, C. (2010) *Understanding Schemas and Emotion in Early Childhood*. London: Paul Chapman Publishing.

Askeland, N. and Maagero, E. (2010) Tasting words and letting them hang in the air: about subject-oriented language in kindergarten. *European Early Childhood Education Research Journal*, 18(1): 75–91.

Athey, C. (1990) *Extending Thought in Young Children*. London: Paul Chapman Publishing.

Athey, C. (2007) *Extending Thought in Young Children* (2nd edition). London: Paul Chapman Publishing.

Azmitia, M. and Hesser, J. (1993) Why siblings are important agents of cognitive development: a comparison of siblings and peers. *Child Development*, 64(2): 430–444.

Ball, C. (1994) *Start Right: The Importance of Early Learning*. London: Royal Society of Arts.
Barbatis, G., Camacho, M. and Jackson, L. (2004) Does it speak to me? Visual aesthetics and the digital divide. *Visual Studies*, 19(1): 36–51.
Bartlett, F. (1932) *Remembering: A Study in Experimental and Social Psychology*. Cambridge: Cambridge University Press.
Beals, D. (1998) Re-appropriating schema: conceptions of development from Bartlett and Bakhtin. *Mind, Culture and Activity*, 5(1): 5–24.
Bellagamba, F. and Tomasello, M. (1999) Re-enacting intended acts: comparing 12- and 18-month-olds. *Infant Behaviour and Development*, 22(2): 277–282.
Bennett, J. (2003) Starting strong: the persistent division between care and education. *Journal of Early Childhood Research*, 1: 21.
BERA (British Educational Research Association) (2004) *Revised Ethical Guidelines for Educational Research*. London: BERA.
Berger, S. and Nuzzo, K. (2008) Older siblings influence younger siblings' motor development. *Infant and Child Development*, 17(6): 607–615.
Bilton, H. (1998) *Outdoor Play in the Early Years: Management and Innovation*. London: David Fulton.
Birbeck, D.J. and Drummond, M.J.N. (2005) Research with young children: contemplating methods and ethics. *Journal of Educational Enquiry*, 7(2): 21–31.
Blaikie, A. (2001) Photographs in the cultural account: contested narratives and collective memory in the Scottish Islands. *The Sociological Review*, 49(3): 345–367.
Bornstein, M., Haynes, M., Legler, J., O'Reilly, A. and Painter, K. (1997) Symbolic play in childhood: interpersonal and environmental context and stability. *Infant Behaviour and Development*, 20(2): 197–207.
Bowlby, J. (1965) *Child Care and the Growth of Love* (2nd edition). London: Penguin.
Boyce, E. (1935) An educational experiment: play, work and the bridge between. *Child Life*, 5(May): 66–67.
Brewer, J. (2000) *Ethnography*. Buckingham: Open University Press.
Brierley, J. (1994) *Give Me a Child until He is Seven: Brain Studies and Early Childhood Education*. London: Routledge Falmer.
Broadhead, P. (2004) *Early Years Play and Learning: Developing Social Skills and Cooperation*. London: Routledge Falmer.
Broadhead, P. (2006) Developing an understanding of young children's learning through play: the place of observation, interaction and reflection. *British Educational Research Journal*, 32(2): 191–207.
Bronfenbrenner, U. (1970) *Two Worlds of Childhood*. New York: Russell Sage Foundation.
Brooker, L. (2011) Taking children seriously: an alternative agenda for research? *Journal of Early Childhood Research*, 9: 137.
Bruce, T. (2005) *Early Childhood Education* (3rd edition). London: Hodder Arnold.
Bruner, J. (1966) On cognitive growth. In J. Bruner, R. Oliver and P. Greenfield et al. (eds), *Studies in Cognitive Growth*. London: John Wiley & Sons.
Bruner, J. (1997) Celebrating divergence: Piaget and Vygotsky. *Human Development*, 40(2): 63–73.
Bruner, J. (1999) *The Myth of the First Three Years*. New York: Free Press.
Bryman, A. (2001) *Research Methods and Organisation Studies*. London: Routledge.
Buchbinder, M., Longhofer, J., Barrett, T., Lawson, P. and Floersch, J. (2006) Ethnographic approaches to child care research: a review of the literature, *Journal of Early Childhood Research*, 4(1): 45–63.
Burton, D. and Bartlett, S. (2005) *Practitioner Research for Teachers*. London: Paul Chapman Publishing.

Bush, J. and Phillips, D. (1996) International approaches to defining quality. In S. Kagan and N. Cohen (eds), *Reinventing Early Care and Education: A Vision for a Quality System*. San Francisco: Jossey-Bass.

Cameron, H. (2005) Asking the tough questions: a guide to ethical practices in interviewing young children. *Early Child Development and Care*, 175(6): 597–610.

Carr, M., Jones, C. and Lee, W. (2005) Beyond listening: can assessment practice play a part? In A. Clarke, T. Kjorholt and P. Moss (eds), *Beyond Listening: Children's Perspectives on Early Childhood Services*. Bristol: Policy Press.

Cheng, P.W. and Holyoak, K. (1985) Pragmatic reasoning schemas. *Cognitive Psychology*, 17: 391–416.

Chesterton, G.K. (1911) The innocence of Father Brown. In E. Waugh (1945) *Brideshead Revisited*. Boston, MA: Little, Brown and Co.

Christensen, H.P. (2004) Children's participation in ethnographic research: issues of power and representation. *Children and Society*, 18: 165–76.

Christensen, P. and James, A. (2000) Researching children and childhood: cultures of communication. In P. Christensen and A. James (eds), *Research with Children: Perspectives and Practices*. London: Routledge Falmer.

Clarke, A. (2005) Ways of seeing: using the Mosaic approach to listen to young children's perspectives. In A. Clarke, T. Kjorholt and P. Moss (eds), *Beyond Listening: Children's Perspectives on Early Childhood Services*. Bristol: Policy Press.

Clarke, A. (2007) A hundred ways of listening: gathering children's perspectives of their early childhood environment. *Young Children*, 62(3): 76–81.

Clarke, A. and Clarke, A. (1998) Early experience and the life path. *The Psychologist*, 11: 433–436.

Clough, P. and Nutbrown, C. (2007) *A Student's Guide to Methodology* (2nd edition). London: Sage.

Coates, E. (2002) 'I forgot the sky!' Children's stories contained within their drawings. *International Journal of Early Years Education*, 10(1): 21–35.

Coates, E. and Coates, A. (2006) Young children talking and drawing. *International Journal of Early Years Education*, 14(3): 221–241.

Cocks, A.J. (2006) The ethical maze: finding an inclusive path towards gaining children's agreement to research participation. *Childhood*, 13(2): 247–66.

Coffey, A. (2002) Ethnography and self: reflections and representations. In T. May (ed.), *Qualitative Research in Action*. London: Sage.

Cohen, L. and Kim, Y. (1999) Piaget's equilibration theory and the young gifted child: a balancing act. *Roeper Review*, 21(3): 201–206.

Cohen, L., Manion, L. and Morrison, K. (2007) *Research Methods in Education* (6th edition). London: Routledge Falmer.

Coles, A. and McGrath, J. (2010) *Your Education Research Project Handbook*. London: Pearson Education.

Conrad, P. and Reinharz, S. (1984) Computers and qualitative data: Editor's introductory essay. *Qualitative Sociology*, 7(1–2): 3–13.

Conroy, H. and Harcourt, D. (2008) Informed agreement to participate: beginning the partnership with children in research. *Early Childhood Development and Care*, 179(2): 157–165.

Corbetta, D. and Snapp-Childs, W. (2009) Seeing and touching: the role of sensory-motor experience on the development of infant reaching. *Infant Behaviour and Development*, 32: 44–58.

Corsaro, W. and Molinari, L. (2000) Entering and observing in children's worlds: a reflection on a longitudinal ethnography of early education in Italy. In P. Christensen and

A. James (eds), *Research with Children: Perspectives and Practices*. London: Routledge Falmer.
Cox, S. (2005) Intention and meaning in young children's drawing. *International Journal of Art and Design Education*, 24(2): 115–125.
Cremin, H. and Slatter, B. (2004) Is it possible to access the 'voice' of pre-school children? Results of a research project in a pre-school setting. *Educational Studies*, 30(4): 457–471.
Creswell, J. (2008) *Educational Research: Planning, Conducting, and Evaluating Quantitative and Qualitative Research* (3rd edition). London: Pearson Education.
Crowe, D. (2003) Objectivity, photography and ethnography. *Cultural Studies–Critical Methodologies*, 3(4): 470–485.
Cruickshank, I. and Mason, R. (2003) Using photography in art education research: a reflexive enquiry. *International Journal of Art & Design Education*, 22(1): 5–22.
Curran, H. V. (1988) Relative universals: perspectives on culture and cognition. In G. Claxton (ed.), *Growth Points in Cognition*. London: Routledge.
Curtis, A. (1996) Do we train our early childhood educators to respect children? In C. Nutbrown (ed.), *Respectful Educators – Capable Learner: Children's Rights and Early Education*. London: Paul Chapman Publishing.
Dahlberg, G., Moss, P. and Pence, A. (2007) *Beyond Quality in Early Childhood Education and Care* (2nd edition). London: Falmer.
Darbyshire, P., Schillera, W. and MacDougall, C. (2005) Extending new paradigm childhood research: meeting the challenges of including younger children. *Early Child Development and Care*, 175(6): 467–472.
David, T. (1999) Changing minds: young children learning. In T. David (ed.), *Young Children Learning*. London: Paul Chapman Publishing.
David, T. and Powell, S. (1999) Changing childhoods, changing minds. In T. David (ed.), *Young Children Learning*. London: Paul Chapman Publishing.
Davis, B. (2011) Open listening: creative evolution in early childhood settings. *International Journal of Early Childhood*, 43: 119–132.
Davis, J., Watson, N. and Cunningham-Burley, S. (2000) Learning the lives of disabled children: developing a reflexive approach. In P. Christensen and A. James (eds), *Research with Children: Perspectives and Practices*. London: Routledge Falmer.
DCSF (Department for Children, Schools and Families) (2007) *The Children's Plan: Building Brighter Futures*. London: TSO.
DCSF (Department for Children, Schools and Families) (2008a) *Statutory Framework for the Early Years Foundation Stage*. Nottingham: DCSF Publications.
DCSF (Department for Children, Schools and Families) (2008b) *Play Strategy*. Nottingham: HMSO.
DCSF (Department for Children, Schools and Families) (2009a) *Next Steps for Early Learning and Childcare: Building on the 10-Year Strategy*. Nottingham: DCSF Publications.
DCSF (Department for Children, Schools and Families) (2009b) *Learning, Playing and Interacting Good Practice in the Early Years Foundation Stage*. Nottingham: HMSO.
De Lisi, R. (2002) From marbles to instant messenger: implications of Piaget's ideas about peer learning. *Theory into Practice*, 41(1): 5.
Denzin, N. (1997) *Interpretive Ethnography: Ethnographic Practices for the 21st Century*. Thousand Oaks, CA; London: Sage.
Dex, S. and Joshi, H. (2005) *Children of the 21st Century: From Birth to Nine Months*. Bristol: Policy Press.
DES (Department for Education and Science) (1990) *Starting with Quality: Report of the Committee of Enquiry into the Quality of Education Experience Offered to Three and Four Year Olds* (The Rumbold Report). London: HMSO.

DfE (2011) *The Early Years: Foundations for Life, Health and Learning: An Independent Report on the Early Years Foundation Stage to Her Majesty's Government*. London: DfE.
DfE (2012) *Statutory Framework for the Early Years Foundation Stage: Setting the Standards for Learning, Development and Care for Children from Birth to Five*. London: DfE.
DfES (Department for Education and Skills) (2003) *Birth to Three Matters: A Framework to Support Our Youngest Children*. London: DfES/Sure Start.
DfES (2004a) *The Children Act 2004*. London: HMSO.
DfES (2004b) *Every Child Matters: Change for Children*, ref 1081/2004. Nottingham: DfES Publications.
DfES (2005) *Childcare Bill*. Nottingham: HMSO.
DfES (2007a) *National Evaluation of the Neighbourhood Nurseries Initiative: Integrated Report*. London: DfES/Sure Start.
DfES (2007b) *Statutory Framework for the Early Years Foundation Stage: Setting the Standards for Learning, Development and Care for Children from Birth to Five*. Nottingham: DfES Publications.
Dicks, B., Soyinka, B. and Coffey, A. (2006) Multimodal ethnography. *Qualitative Research*, 6(1): 77–96.
Dietrich, S. (2005) A look at the friendships between pre-school aged children with and without disabilities in two inclusive classrooms. *Journal of Early Childhood Research*, 3(2): 193–215.
Dockett, S. and Perry, B. (2004) Starting school: perspectives of Australian children, parents and educators. *Journal of Early Childhood Research*, 2(2): 171–189.
Dockett, S. and Perry, B. (2005) Researching with children: insights from the Starting School research project. *Early Child Development and Care*, 175(6): 507–521.
Dockett, S. and Perry, B. (2007) Trusting children's accounts in research. *Journal of Early Childhood Research*, 5(1): 47–63.
Donaldson, M. (1978) *Children's Minds*. London: HarperCollins.
Driscoll, V. and Rudge, C. (2005) Channels for listening to young children and parents. In A. Clark, T. Kjorholt and P. Moss (eds), *Beyond Listening: Children's Perspectives on Early Childhood Services*. Bristol: Policy Press.
Dunphy, E. (2007) Effective and ethical and interviewing of young children in pedagogical context. *European Early Childhood Education Research Journal*, 15 June 2007. Available online at: www.tandfonline.com/loi/recr20.
Dunsmuir, S. and Blatchford, P. (2004) Predictors of writing competence in 4- to 7-year old children. *British Journal of Educational Psychology*, 74: 461–483.
Dyer, P. (2002) A 'Box Full of Feelings': developing emotional intelligence in a nursery community. In C. Nutbrown (ed.), *Research Studies in Early Childhood Education*. Stoke-on-Trent: Trentham Books.
Einarsdottir, J. (2005) Playschool in pictures: children's photographs as a research method. *Early Child Development and Care*, 175(6): 523–541.
Einarsdottir, J., Dockett, S. and Perry, B. (2009) Making meaning: children's perspectives expressed through drawings. *Early Child Development and Care*, 179(2): 217–232.
Elfer, P. (2007) What are nurseries for? The concept of primary task and its application in differentiating roles and tasks in nurseries. *Journal of Early Childhood Research*, 5: 169.
Elkind, D. (2007) *The Power of Play: Learning What Comes Naturally*. Cambridge, MA: Da Capo Press; London: Perseus Books Group (distributor).
Elfer, P., Goldschmied, E. and Selleck, D. (2003) *Key Persons in the Nursery: Building Relationships for Quality Provision*. London: David Fulton.
Empson, J. M. and Nabuzoka, D., with Hamilton, D. (2004) *Atypical Development in Context*. Basingstoke; New York: Palgrave Macmillan.
Erikson, E. (1963) *Childhood and Society*. New York and London: W.W. Norton & Co.

Erikson, E. (1972) Play and actuality. In J. Bruner, A. Jolly and K. Sylva (eds), *Play: Its Role in Development and Evolution*. New York: Basic Books.

Fargas-Malet, M., McSherry, D., Larkin, E. and Robinson, C. (2010) Research with children: methodological issues and innovative techniques. *Journal of Early Childhood Research*, 8: 175.

Farrell, A. (2005) New possibilities for ethical research with children. In A. Farrell (ed.), *Ethical Research with Children*. Maidenhead: Open University Press.

Fawcett, B. and Hearn, J. (2004) Researching others: epistemology, experience, standpoints and participation. *International Journal of Social Research Methodology*, 7(3): 201–218.

Fetterman, D. (1998) *Ethnography*. London: Sage.

Filer, A. and Pollard, A. (1998) Developing the identity and learning programme: principles and pragmatism in a longitudinal ethnography of pupil careers. In G. Walford (ed.), *Doing Research about Education*. London: Falmer Press.

Filippini, T. and Vecchi, V. (1996) *The Hundred Languages of Children: The Exhibit*. Reggio Emilia: Reggio Children.

Finlay, L. and Gough, B. (eds) (2003) *Reflexivity: A Practical Guide for Researchers in Health and Social Sciences*. Oxford: Blackwell.

Fisher, R. (1990) *Teaching Children to Think*. London: Basil Blackwell.

Flavell, J. (1963) *The Developmental Psychology of Jean Piaget*. Letchworth: The Garden City Press.

Flewitt, R. (2005) Conducting research with young children: some ethical considerations. *Early Child Development and Care*, 175(6): 553–565.

Flick, U. (1998) *An Introduction to Qualitative Research*. London: Sage.

Forman, G. (1994) Different media, different languages. In L.G. Katz and B. Cesarone (eds), *Reflections on the Reggio Emilia Approach*. Chicago: ERIC Clearinghouse on Elementary Early Childhood Education pp. 41–54.

Forman, G. and Fosnot, C. (1982) The use of Piaget's constructivism in early childhood education programs. In B. Spodek (ed.), *Handbook of Research in Early Childhood Education*. New York: Free Press, pp. 185–211.

Friedman, D. (2006) *What Science is Telling Us: How Neurobiology and Developmental Psychology are Changing the Way Policymakers and Communities Should Think about the Developing Child*. Cambridge, MA: National Scientific Council on the Developing Child (Harvard University).

Gallard, D. (2010) The psychology of the child: mind games. In D. Kassem, L. Murphy and E. Taylor (eds) *Key Issues in Childhood and Youth Studies*. London: Routledge.

Garcia-Horta, J. and Guerra-Ramos, M. (2009) The use of CAQDAS in educational research: some advantages, limitations and potential risks. *International Journal of Research and Method in Education*, 32(2): 151–165.

Gardner, H. (1984) *Frames of Mind: The Theory of Multiple Intelligences*. London: Heinemann.

Gardner, R.A. (1997) *Recommendations for Dealing with Parents who Induce a Parental Alienation Syndrome in their Children*. Cresskill, NJ: Creative Therapeutics.

Gauvain, M. (2001) *The Social Context of Cognitive Development*. New York: Guilford Press.

Gibbs, A. (1997) *Social Research Update 19: Focus Groups*. Guildford: University of Surrey.

Ginsburg, H. and Opper, S. (1969) *Piaget's Theory of Intellectual Development: An Introduction*. London: Prentice-Hall.

Gleitman, H., Friedman, A. and Reisberg, D. (1999) *Psychology*. New York and London: W.W. Norton & Co.

Goldschmied, E. and Jackson, S. (2004) *People under Three* (2nd edition). London: Routledge.

Goodley, D. and Runswick-Cole, K. (2010) Emancipating play: dis/abled children, development and deconstruction. *Disability & Society*, 25(4): 499–512.

Goouch, K. and Lambirth, A. (2010) *Teaching Early Reading and Phonics: Creative Approaches to Early Literacy*. London: Sage.

Gopnik, A., Meltzoff, A. and Kuhl, P. (1999) *How Babies Think*. London: Phoenix.

Gordon, T. and Lahelma, E. (2003) From ethnography to life history: tracing transitions of school students. *International Journal of Social Research Methodology*, 6(3): 245–254.

Grace, D. and Brandt, M. (2006) Ready for success in kindergarten: a comparative analysis of teacher, parent, and administrator beliefs in Hawaii. *Journal of Early Childhood Research*, 4: 223.

Graue, M. and Walsh, D. (1998) Ethics: being fair. In M. Graue and D. Walsh (eds), *Studying Children in Context: Theories, Methods and Ethics*. Thousand Oaks, CA: Sage, pp. 55–69.

Green, D. (1988) Problem-solving: representation and discovery. In G. Claxton (ed.), *Growth Points in Cognition*. London: Routledge.

Greene, S. and Hill, M. (2005) Researching children's experience: methods and methodological issues. In S. Greene and D. Hogan (eds), *Researching Children's Experience: Approaches and Methods*. London: Sage, pp. 1–21.

Greig, A., Taylor, J. and MacKay, T. (2007) *Doing Research with Children*. London: Sage.

Grieshaber, S. and McArdle, F. (2010) *The Trouble with Play*. Maidenhead: Open University Press.

Griffin, B. (1997) 'The child should feel good enough': nurturing a sense of self in young people. In L. Abbott and H. Moylett (eds), *Working with the Under-3s: Responding to Children's Needs*. Buckingham: Open University Press.

Grover, S. (2004) Why won't they listen to us? On giving power and voice to children participating in social research. *Childhood*, 11(1): 81–93.

Hammersley, M. and Atkinson, P. (1983) *Ethnography: Principles on Practice*. London: Methuen.

Hannon, P. (2003) Developmental neuroscience: implications for early childhood. *Intervention and Education Current Paediatrics*, 13(1): 58–63.

Harcourt, D. and Conroy, H. (2005) Informed assent: ethics and processes when researching with young children. *Early Child Development and Care*, 175(6): 567–577.

Harms, T., Cryer, D. and Clifford, R.M. (2003) *Infant/Toddler Environment Rating Scale (ITERS-R)* (revised edition). New York: Teachers College Press.

Hastrup, K. (1993) The native voice – and the anthropological vision. *Social Anthropology*, 1: 173–186.

Haudrup, P. (2004) Children's participation in ethnographic research: issues of power and representation. *Children & Society*, 18: 165–176.

Heywood, C. (2001) *A History of Childhood: Children and Childhood in the West from Medieval to Modern Times*. Cambridge: Polity Press.

HM Treasury (HMT) (2004) *Choice for Parents: The Best Start for Children – A Ten Year Strategy for Childcare*. London: HMSO.

Hofer, T., Hohenberger, A., Hauf, P. and Aschersleben, G. (2008) The link between maternal interaction style and infant action. *Understanding Infant Behaviour and Development*, 31: 115–126.

Hohmann, M. and Weikart, D. (2002) *Educating Young Children*. Ypsilanti: High/Scope Press.

Holliday, E., Harrison, L. and McLeod, S. (2009) Listening to children with communication impairment talking through their drawings. *Journal of Early Childhood Research*, 7: 244.

Holliday, R. (2000) We've been framed: visualising methodology. *The Sociological Review*, 48(4): 503–521.
Howard, R. (1987) *Concepts and Schemata*. London: Cassell Education.
Hurst, V. and Joseph, J. (1998) *Supporting Early Learning: The Way Forward*. Buckingham: Open University Press.
Inhelder, B. and Piaget, J. (1964) *The Early Growth of Logic in the Child: Classification and Seriation*. London: Routledge and Kegan Paul.
Irwin, L., Johnson, A., Henderson, V., Dahinten,V. and Hertzman, C. (2007) Examining how contexts shape young children's perspectives of health. *Child: Care, Health and Development*, 33(4): 353–359.
Isaacs, S. (1930) *Intellectual Growth in Young Children*. London: Routledge and Kegan Paul.
Jenkins, J., Franco, F., Dolins, F. and Sewell, A. (1995) Toddlers' reactions to negative emotion displays: forming models of relationships. *Infant Behaviour and Development*, 18: 273–281.
Jenks, C. (2000) Zeitgeist research on childhood. In P. Christensen and A. James (eds), *Research with Children: Perspectives and Practices*. London: Routledge Falmer.
Jones, A. and Bugge, C. (2006) Improving understanding and rigour through triangulation: an exemplar based on patient participation in interaction. *Journal of Advanced Nursing*, 55(5): 612–621.
Kellett, M. and Ding, S. (2004) Middle childhood. In S. Fraser, V. Lewis, S. Ding, M. Kellet and C. Robinson (eds), *Doing Research with Children and Young People*. London: Sage/The Open University, pp. 161–174.
Kellmer Pringle, M. (1986) *The Needs of Children: A Personal Perspective*. London: Hutchinson.
Kellogg, R. (1969) *Analyzing Children's Art*. Mountain View, CA: Mayfield Publishing Co.
Keddie, A. (2005) Research with young children: the use of an affinity group approach to explore the social dynamics of peer culture. *British Journal of Sociology of Education*, 25(1): 35–51.
Kinney, L. (2005) Small voices…powerful messages. In A. Clarke, T. Kjorholt and P. Moss (eds), *Beyond Listening: Children's Perspectives on Early Childhood Services*. Bristol: Policy Press.
Kjorholt, T., Moss, P. and Clark, A. (2005) Beyond listening: future prospects. In A. Clarke, T. Kjorholt and P. Moss (eds), *Beyond Listening: Children's Perspectives on Early Childhood Services*. Bristol: Policy Press.
Koch, T. and Harrington, A. (1997) Reconceptualizing rigour: the case for reflexivity. *Journal of Advanced Nursing*, 28(4): 882–890.
Komulainen, S. (2007) The ambiguity of the child's 'voice'. *Social Research Childhood*, 14(1): 11–28.
Krahenbuhl, S. and Blades, M. (2006) The effect of interviewing techniques on young children's responses to questions. *Child: Care, Health and Development*, 32(3): 321–331.
Laevers, F. (1976) The Project Experiential Education: Concepts and Experiences at the Level of Context, Process and Outcome. Available at: https://www.european-agency.org/agency-projects/assessment-resource-guide/documents/2008/11/Laevers.pdf/view?searchterm=laevers (accessed October 2012).
Lahman, M.K.E. (2008) Always Othered: ethical research with children. *Journal of Early Childhood Research*, 6(3): 281–300.
Lancaster, P. (2006) Listening to young children: respecting the voice of the child. In G. Pugh and B. Duffy (eds), *Contemporary Issues in the Early Years* (4th edition). London: Sage.

Lansdown, G. (1996) The United Nations Convention on the Rights of the Child: Progress in the United Kingdom. In C. Nutbrown (ed.), *Respectful Educators – Capable Learners: Children's Rights and Early Education*. London: Paul Chapman Publishing.

Learning and Teaching Scotland (2005) *Birth to Three: Supporting Our Youngest Children*. Edinburgh: Learning and Teaching Scotland.

LeCompte, M. (2002) The transformation of ethnographic practice: past and current challenges. *Qualitative Research*, 2(3): 283–299.

Legerstee, M., Markova, G. and Fisher, T. (2007) The role of maternal affect attunement in dyadic and triadic communication. *Infant Behaviour and Development*, 30: 296–306.

Lewis, C., Lewis, M. and Ifekwunigue, M. (1978) Informed consent by children and participation in an influenza vaccine trial. *American Journal of Public Health*, 68(11): 1079–1082.

Lincoln, Y.S. and Guba, E.G. (2003) Paradigmatic controversies, contradictions, and emerging confluences. In N. Denzin and Y.S. Lincoln (eds), *The Landscape of Qualitative Research Theories and Issues*. Thousand Oaks, CA: Sage.

Locke, J. (1947) *Essay Concerning Human Understanding*. Oxford: Oxford University Press (original work published 1690).

Loreman, T. (2009) *Respecting Childhood*. London: Continuum.

Lowenfeld, V. and Brittain, W. (1982) *Creative and Mental Growth*. London: Collier Macmillan.

Maggs-Rapport, F. (2000) *Combining Methodological Approaches in Research: Ethnography and Interpretive Phenomenology*. Oxford: Blackwell Science.

Malaguzzi, L. (1998) *Children, Spaces, Relations: Metaproject for an Environment for Young Children*. Domus Academy Research Center: Reggio Children.

Malmberg, L., Stein, A., West, A., Lewis, S., Barnes, J., Leach, P. and Sylva, K. (2007) Parent–infant interaction: a growth model approach. *Infant Behaviour and Development*, 30: 615–630.

Manias, E. and Street, A. (2000) Rethinking ethnography: reconstructing nursing relationships. *Journal of Advanced Nursing*, 31(1): 234–242.

Mansson, A. (2011) Becoming a preschool child: subjectification in toddlers during their introduction to preschool, from a gender perspective. *International Journal of Early Childhood*, 43: 7–22.

Mason, J. (2002) *Qualitative Researching* (2nd edition). London: Sage.

Mason, P. (2005) Visual data in applied qualitative research: lessons from experience. *Qualitative Research*, 5(3): 325–346.

Mayall, B. (2000) Conversations with children: working with generational issues. In P. Christensen and A. James (eds), *Research with Children: Perspectives and Practices*. London: Routledge Falmer.

McKechnie, L. (2006) Observations of babies and toddlers in library settings. *Library Trends*, 55(1): 190–201.

McVee, M., Dunsmore, K. and Gavelek, J. (2005) Schema theory revisited. *Review of Educational Research*, 75(4): 531–566.

Meade, A. and Cubey, P. (2008) *Thinking Children: Learning about Schemas* (2nd edition). Wellington: New Zealand Council for Educational Research and Institute for Early Childhood Studies, Wellington College of Education/Victoria University of Wellington.

Meltzoff, A. and Moore, M. (1998) Object representation, identity, and the paradox of early permanence: steps toward a new framework. *Infant Behaviour and Development*, 21(2): 201–235.

Messiou, K. (2006) Understanding marginalisation in education: the voice of children. *European Journal of Psychology of Education*, 21(3): 305–318.

Miller, A. (2003) *Never Too Young: How Young Children Can Take Responsibility and Make Decisions*. London: National Early Years Network/Save the Children.

Montessori, M. (1988) *The Absorbent Mind*. Trans C. Claremont. Oxford: Clio Press.

Moyles, J. (1989) *Just Playing? The Role and Status of Play in Early Childhood Education*. Milton Keynes: Open University Press.

Moyles, J. (ed.) (2010) *The Excellence of Play* (3rd edition). Maidenhead: McGraw-Hill/Open University Press.

Neisser, U. (1976) *Cognition and Reality: Principles and Implications of Cognitive Psychology*. San Francisco: Freeman & Co.

New, R. (1998) Theory and praxis in Reggio Emilia: they know what they are doing and why. In C. Edwards, L. Gandini and G. Forman (eds), *The Hundred Languages of Children: The Reggio Emilia Approach – Advanced Reflections*. Norwood, NJ, and London: Ablex.

Newby, P. (2010) *Research Methods for Education*. Harlow: Pearson Education.

Nurse, A. and Headington, R. (1999) Balancing the needs of children, parents and teachers. In T. David (ed.), *Young Children Learning*. London: Paul Chapman Publishing.

Nutbrown, C. (ed.) (1996) *Respectful Educators – Capable Learners: Children's Rights and Early Education*. London: Paul Chapman Publishing.

Nutbrown, C. (1998) *The Lore and Language of Early Education*. London: University of Sheffield, Department of Educational Studies.

Nutbrown, C. (1999) *Threads of Thinking: Young Children Learning and the Role of Early Education* (2nd edition). London: Paul Chapman Publishing.

Nutbrown, C. (2001) Watching and learning: the tools of assessment. In G. Pugh (ed.), *Contemporary Issues in the Early Years: Working Collaboratively for Children*. London: Paul Chapman Publishing.

Nutbrown, C. (2002) Early childhood education in contexts of change. In C. Nutbrown (ed.), *Research Studies in Early Childhood Education*. Stoke-on-Trent: Trentham Books.

Nutbrown, C. (2006) *Threads of Thinking: Young Children Learning and the Role of Early Education* (3rd edition). London: Paul Chapman Publishing.

Nutbrown, C. (2010) Naked by the pool? Blurring the image: ethical issues in the portrayal of young children in arts-based educational research. *Qualitative Inquiry*, 17(1): 3–14.

Nutbrown, C. (2011) *Threads of Thinking: Young Children Learning and the Role of Early Education* (4th edition). London: Paul Chapman Publishing.

Nutbrown, C. (2012) *Foundations for Quality: The Independent Review of Early Education and Childcare Qualifications Final Report*. London: DfE Publications.

Nutbrown, C. and Abbott, L. (2001) Experiencing Reggio Emilia. In C. Nutbrown and L. Abbott (eds), *Experiencing Reggio Emilia: Implications for Pre-School Provision*. Buckingham: Open University Press.

Nutbrown, C. and Hannon, P. (2003) Children's perspectives on family literacy: methodological issues, findings and implications for practice. *Journal of Early Childhood Literacy*, 3(2): 115–145.

Nutbrown, C. and Page, J. (2008) *Working with Babies and Children from Birth to Three*. London: Sage.

O'Kane, C. (2000) The development of participatory techniques: facilitating children's views about decisions which affect them. In P. Christensen and A. James (eds), *Research with Children: Perspectives and Practices*. London: Routledge Falmer.

Osgood, J. (2004) Approaches to professionalism: time to get down to business? The responses of early years practitioners to entrepreneurial approaches to professionalism. *Journal of Early Childhood Research*, 2: 157–169.
Palmer, S. (2006) *Toxic Childhood: How the Modern world is Damaging our Children and what we can Do about H.* London: Orion Books.
Park, J. and Kwon, Y. (2009) Parental goals and parenting practices of upper-middle-class Korean mothers with preschool children. *Journal of Early Childhood Research*, 7: 58–75.
Parker-Rees, R. (1999) Protecting playfulness. In L. Abbott and H. Moylett (eds) *Early Education Transformed*. London: Falmer Press.
Parker-Rees, R. (2010) Developing communication: enjoying the company of other people. In R. Parker-Rees, C. Leeson, J. Willan and J. Savage (eds), *Early Childhood Studies* (3rd edition). Exeter: Learning Matters.
Pascal, C. and Bertram, T. (2009) Listening to young citizens: the struggle to make real a participatory paradigm in research with young children. *European Early Childhood Education Research Journal*, 17(2): 249–262.
Payne, G. and Payne, J. (2004) *Key Concepts in Social Research*. London: Sage.
Penn, H. (1994) Working in conflict: developing a dynamic model of quality. In P. Moss and A. Pence (eds), *Valuing Quality in Early Childhood Services*. London: Paul Chapman Publishing.
Penn, H. (2005) *Understanding Early Childhood*. Maidenhead: Open University Press.
Piaget, J. (1950) *The Psychology of Intelligence*. London: Routledge and Kegan Paul.
Piaget, J. (1952a) *The Child's Conception of Number*. London: Routledge and Kegan Paul.
Piaget, J. (1952b) *The Origin of Intelligence in the Child*. London: Routledge and Kegan Paul.
Piaget, J. (1954) *The Construction of Reality in the Child*. London: Routledge and Kegan Paul.
Piaget, J. (1959) *The Language and Thought of the Child*. London: Routledge and Kegan Paul.
Piaget, J. (1969) *The Mechanisms of Perception*. London: Routledge and Kegan Paul.
Piaget, J. and Inhelder, B. (1956) *The Child's Conception of Space.* London: Routledge and Kegan Paul.
Piaget, J. and Inhelder, B. (1969) *The Psychology of the Child*. London: Routledge and Kegan Paul.
Piaget, J. and Inhelder, B. (1971) *Mental Imagery in the Child: A Study of the Development of Imaginal Representation*. London: Routledge and Kegan Paul.
Pink, S. (2001) More visualising, more methodologies: on video, reflexivity and qualitative research. *The Sociological Review*, 48(4): 586–599.
Plaskow, D. (1972) *The Crucial Years*. London: Society for Education Through Art.
Pole, C. (2007) Researching children and fashion: an embodied ethnography. *Childhood*, 14(1): 67–84.
Pole, K. (2007) Mixed method designs: a review of strategies for blending quantitative and qualitative methodologies. *Mid-Western Educational Researcher*, 20(4): 35–38.
QCA/DfEE (Qualifications and Curriculum Authority/Department for Education and Employment) (2000) *Curriculum Guidance for the Foundation Stage*. London: Qualifications and Curriculum Authority.
Riley, R. and Manias, E. (2003) Snap-shots of live theatre: the use of photography to research governance in operating room nursing. *Nursing Inquiry*, 10(2): 81–90.
Rinaldi, C. (1999) *In Dialogue with Reggio Emilia: Listening, Researching, and Learning*. London; New York: Routledge.

Rinaldi, C. (2005) Documentation and assessment: what is the relationship? In A. Clarke, T. Kjorholt and P. Moss (eds), *Beyond Listening: Children's Perspectives on Early Childhood Services*. Bristol: Policy Press.

Rinaldi, C. (2006) *In Dialogue with Reggio Emilia*. London: Routledge.

Riojas-Cortez, M. and Bustos Flores, B. (2009) Supporting preschoolers' social development in school through funds of knowledge. *Journal of Early Childhood Research*, 7: 185.

Roberts, H. (2000) Listening to children, and hearing them. In P. Christensen and A. James (eds), *Research with Children: Perspectives and Practices*. London: Routledge Falmer.

Rogoff, B. (1990) *Apprenticeship in Thinking: Cognitive Development in Social Context*. Oxford: Oxford University Press.

Rose, G. (2007) *Visual Methodologies: An Introduction to the Interpretation of Visual Materials* (2nd edition). London: Sage.

Rosen, R. (2010) We got our heads together and came up with a plan: young children's perceptions of curriculum development in one Canadian preschool. *Journal of Early Childhood Research*, 8: 89–108.

Samuelsson, I., Sheridan, S. and Williams, P. (2006) Five preschool curricula: a comparative perspective. *International Journal of Early Childhood*, 38(1): 11.

Sanchez-Jankowski, M. (2002) Representation, responsibility and reliability in participant observation. In T. May (ed.), *Qualitative Research in Action*. London: Sage.

Sandberg, A. and Heden, R. (2011) Play's importance in school. *Education*, 3(13): 317–329.

Schiller, P. and Willis, C. (2008) Using brain-based teaching strategies to create supportive early childhood environments that address learning standards. *Young Children*, 63(4): 1–6.

Selbie, P. and Wickett, K. (2010) Providing an enabling environment. In R. Parker-Rees, C. Leeson, J. Willan and J. Savage (eds), *Early Childhood Studies* (3rd edition). Exeter: Learning Matters.

Selleck, D. (2001) Being under 3 years of age: enhancing quality experiences. In G. Pugh (ed.), *Contemporary Issues in the Early Years: Working Collaboratively for Children*. London: Paul Chapman Publishing.

Selleck, D. and Griffin, S. (1996) Quality for the under threes. In G. Pugh (ed.), *Contemporary Issues in the Early Years: Working Collaboratively for Children* (2nd edition). London: Paul Chapman Publishing.

Sellers, K., Russo, T., Baker, I. and Dennison, B. (2005) The role of childcare providers in the prevention of childhood overweight. *Journal of Early Childhood Research*, 3: 227.

Sheridan, S. and Schuster, K.M. (2001) Evaluation of pedagogical quality in early childhood education: a cross-national perspective. *Journal of Research in Childhood Education*, 16(1): 109–124.

Shore, R. (1997) Baby's brain: important findings. *The Futurist*, 31(6) 51

Silverman, D. (2000) *Doing Qualitative Research: A Practical Handbook*. London: Sage.

Siraj-Blatchford, I., Sylva, K., Muttock, S., Gilden, R. and Bell, D. (2002) *Researching Effective Pedagogy in the Early Years*. Research Report No. 356. London: Department for Education and Skills.

Siraj-Blatchford, I., Sylva, K., Taggart, B., Sammons, P., Melhuish, E. and Elliot, K. (2003) *The Effective Provision of Pre-School Education (EPPE) Project: Technical Paper 10 – Intensive Case Studies of Practice across the Foundation Stage*. London: DfES and Institute of Education, University of London.

Smidt, S. (2006) *The Developing Child in the 21st Century: A Global Perspective on Child Development*. London: Routledge.

Smidt, S. (2011) *Playing to Learn: The Role of Play in the Early Years*. London: Routledge.
Smith, A., Duncan, J. and Marshall, K. (2005) Children's perspectives on their learning: exploring methods. *Early Child Development and Care*, 175(6): 473–487.
Stanczak, G.C. (2007) Introduction: images, methodologies, and generating social knowledge. In G.C. Stanczak (ed.), *Visual Research Methods: Image, Society, and Representation*. Thousand Oaks, CA: Sage, pp. 1–21.
Stenhouse, L. (1975) *An Introduction to Curriculum Research and Development*. London: Heinemann.
Stephenson, A. (2009) Horses in the sandpit: photography, prolonged involvement and 'stepping back' as strategies for listening to children's voices. *Early Child Development and Care*, 179(2): 131–141.
Swain, J. (2006) An ethnographic approach to researching children in junior school. *International Journal of Social Research Methodology*, 9 (July): 199–213.
Swanson J., Raab M. and Dunst, C. (2011) Strengthening family capacity to provide young children everyday natural learning opportunities. *Journal of Early Childhood Research*, 9: 66.
Sylva, K. (1994) The impact of learning on children's later development. In C. Ball (ed.), *Start Right: The Importance of Early Learning*. London: Royal Society for the Arts, pp. 84–96 (Appendix C).
Sylva, K., Melhuish, E., Sammons, P., Siraj-Blatchford, I. and Taggart, B. (2011) Pre-school quality and educational outcomes at age 11. *Journal of Early Childhood Research*, 9: 109.
Sylva, K. and Taylor, H. (2006) Effective settings: evidence from research. In G. Pugh and B. Duffy (eds), *Contemporary Issues in the Early Years* (4th edition). London: Sage.
Thomas, N. and O'Kane, C. (1998) The ethics of participatory research with young children. *Children and Society*, 12: 336–348.
Tickell, C. (2011) *The Early Years: Foundations for Life, Health and Learning*. An Independent Report on the Early Years Foundation Stage to the Majesty's Government. London: DfE.
Tovey, H. (2007) *Playing Outdoors*. Maidenhead: Open University Press.
United Nations (1989) *The UN Convention on the Rights of the Child*. New York: United Nations.
Verma, G. and Mallick, K. (1999) *Researching Education: Perspectives and Techniques*. London: Falmer Press.
Vygotsky, L. (1978) *Mind in Society: The Development of Higher Psychological Processes*. Cambridge, MA: Harvard College.
Walker, R. (2004) Editorial. *Cambridge Journal of Education*, 34(2): 139–142.
Wang, X., Bernas, R. and Eberhard, P. (2005) Maternal teaching strategies in four cultural communities: implications for early childhood teachers. *Journal of Early Childhood Research*, 3: 269.
Warash, B., Curtis, R., Hursh, D. and Tucci, V. (2008) Skinner meets Piaget on the Reggio playground: practical synthesis of applied behaviour analysis and developmentally appropriate practice orientations. *Journal of Research in Childhood Education*, 22(4): 441–453.
Weikart, D. (1972) Relationship of curriculum, teaching, and learning in pre-school education. In J. Stanley (ed.), *Preschool Programs for the Disadvantaged*. Baltimore, MD: Johns Hopkins University Press, pp. 22–67.
Wells, G. (1987) *The Meaning Makers: Children Learning Language and Using Language to Learn*. London: Hodder & Stoughton.
Whalley, M. (2001) *Involving Parents in their Children's Learning*. London: Paul Chapman Publishing.

Willan, J. (2010) Research projects in early childhood studies: students' active explorations of children's worlds. In R. Parker-Rees, C. Leeson, J. Willan and J. Savage (eds), *Early Childhood Studies* (3rd edition). Exeter: Learning Matters.

Willattes, P. (1984) The Stage IV: infants' solution of problems requiring the use of supports. *Infant Behaviour and Development*, 7: 125–134.

Winnicott, D.W. (1971) *Playing and Reality*. London: Tavistock.

Wood, D. (1988) *How Children Think and Learn*. Oxford: Blackwell.

Wood, E. and Attfield, J. (1996) The role of the educator in children's play. In E. Wood and J. Attfield, *Play, Learning and the Early Childhood Curriculum*. London: Paul Chapman Publishing, pp. 98–173.

Woodhead, M. (1998) Quality in early childhood programmes: a contextually appropriate approach. *International Journal of Early Years Education*, 6(1): 5–17.

Woodhead, M. and Faulkner, D. (2000) Subjects, objects or participants? Dilemmas of psychological research with children. In P. Christensen and A. James (eds), *Research with Children: Perspectives and Practices*. London: Routledge Falmer.

Woods, P. (1986) *Inside Schools: Ethnography in Educational Research*. London: Routledge.

Xu, Y. (2005) Toddlers' emotional reactions to separation from their primary caregivers: successful home–school transition. *Early Child Development and Care*, 176(6): 661–674.

Zimmermann, A. and Morgan, J. (2011) The possibilities and consequences of understanding play as dialogue. *Sport, Ethics and Philosophy*, 5(1): 46–62.

# AUTHOR INDEX

Abbott, 22
Amith, 8
Angelides, 82
Anning, 84, 85, 127, 132
Arnold, 14, 23, 102, 111, 177, 189
Athey, x, 8, 10, 12, 15, 16, 19, 23, 29, 31, 41, 42, 44, 48, 49, 52, 53, 54, 57, 60, 62, 64, 66, 69, 70, 73, 74, 75, 76, 77, 78, 79, 80, 82, 83, 86, 87, 88, 90, 95, 98, 102, 104, 107, 108, 115, 118, 124, 128, 136, 138, 141, 142, 144, 146, 149, 156, 159, 163, 166, 170, 171, 177, 183, 184, 186, 187, 188, 189

Ball, 16
Bartlett, 9, 12, 186
Beales, 9
Bennett, 19
Bilton, 158
Birbeck, 10
Blaikie, 29
Bornstein, 105
Boyce, 106
Brewer, 27
Brierley, 6, 7, 8, 27, 107, 129
Broadhead, 15
Bronfenbrenner, 20
Bruce, 61, 108, 109, 189
Bruner, 11, 12, 37, 67, 100, 103, 149
Bush, 19

Cameron, 6
Carr, 13
Cheng, 10, 102
Chesterton, 168
Christensen, 27
Clarke, 6, 8, 53
Clough, 171, 188
Coates, 78, 79, 82, 89
Conroy, 20
Corbetta, 11, 54, 97

Cox, 83
Cruickshank, 30

Dahlberg, 19
David, 5
Davis, 21
DCSF, 18
Denzin, 30
Department for Children, Schools and Families, 7, 105
Department for Education and Science, 16, 17
Department for Education, 8, 18, 66, 95, 101, 102, 104, 105, 106, 118, 130, 131, 133, 134, 136, 146, 151, 156, 157, 165, 166, 189
Department of Children Schools and Families, 163
Dicks, 31
Dockett, 27, 78
Donaldson, 10, 37, 39, 40, 45, 100, 123, 143
Dunsmuir, 90

Elfer, 13, 14
Elkind, 139
Empson, 179
Erikson, 105, 167, 182

Fargas-Malet, 82
Fetterman, 27
Filippini, 127, 128
Flavell, 12, 100
Flewitt, 26, 27, 29, 30
Forman, 22, 41, 42, 107
Friedman, 6, 103

Gallard, 144
Gardner, 7, 8, 9, 10, 66, 139, 158, 161
Gauvain, 163, 167
Gleitman, 142

Goldschmied, 7, 95, 103
Goodley, 12
Goouch, 127, 128
Gopnik, 6, 7, 61
Grace, 11, 19
Green, 9, 12
Grieshaber, 167

Hannon, 6, 8
Harms, 17
Hastrup, 27
Haudrup, 20
Heywood, 89
HM Treasury, 17
Hofer, 61
Hohmann, 22
Holliday, 78, 188
Howard, 64, 100

Inhelder, 48
Isaacs, 123, 124, 158

Jenkins, 20

Kellmer Pringle, 37
Kellogg, 74, 75, 76, 77, 79, 80, 81, 82, 84, 89
Kinney, 15
Kjorholt, 15

Laevers, 57, 101
Lahman, 14, 26
LeCompte, 28
Loreman, 144
Lowenfeld, 74, 75, 86

Malaguzzi, 5, 106
Malmberg, 105
McVee, 8, 9
Meade, 12, 23, 54, 70, 90, 100, 108, 129, 139, 144, 164, 172, 187, 189
Meltzoff, 7, 11, 97, 161, 183
Montessori, 158, 163, 164
Moyles, 106, 126

Neisser, 9, 63, 102, 161
Nurse, 5
Nutbrown, 5, 8, 12, 14, 16, 18, 19, 21, 22, 23, 24, 26, 29, 42, 45, 56, 57, 60, 63, 67, 70, 80, 87, 100, 11, 129, 143, 144, 148, 149, 128, 139, 155, 158, 170, 172, 182, 189, 190

Palmer, 179
Parker-Rees, 41, 129
Penn, 8, 19
Piaget, 10, 11, 12, 23, 24, 44, 45, 50, 51, 52, 55, 63, 64, 65, 66, 67, 68, 69, 73, 74, 76, 78, 81, 85, 88, 90, 98, 100, 104, 105,115, 116, 117, 118, 122, 123, 124, 128, 132, 133, 141, 142, 149, 161
Plaskow, 74

QCA/DfEE, 17

Riley, 29
Rinaldi, 15, 20, 42
Rogoff, 9, 13, 15, 123, 179
Rosen, 7, 19

Samuelsson, 18, 19, 21
Sandberg, 13
Schiller, 6
Selbie, 107
Selleck, 7, 102
Sellers, 19
Sheridan, 19, 21
Shore, 6, 7, 103
Siraj-Blatchford, 13, 20, 21, 22
Smidt, 6, 12, 121, 128, 174
Smith, 7
Stanczak, 29
Stephenson, 21
Swanson, 29
Sylva, 7, 21, 22

Tickell, 189
Tovey, 52, 53

United Nations, 134

Verma, 25
Vygotsky, 123, 162, 166

Wang, 6
Wells, 171, 172, 184, 188
Whalley, 23
Willattes, 11, 98
Williams, 19
Winnicott, 41, 42, 45
Wood, 22, 122
Woodhead, 19

# SUBJECT INDEX

Action representations, 76
Action, 11, 12, 66
Addition, 142
Adult, 14, 41, 103
Affordance, 41
Application, 53
*Areas of learning and development*, 150
Assessments, 93, 105
Attunement, 65

Babies, 6
Back and forth schema, 47–58, 87
*Birth to Three Matters*, 17
Brain, 6

Capacity, 106
Care, 16
Causal connections, 68
Cause and effect relationships, 52
*Characteristics of effective learning*, 101, 105, 133, 156, 165
Childhood, 19
Children, 25, 30
Circular rotation, 101
Classification, 53
Clusters of schemas, 70
Co-ordination, 183
Co-ordinations, 70
Cognitive competence, 52
Cognitive concerns, 71
Cognitive structures, 65
Cognitive, 21
Collaboration, 179
Communication and language, 130, 157, 165
Communication, 23, 64, 96, 102, 129
Conceptual understanding, 80
Confidentiality, 28
Constructivism, 42

Containing and enveloping schema 35–46, 95–135, 130, 109, 110, 115, 117, 118, 124, 127, 128, 129, 133, 142, 145, 164, 172, 180
Containment, 77
Content related exchanges, 89
Content, 23, 63, 87, 159
Conversations, 30, 31
Coordination of actions, 74
Creativity, 106, 107
Curriculum, 18, 19

Definitions of schema, 8, 9, 13
Development, 16, 23, 31
Developmental journeys, 93
Discovery, 62
Disembedded thinking, 44
Dispositions, 11
Dynamic back and forth, 183
Dynamic representations, 59–72, 77, 101, 150–169, 174, 176, 177

Early childhood education, 18
Early childhood intervention, 29
Early Years Foundation Stage, 156, 165
Emotion, 29
Emotional development, 14
Enclosing and enveloping, 173, 177, 178
Environment, 6, 13, 14, 20, 42, 44, 49, 67, 90, 103, 111, 148, 158
Ethical philosophy, 22
Ethnographic research, 27
Ethos, 19
Experimentation, 62, 67
*Expressive Arts and Design*, 96, 106, 134, 157, 165
Expressive arts, 131

Figurative patterns, 90
Figurative representation, 78, 85

Figurative, 66, 73
Form of thinking, 10, 31, 35, 53, 43, 48, 50, 51, 62, 69, 78, 82, 83, 87, 90, 95, 102, 109, 111, 124, 129, 132, 139, 141, 148, 155, 159, 161, 164, 176
Form, 23, 63, 74, 79, 80, 84, 87, 89
*Foundations for Quality*, 16
*Froebel Early Education Project*, 23
Functional dependency relationship, 43, 44, 51, 52, 64, 66, 70, 73, 96, 119, 122, 145, 166

Going through a boundary, 101, 115, 136–149
Going through, 138, 141, 145
Graphic collection, 48
Graphic representations, 87

Holistic development, 11
Holistic, 15
Home environment, 23, 29
Home, 25
Horizontal, 48

Images, 29
Insideness, 73, 115, 124
Intelligence, 6
Interaction, 14, 23
Intimacy, 14, 15
Interactions, 61

Language of form, 36
Language, 54, 146
Learning environment, 8, 15, 16, 17, 22, 26, 35, 46, 61, 63, 105, 168
Learning experiences, 18
Learning journey, 21
Learning, 5, 16, 21, 23, 24
Listening, 28
Literacy, 96

Mark making, 73
Match and mismatch, 10
Match, 23, 82
Mathematical discovery, 56
*Mathematics*, 66, 96, 130, 134, 157, 165
Mind, 13
Motivation, 57
Motor functioning, 83
Motor level , 137, 158, 166, 181
Motor level actions, 38, 44, 47, 96
Movements, 59
Multi modal approach, 84

Observation, 15, 16, 26, 27, 28, 29, 30, 40, 42, 66, 73, 95, 127, 132, 137, 142, 156, 164
Operative, 66, 73

Parents, 18, 25, 26, 27, 29, 30, 172, 184
Partnership, 21
Pattern of action, 161
Pattern of thought, 85, 127
Patterns of behaviour, 24
Patterns, 35
Pedagogy, 22
*Personal, social and emotional development*, 13, 96, 130, 133, 156, 165
Philosophy, 14
Photographs, 25, 29, 30, 31
Physical development, 96, 102, 134, 157, 165
Physical, 6
Planning, 14
Play based learning, 18
Play, 8, 22, 38, 64, 71, 87, 95, 126, 132, 139, 155, 182
Play,
Playful, 57
Playfulness, 126, 134
Policy, 20
Power, 26
Practitioner, 6, 19, 26, 30
Preciousness, 5, 6, 8
Professional adults, 19, 106
Professional educators, 172
Professional understanding, 168
Professionals, 14, 25

Quality, 16, 17, 18, 19, 20, 21

Reflection, 15
Reflexive questioning, 15
Relationships, 13, 14, 19, 20, 21, 24, 26, 27, 31, 42, 61
Repeated actions, 68
Representation, 11
*Researching Effective Pedagogy in the Early Years* (REPEY), 20
Respect, 29
Respectful relationships, 20
Rotation, 70

Schema conversations, 171
Sensori-motor co-ordinations, 98
Sensory experience, 107
Sensory exploration, 97
Seriation, 53
Significant adult, 36
Size, 69
Social construction of knowledge, 44
Speech, 59, 62, 89
*Starting with Quality*, 16
*Statutory Framework for The Early Years Foundation Stage*, 17, 105, 118, 146, 156

Stories from home, 28, 170, 172
Subtraction, 142
Sustained, shared understanding, 22
Symbolic functioning, 52, 83
Symbolic level observations, 143
Symbolic level, 96
Symbolic representation, 50
Symbolic thinking, 93
Symbolic, 42
Systems of thought, 139

Talk, 71
Theoretical situatedness, 30
Thinking, 12, 15, 23, 24
Toddlers, 20
Trajectories, 74
Trajectory behaviour, 49, 51, 53, 54, 55, 56, 62, 148

Trajectory motor experiences, 61
Trajectory, 70
Transportability, 48
Treasure basket, 103

UN Convention on the Rights of the Child, 134
*Understanding the world,* 96, 104, 130, 134, 157, 165
Understanding, 31

Voices, 25

Watching, 28
Weight, 69
Well being, 19
'Why' questions, 24

*Zone of Proximal development*, 123